CROSSCURRENTS *Modern Critiques*

CROSSCURRENTS *Modern Critiques*
Harry T. Moore, *General Editor*

EDITED BY
David Madden, 1933 —

Proletarian Writers
of the Thirties

WITH A PREFACE BY
Harry T. Moore

Carbondale and Edwardsville

SOUTHERN ILLINOIS UNIVERSITY PRESS

FEFFER & SIMONS, INC.

London and Amsterdam

In memory of John Gassner

Copyright © 1968 by Southern Illinois University Press
All rights reserved
Library of Congress Card Number 68–11423
Printed in the United States of America
Designed by Andor Braun

PREFACE

THIS IS A COMPANION VOLUME to Tough Guy Writers of the Thirties, also in the Crosscurrents/Modern Critiques series and also edited by Professor David Madden of Ohio University.

As in the case of the other book, Mr. Madden has here assembled a star cast of critics, several of them among the finest in the country. The reader has only to look at the table of contents to see what I mean.

One particularly interesting feature of the book is the double inclusion of Jack Conroy. He appears not only as one of the contributors, but also as one to whom a chapter is devoted because of his novel The Disinherited. This is one of the many depression items reprinted in recent years because of the rising interest in the American 1930's.

Before such books of that decade went out of print, who read them? Surely there couldn't have been a great audience among the proletarians themselves, who were busy with the assembly lines, the bread lines, and the picket lines. And certainly there was little interest in such novels on the part of the wide public that was glutting itself on such books as Gone with the Wind.

No, the readers of the proletarian novel, outside committed Party members, were the bourgeois intellectuals (in those days both elements of that term were pejorative) who were often sympathetic to left-wing causes, and just as often known as simps. They were generally at a remove from the proletariat but, during the days of the United

Front, they were ardently in favor of the Loyalists. In the present volume, Leslie Fiedler mentions the importance of that war at the time. Many of the bourgeois intellectuals felt guilty over not signing up to fight in the Spanish trenches. The day Franco took Barcelona was a black day indeed.

But what did these bourgeois intellectuals really do during the depression years? Some worked on the Federal Writers' Project. Those who were not with the WPA in Chicago used to hear, from their friends who were, about a Negro of brilliant promise, Richard Wright, also the subject of an essay in this volume. Wright was a genuine proletarian writer and can be categorized more easily than some of his fellows, as we see in the present book.

Another center of activity, besides teaching, for the bourgeois intellectuals in the depression years was the encyclopedia industry. It was a fairly large industry in Chicago and one of the places where anyone who was literate and knew a few things could get a job.

In 1936 one group, including WPA and encyclopedia workers, organized a magazine, Midwest, edited from Minneapolis by Meridel LeSeuer and Dale Kramer. Because of Chicago's central location, the editorial meetings were generally held there. The staff included Mitchell Siporin (art editor), Jack Conroy, Weldon Kees, and Kerker Quinn. We had a lively time, but we couldn't afford to keep the magazine going and it soon disappeared. It had some good proletarian items; I particularly remember a fine account of the railroad "gandy dancers."

But—enough of the pieties of history. For now those hectic days of the 1930's are being lived again, through volumes such as the present one and the recent anthology by Jack Salzman and Barry Wallenstein, Years of Protest (Pegasus, 1967). This includes more than a mere sampling of the writings of the time, proletarian and otherwise. There is also Malcolm Cowley's Think Back on Us . . . (Southern Illinois University Press, 1967), a collection of the fine causeries which Malcolm Cowley wrote each week for The New Republic. And there will be other books from and about the 1930's, though it would be hard to imagine a finer survey collection of criticism than Mr. Madden's.

It deals with a number of separate authors as well as with general characteristics of the movement, and it contains fascinating biographical studies of Louis C. Fraina (Lewis Corey) and Michael Gold, two of the outstanding figures of the period. There is also a valuable chapter on proletarian poetry. Mr. Madden's Introduction is ample, sensible, and extremely useful.

Old-timers will find this volume a quickening reminder of past days, and newcomers to the subject will discover an invaluable guide. Only one of these essays has been printed before; Gerald Green's appeared in The Partisan Review.

Occasionally the chapters overlap, so that one writer or book may be discussed several times between these covers. This is all to the good, the many-mirrors approach that will provide different perspectives and help build toward the total picture.

HARRY T. MOORE

Southern Illinois University
October 31, 1967

DAVID MADDEN is the author of two literary studies, *James M. Cain* and *Wright Morris*, and of a novel, *The Beautiful Greed*. His literary essays have appeared in *Prairie Schooner*, *Antioch Review*, *Journal of Aesthetics*, *Modern Fiction Studies*, *Studies in Short Fiction*, and *The University Review*. Other articles and film criticism have appeared in *The Appalachian Review*, *Film Quarterly*, and *Film Heritage*. His stories and poems have been published in such journals as *The Kenyon Review*, *Botteghe Oscure*, *The Southwest Review*, and *Ante*. His prize-winning plays have had many productions and several have been published in *New Campus Writing #2* and *First Stage*. Former assistant editor of *The Kenyon Review*, he is associate editor of *Film Heritage*, and teaches creative writing at Ohio University, Athens.

LESLIE FIEDLER's critical writings include *Love and Death in the American Novel*, *An End to Innocence*, *No! in Thunder*; his novels are *Waiting for the End*, *The Second Stone*, and *Back to China*; his stories appeared under the title *Put Down Vanity*; he has contributed essays to *The Partisan Review*, *Poetry*, *Ramparts*, *Commentary*, *The New Republic*, and *The Kenyon Review*.

GERALD GREEN has been a producer-writer for NBC since 1950, working on "Today," "Wide Wide World," and numerous documentaries. His novels are well-known: *His Majesty O'Keefe*, *The Last Angry Man*, *The Lotus Eaters*, *The Heartless Light*, and most recently *The Legion of Noble*

Christians. He is working now on a novel of the Depression, set in Brooklyn.

LEO GURKO is a Professor of English at Hunter College and author of *The Angry Decade; Heroes, Highbrows, and the Popular Mind; Tom Paine, Freedom's Apostle; Joseph Conrad: Giant in Exile;* and *The Two Lives of Joseph Conrad.* Soon to appear are a volume of Shelley's selected poems and a critical study of Ernest Hemingway.

JULES CHAMETZKY, Associate Professor of English at the University of Massachusetts and coeditor of *The Massachusetts Review,* has published articles on writers of the Thirties in *The Nation, The Progressive, Midstream, New England Quarterly,* and *The Massachusetts Review.* At present he is writing a short book on Abraham Cahan's literary work.

JACK CONROY's first novel, *The Disinherited,* a classic proletarian novel, was published in 1933 and reissued in 1963. *A World To Win* appeared in 1935. He edited *The Rebel Poet, The Anvil,* and *The New Anvil* magazines, and has contributed book reviews to magazines and to Chicago newspapers. A lecturer on literature and folklore, he has recently returned to his birthplace, Moberly, Missouri, to write his memoirs.

ERLING LARSEN is the author of *Minnesota Trails: A Sentimental History,* which is illustrated with his own photographs. He teaches English at Carleton College and is editor of *The Carleton Miscellany.* His short stories and essays have appeared in various magazines.

IRVING HOWE is Professor of English at Hunter College. He is the editor of *Dissent* and a contributing editor of *The New Republic.* His books include *Politics and the Novel; The UAW and Walter Reuther* (with B. J. Widick); *Sherwood Anderson: A Critical Biography; The American Communist Party: A Critical History* (with Lewis Coser). His most recent book is *Steady Work.*

LEONARD KRIEGEL, Assistant Professor of English at the City College of New York, has written scholarly and critical articles, short stories, and reviews, appearing in such magazines as *The Nation, Commonweal, American Judaism,* and *The Reconstructionist,* and an autobiographical narrative, *The Long Walk Home.* At present he is working on a political novel and a study of Edmund Wilson.

CHARLES H. MILLER, free-lance writer who sometimes lives in a hut in Mexico, has published in *Evergreen Review, Texas Quarterly, Michigan Quarterly Review,* the New York *Times,* and *Siempre!* At present he is writing a full critical study of B. Traven's books, with the mysterious Traven's own approval and assistance.

MARCUS KLEIN, Associate Professor of English at the State University of New York at Buffalo, is the author of *After Alienation: American Novels in Mid-Century.* His essays, fiction, and reviews have appeared in such magazines as *The Kenyon Review, The New Leader, The Reporter,* and *The Nation.* He is now working on a history of American literature from 1932 to the present.

CHESTER E. EISINGER, Professor of English and Chairman of the Committee on American Studies at Purdue University, has held Fulbright lectureships at the University of Cairo in Egypt and Innsbruck University in Austria. He has written articles on American agrarianism and the freehold concept and on twentieth-century American fiction. In 1963, his *Fiction of the Forties* appeared, and he is editor of *The 1940's,* a volume which will appear soon.

FREDERICK J. HOFFMAN is Distinguished Professor of English at the University of Wisconsin and author of numerous literary essays and books, including *The Mortal No: Death and the Modern Imagination* and *The Art of Southern Fiction.* Soon to appear is *The Imagination's New Beginning: Theology and Modern Literature.*

LEE BAXANDALL, an editor of *Studies on the Left,* has published in *The Journal of Aesthetics and Art Criticism, Modern Drama, Tulane Drama Review, Encore,* and elsewhere, and is presently coediting *Marxists on Art and Literature.* He is also a playwright.

MICHAEL BREWSTER FOLSOM, Assistant Professor of Literature at Massachusetts Institute of Technology, is the son of literary radicals (his father was executive secretary of the League of American Writers). He has reviewed for *The Nation* and other periodicals and is now working on studies of Middle English literature and of radical literature in the United States before the 1930's.

ALLEN GUTTMANN, Associate Professor of English and American Studies at Amherst College, has published *The Wound in the Heart: America and the Spanish Civil War* and *American Democracy and the Conservative Imagination* and several dozen essays on American literature and politics.

CONTENTS

INTRODUCTION

SINCE NOT ALL the writers discussed in this volume are "proletarian" by any general definition, its title, one may charge, only compounds the confusion which the use and misuse of the term has caused. The term dissatisfies those few who write about the genre, while revealing little to the many whose understanding of it is vague. This book does not set out to whitewash a label that has, some claim, blackened many good novels. In a letter in which she declined to write an essay for this volume, Josephine Herbst, regarded as one of the finest of the radical novelists of the Thirties, expressed an apprehension that may be representative. "I do think it is stupid to select and warp out of shape a writer's actual work and development." "Who made the demarcations for the works you put into this category? It seems to me arbitrary. I have felt that my own work has been considerably damaged by the category, and that the term since the Second World War has been used more as blackmail than as a definitive term with any valid meaning. I think the whole thing needs a more fundamental approach. Where are the roots to the writing in the thirties? Was it all political?"

As the revival of interest in the Thirties gets underway, we must avoid the preconception that it was primarily an era of radical action, thinking, and literature. This impression was made persuasive by the appearance in 1956 and the reissue in 1965 of Walter B. Rideout's invaluable *The Radical Novel in the United States 1900–1954: Some In-*

terrelations of Literature and Society (Harvard University Press) and of Daniel Aaron's quite different *Writers on the Left* in 1961 (Avon paperback, 1965). Produced by a "crisis generation," proletarian literature is the most visible and identifiable of genres in the Thirties, and certainly the one which the "protest" fraction of the present generation will find most relevant. In a lecture in 1965, Granville Hicks spoke of both the necessity and the danger of reassessment. "The writers of the 30's are largely unknown today," but it "is a mistake to consider all the literature of the decade as unimportant." Few would disagree with his assertion that the greatest novels were written by Faulkner, who, writing out of an agrarian culture, was unaffected by the problems of an industrial society. Both Rideout and Aaron suggest a wider scope by showing that even the good radical literature was written by both the writers who embraced communism and those who wrote out of what Chester Eisinger calls "the ambience of Marxism." The contents of Harvey Swados' excellent anthology *The American Writer and the Great Depression* (1966) suggest a broader approach to the literature of the Thirties, including with the radical or proletarian many other writers not listed in Rideout's bibliography: Wolfe, Agee, Steinbeck, Caldwell, Nathanael West. During this decade also appeared *The Autobiography of Alice B. Toklas* and other Stein works; John P. Marquand's *The Late George Apley*; Fitzgerald's *Tender Is the Night*; Ellen Glasgow's *Vein of Iron*; Willa Cather's *Shadows on the Rock* and *Lucy Gayheart*; Wilder's *Heaven's My Destination*; and most of Katherine Anne Porter's stories. Then also appeared the popular novels, dealing with the historical past and with the exotic, and the tough guy novels. While focussing on proletarian novelists, poets, and critics, the present volume is concerned with writers in the "ambience" as well.

But Josephine Herbst will not let us rest so easily. The problems raised by the term are there. Something there is that doesn't tolerate a label. Let us listen to Miss Herbst at some length.

This [term] seems to have sprung up—where? Like . . . college courses or the text books? Who thinks up these things and makes the selections? Who says what is what? There were actually arguments about the word "proletarian" when it was pitched in, during the thirties. I thought of the writing as 'revolutionary' in the sense that the whole century was going to be involved, in one way or another, with revolution, and I think this is quite right. But proletarian was a narrow word, and part of the jargon. I do not believe that I can write anything for this project as, among other things, it starts off with a cliché. If this question of what is called "proletarian" novels is really going to be examined intensively as you say, then I suggest they begin by looking into the sources of the naming of this particular body of work and question some of the demarcations they have made.

While several take up the problem the term poses for criticism, a few attack it, and none attempt to justify or defend it, most of the contributors either accept it as harmless and serviceable, or write with no particular awareness of it. "The label will be examined carefully," I assured Miss Herbst, "not sanctified. . . . *Everyone* knows the label is no damn good, perhaps harmful, but you don't make it go away by ignoring it; we're stuck with it; let's look at it, and invest it with meaning, and use it, fully aware of the weaknesses of the term; such use can have good results; let's not use it glibly, but it's impossible to destroy it. . . . We ought to examine the genesis of the term, its strengths, and expose its weaknesses." One may begin this task by looking, as Frederick Hoffman does, at Rideout's careful, detailed account of the origin of the term and the controversy among radicals over its proper definition (pp. 165–70).

Rideout calls it "the most important critical term among radical literary groups of the early thirties" (See also Aaron's account, pp. 310–12, Avon paperback.) In his essay on Michael Gold, Michael Folsom shows that the young Marxist critic was the first to make "proletarian literature" synonymous with "radical literature." He planted the term in 1921, it flowered in the early Thirties, and, as disenchantment with communism created an ideological wasteland, went to seed in the Forties. V. F. Calverton in 1932 declared that the major distinction between proletarian and bourgeois writers is that the former, regardless of class origin, "have adopted the revolutionary point of view of the proletarian ideology," and "express that ideology in their work." In 1934, E. A. Schachner, who, unlike Calverton, spoke as a communist, made a distinction between the revolutionary novel, "which consciously supports the movement for the revolutionary destruction of Capitalism," and the proletarian novel, which merely "reflects the life of any typical cross section of the proletariat and need not be more revolutionary than the proletariat itself is at the time the novel is written." In 1935, at the first of three American Writers' Congresses, an angry debate developed over the nature and function of proletarian literature, then enjoying its greatest popularity. Expressing a rather intellectual point of view, Waldo Frank declared that if the writer's "vision be sound, it will make—*whatever his subject*—the material for revolutionary art. . . . A story of middle-class or intellectual life, or even of mythological figures, if it is alight with revolutionary vision, is more effective proletarian art—and more effective art for proletarians—than a shelffull of dull novels about stereotyped workers." The definition "most frequently accepted in both theory and practice" was the one stated by Calverton, Frank, and Gold: literature "written from a Marxist viewpoint." Just as heretofore the novel had reflected bourgeois values, the proletarian novel, Rideout sums up, "would reflect proletarian values, would bring the worker to class-consciousness, steel him for the coming revolution, prepare him for the role he would play in the next stage of history. Art was a form of politics; it was a weapon in the class war." Rideout, who discusses the socialist novel also (1900–1919), points out that the term "proletarian literature" was not used among socialist writers; while *they* rejected violence in favor of social evolution, the proletarian writer subscribed to the inevitability of "cataclysmic" class struggle.

Literary terms often slight the suburbs of their province.

For instance, what are we to make of writers who, with no identifiable ideological preconceptions, depict the life of the poor (Daniel Fuchs, Henry Roth) or portray the loneliness of men who do cleave to an ideology, as Carson McCullers does in *The Heart Is a Lonely Hunter*—Jake Blount and Doctor Copeland represent both white and Negro radicals, but McCullers expounds no ideology of her own. Since all literary terms, being relative, are inadequate, they require, if they are to be useful, constant watchfulness and re-evaluation.

Again, Miss Herbst's misgivings must be heeded.

> When I was writing my trilogy I never thought of it as "proletarian"—in fact I hated the term, and thought it never comprehensive enough. Actually the Soviet Union gave it up early in the thirties for the equally ambivalent and never defined term of social realism. Still, there is more sense to that than to proletarian.
>
> .   .   .   .
>
> It may be true that we are stuck with the label "proletarian" but who did the sticking? I had nothing to say about it and neither did any of the fiction writers of the period. Maybe some of the folks writing tracts liked it. Quite possibly. But it's odd that Louis Aragon, a party liner, never got stuck with such a label in France for all his novels. Nor Silone in Italy either. They don't use such terms. No, it took this country, the least likely place to produce a genuine proletariat in the genetic sense of the word, to find that label. I guess I hate it because I always proposed to write about what I knew something of and I didn't know the proletariat. The poor aren't proletariat and we have about as many poor now as we did in the thirties but they are all mixed up, unclassified. Only the communist *The Worker* could make an organic proletariat out of them. I think the better of the books of the thirties could be classified as vehicles for protest and engines for change. Some of them were more sharply focused than others as to the kind of change the era seemed to imply.
>
> .   .   .   .
>
> *Language*—sex, the exalted role of the body—the confluence of so many diverse elements—how can it be nailed down to Marx or to an angled proletarian?

. . . .

Language played a role and the revolution in language, as in sex, preceded the social revolution in this country at least. I really don't think I should enter into this series as I am going to attack a good deal of the preconceptions [in her autobiography, near completion] and there isn't any use in doing it in more than one place. I never was a penitent. I am not sorry for anything in that sphere; my sorrows are private ones. Mistakes aren't crimes. I never thought I was God, seeing all, knowing all.

She says that she does not see any of the writers she knew apart from their own special circumstances and development.

What Miss Herbst says about her *own* special circumstances and development substantiates her claim that "proletarian" is an imprecise term.

What interests me in my own trilogy is the language (as well as the substance; I think it is sound for what it attempted though I can't say I like it either) but I did have a mastery of the idiom (and was credited for it, too) but it ran away from me. In fact the period was overwhelming and there was not enough of a solid body of intellectual or literary life behind anyone to help much.

. . . .

I began with trying to understand how I had evolved from a long family line, in this country since 1700 and beginning by being big landowners and prosperous. The family was disappearing, its allegiances no longer held the center. As it turned out, emotionally, the tie was stronger than individuals thought. But the first volume, *Pity Is Not Enough*, was using the past as the narrative, taking the time directly following the Civil War as a counterpoise to my time, directly following World War 1—and the insert pieces were posed in the present. That is, in the present of someone mature in the thirties. In the second volume, *The Executioner Waits*, the past of the old ties had been crushed by the realities of the present, and the inserts dealt with the explosive episodes which related to the development of the one character who was continuous in the trilogy. All episodes in this book related to USA but in the third volume, the international aspect had moved in, and the inserts related to Cuba, Germany and other points. The whole trilogy was an attempt to relate the urgency of the issues which projected the nation into the world, but this was done in terms of a single group and a few individuals as the main body of the work. Nothing of the significance I had intended ever came through, as it was never published as a complete volume. The last volume, *Rope of Gold*, also has intimations of the breakdown of the international hope, as signified within certain of the characters, their doubts, their fears.

There is a lot of the didactic in the last two books of the trilogy. I wasn't against it then, and in fact, nourished as I mostly was in the literary sense by Russian works of the 19th century, I wasn't afraid of it. . . . So we weren't afraid of being didactic and I wasn't afraid of being subversive. In fact, I intended to be. . . . I wouldn't write those two books in the same way—even then—if I could have written them otherwise. But that's the way I felt. And the books contain some first hand documentation, for I never wrote about anything I hadn't some understanding of first hand. I think that is true of a number of the books [of the Thirties]. The urgency of the times crumpled much that would have made the works more valid but there was never time or space. The whole business of that kind of world view and type of writing needed room for development which never came.

While the term "proletarian" does seem inadequate for Miss Herbst's trilogy, these novels exemplify Waldo Frank's definition, which allowed for the middle class as subject, if it is "alight with revolutionary vision."

Miss Herbst suggests a problem which this book will share with others that deal with the Thirties. "I never read anything about the past that I wholly agree with." She disagrees with the way the authors of recent books on the era look at certain issues.

Aaron did nothing about writing actually. His heroes were the entrepreneurs of writing, the head-boys who have also been mostly responsible for the rehashes. The imaginative world was done in, and the critical world and the critics were the most vocative. The causes for this go far deeper than any discussion of the thirties can evaluate. The entrepreneurs whom Dan Aaron wrote about were all stuck in the claustrophobia of New York City and it was clear that what was going on in the world wasn't going to be decided by the literati anyhow. That's why I was always leaving for Germany, Cuba, Mexico, Latin America, the midwest and Spain. New York became a tempest in a teapot, or pisspot, as we actually said. The Trotsky crowd vs. Stalin crowd. It was never that simple. The communist press wrote jargon for farmers and for "workers" most of the time and in the midwest they had no circulation worth a damn.

Turning away in disgust and despair from the capitalist government's accommodation of European fascism and from fascist tendencies in the handling of problems created by the collapse of capitalism in this country, American writers in various ways accepted the leadership of Soviet Russia, unable to see there the workings of communism as they so keenly experienced the malfunction of capitalism here. And their own words roused no significant popular support for radicalism or communism among the masses at home. It is one thing to experience as nightmare something as tenuous as the American dream—capitalism had always visibly contradicted the dream anyway—but having pursued the radical cause as a crusade based on the ideal of world brotherhood, the American writer, betrayed by the reality, experienced a disenchantment in the Forties and Fifties that was more bitter than his disaffiliation from capitalism in the Thirties. For some, the demoralization has resulted in an immobilization that has extended into the present. When the creative will and social involvement have been so interactive, no reassessment can set out to satisfy everyone.

Rideout's and Aaron's books have persuaded people to examine more carefully the notion that proletarian novels aren't important. With the never-denied estimation that they are valuable as journalistic mirrors of the times there has seldom been a desire to look deeply into those mirrors.

Perhaps as we actually do venture upon an act of rediscovery, we shall perceive, as have some of the contributors to this volume, *other* values, including, surprisingly, aesthetic ones; at their artistic worst, these novels offer unique negative occasions for analyzing the nature of aesthetics in the novel. And these novels can offer fresher perspectives on finer works the vitality of which we have tended to exhaust by overexplication. Despite her severe apprehensions, Josephine Herbst expresses delight in seeing relatively new ground explored: "Your project is at least on new, if somewhat despised ground (that is, as it has been projected and patronized) but at least you are getting away from prodding the old dead horses for ritual, symbol and myth." Instead of perpetuating duplication and depletion, we need to step back and sight new approaches. The proletarian angle of vision is one of many possibilities; the tough guy is another. Going beyond Rideout, Aaron, and Swados, this book attempts to keep alive an interest excited among general readers, students, critics, writers, and teachers mainly by their three books alone so far.

While the contributors responded to a brief description of the book we hoped to assemble, these essays represent more the interests of the writers than the intention or design of the editor. The design that exists emerged quite naturally out of common interests, not out of a concerted intention to cover ground already covered, or specifically not covered, by Aaron and Rideout. This volume presents what we happened to want to say rather than everything that we all agreed *must* be said on the subject. In the course of these essays, the reader unfamiliar with proletarian writing will be introduced to a great variety of works—novels, criticism, poetry. The multi-leveled vision through which he will see these works offers a chronological cross section: Jack Conroy, Leo Gurko, Erling Larsen, and Frederick J. Hoffman look back on a time in which they lived and wrote; Leslie Fiedler and Irving Howe, who began to write in the Forties, look back on a time when they were children; and very young men like Michael Folsom and Lee Baxandall (who weren't even born until

World War II) and who have only heard, read, and learned about the era, attempt to understand a decade that explains their fathers and that produced certain polit- ical and literary forces which they witness around them today. These writers seem aware of the dangers implicit in their tasks. Belatedly engaged as we are in finishing many of the tasks begun then—civil rights, war on poverty, etc.—we run the risk of glamorizing the Thirties. If we are to achieve a balanced perspective—such as we seem now to have on the works of Fitzgerald, Hemingway, and Faulkner, if not perhaps of Dos Passos and Wolfe—we must avoid making extravagant claims for or against cer- tain novels and attitudes.

The volume opens with general essays by Leslie Fiedler and Gerald Green. In "The Two Memories: Reflections on Writers and Writing in the Thirties," Leslie Fiedler poses the social and moral necessity of "thinking about the Thirties in the second half of the Sixties," not in the "luxury" of "reminiscence and nostalgia," but through "the kind of return to roots and sources so often required for cultural renewal; the re-examination of a past never quite understood—out of an awareness that unless we un- derstand it now we will not understand the present or our own surviving selves." Fiedler himself approaches that task in the personal manner that one has come to expect of him, and his observations and insights range over many novels (focussing on Nathanael West's), plays, movies, poems, and critical points of view.

As his first line suggests, Green's reassessment is even more lyrical than Fiedler's: "Bigger Thomas has been haunting me lately. . . . How clearly I see him—black, ugly, murderous. . . . And he still has the power to scare me silly." Green does not write as a literary critic; his is the kind of novelist-documentarist's sensibility that went into making many of the novels of the Thirties. As an uncommonly articulate reader, he echoes less articulate attitudes and responses of readers in general. He rereads some 19 novels in one great immersion with such intense personal involvement that he seems to reread them for us all. Reacting against the egocentric, subjective, erotic novel and against critics whose overemphasis on style diminishes the importance of what he calls "meaning," Green sees "the realistic novel as a source of information and understanding" and lauds its entertainment function. While one may feel that some of his ideas are wrong-headed, one of the values of his essay is that it represents a widely-held point of view which ought to be kept provocatively in operation as we look more closely at some of the books mentioned in his and in Fiedler's essays. (Except for Green's, none of the essays in this volume have previously appeared in print; as editor of this volume and as assistant editor of *The Kenyon Review*, I asked Green to write the essay for inclusion in both publications.)

Following these two general essays, a focus section offers, in chronological sequence, a close look at eleven novels. Proletarian and many nonideological novels of the Thirties were written, obviously, out of a similar literary and social climate. And different types affected each other in various ways. Steinbeck's *In Dubious Battle* (1936) seems to have been influenced as much by other labor novels as by events themselves. The example of proletarian fiction perhaps persuaded (even, in a sense, intimidated) those writers who were more aesthetically oriented into dealing with immediate social realities; in Hemingway's case, among others, the effect was unfortunate. Scrutiny of some nonproletarian novelists strikingly reveals raw materials, problems, points of view common to the radical novels: Nathanael West, Daniel Fuchs, Carson McCullers, Henry Miller, Thomas Wolfe, Erskine Caldwell, John Steinbeck (none of whom are listed in Rideout). Leo Gurko looks at Dos Passos' spectacular, epic trilogy *U.S.A.* (1930, 1932, 1936). Dos Passos' novels before and after the Thirties demonstrated a radical point of view on the American dream, though his pessimism opposed the optimism of proletarian literature. (One indication of a revival of interest in proletarian and related novels, at least among critics and publishers, is the availability in paperback of *U.S.A.* and most of the other books discussed in this section. It is hoped that discussion and citation of other works in this volume will create among readers a demand which will further induce publishers to reprint these works, for as Irving Howe says in his essay, "reprinting them *is* an act of justice and a welcome one.")

In the Thirties, many books dealing with the wandering "bottom dog" appeared, projecting a sense of Americans uprooted from pastoral and dislocated from industrial settings; certain nonfiction works also expressed this sense of Americans on the move, chronicling their authors' deliberate explorations of the natural and human landscape: Sherwood Anderson's *Puzzled America*, James Rorty's *Where Life Is Better: An Unsentimental American Journey*, Nathan Asch's *The Road: In Search of America*, Louis Adamic's *My America*, Theodore Dreiser's *Tragic America*. Jules Chametzky examines Edward Dahlberg's early autobiographical novels *Bottom Dogs* (1930) and *From Flushing to Calvary* (1932) as phases in the metamorphosis of *Because I Was Flesh* (New Directions, 1964). Dahlberg was of interest to avant-garde writers then, and has been continuously since, because of the "special qualities of his voice," derived in part from a style "a-dazzle with rich metaphor, erudite allusions to religious and pagan mythologies, passionate attention to the rhythms and music of the period." The *word* in Dahlberg transcends the action of the time and ascends to universality.

In 1963, when Hill and Wang reissued his own "classic" proletarian novel, *The Disinherited*, about a wandering worker, Jack Conroy expressed a desire to promote a revival of Robert Cantwell's "classic" novel of protest *Land of Plenty* (1934), a good novel, he felt, by any standards, in any time. This novel is one of many types within the proletarian orbit. Daniel Aaron provides a rich list of these types: novels depicting "the lives of 'Bottom Dogs,' the adventures of young Irish delinquents, the 'Neon Wilderness' of Chicago's North Side Poles, the Negro slum dwellers, the poor East Side Jews, Georgia 'crackers,' California fruit pickers, toilers on the Detroit assembly lines,

Gastonia's textile workers, decaying Southern families, rebellious farmers, department-store wage slaves, or 'boxcar'
hoboes." Conroy praises Cantwell's novel for its accurate
and authentic (and prophetic) depiction of the abortive
seizure of a factory. Writing under the literary influence
of Henry James and the ideological influence of Marx,
Cantwell was "admirably fitted both by experience and
ability to produce an authentic proletarian novel," and he
came closer than any other novelist, Conroy feels, to
meeting Granville Hicks' challenge to writers to produce a
collective novel—one that centers on "a complex of closely
related individuals."

   As word got around that this volume was in the making,
almost a hundred writers contacted me, wanting to write
an essay. I soon perceived that in this country and Mexico
a great underground exists of writers who are still urgently
interested in radical and proletarian fiction. One senses
that a fraternal feeling lingers on among them; they keep
in touch and seem to look out for each other. This sense
of communion and generosity extends to succeeding generations of writers. In his informal, somewhat personal
testimony about the undiminished power of Jack Conroy's
The Disinherited (1933), Erling Larsen talks of Conroy's
encouragement of young writers through his radical literary magazine *The Anvil*. Thus, Willard Motley inscribed
Conroy's copy of *Knock on Any Door* with the words: "To
one who has unselfishly and without envy helped more
aspiring authors than anyone I know." Looking back,
Josephine Herbst feels that "the beauty of the thirties was
its communion among people—its generosity—its willingness to be guilty of folly and its chance to get out of the
constricted *I* in what seemed a meaningful way. Down
under, this ties up with fundamental and eternal impulses,
not related purely to the ideology of the moment. That
the ideology proved a trap is nothing so much as it seems.
That is, not for the individual on any ground he can
control. What is tragic is far more than himself. Far
more." The publications of that time, most of which
figure in the essays in this volume, offered a focus for this

fellow-feeling and a medium through which the "constricted I" expanded itself: *The Partisan Review, The Masses, The New Masses, The Liberator, Poetry, The Daily Worker, Dynamo, Seven Arts, The Marxist Quarterly, Story, New Leader, Americana, The New Republic, The Nation, The American Mercury, People's World, The Worker's Monthly.*

Larsen examines past and present critical attitudes toward *The Disinherited,* concentrating on problems of stylistic artifice, special pleading, and "realism." He suggests that Conroy's short story "Siren" explains the seemingly incongruous lyricism in *The Disinherited.* But if the style was literary, the essence was sweat. In 1965, Conroy described himself as "a working man who wrote about working people, especially to protest injustices." His major aim in the novel was to record his experiences. *My experiences* is the catch phrase of authority in such novels. When parts of the novel appeared in *The American Mercury* as sketches, Mencken announced them with the question, "What Is the Depression Really Like?" As *the man who was there,* Conroy believed that his role was as "a witness of the times" more than as a novelist. The strength of the book, he said in 1963, was that it gave the "feel of what it's like to work, how you handle a machine, and the monotony of it." His purpose was to "show how it feels to be without work, and with the imminent fear of starving, to move people to think about it, and, what's more important, to do something about it." He spoke, as his dedication declared, "for the disinherited and dispossessed of the world." But his attitude was objective, for both unions and employers come off badly in the novel. "I don't like to think that I put any 'philosophy' in the book. It is perhaps true that the book is defective as a novel for that reason. I like what Dan Aaron says in the introduction: 'His tone is bemused and wondering rather than protesting and declamatory, and he is so intent on rendering exactly the texture of his hero's surroundings that he seems to be constantly forgetting the ideological purpose of his narrative.'" In 1963, Conroy felt that if he "succeeded in conveying something of the times, something of the terror and the uncertainty and the actual desperation, then I'm content." He thinks his novel survived because "it made a strong impression on people. They have not only talked about it over the years, but they've written about it." And it has survived because it is "free of the artificialities that most proletarian writers, who observed these things from the outside, filled their books with." If the novels of the Fifties and Sixties are technically better, they also have less to say, Conroy believes. Writers had a higher purpose in the Thirties, and tried "to follow Whitman's injunction of vivifying the contemporary fact." Thus, Conroy testifies to the authenticity of Gerald Green's view of the novelist's role.

Conroy is right about his book—it is no more a novel than is Michael Gold's *Jews Without Money*. But as higher journalism, autobiographically informed, it has its own claim to imaginative truth. In content, form, and intention the distinctions between journalism and fiction became blurred in the Thirties. It is in the American tradition of realism that the journalist longs to soar above the labyrinth of fact. In every time and place, the novel has always had an educative, quasi-journalistic function, which certain times and places stress to satisfy an urgent need. *Let Us Now Praise Famous Men* began as a routine journalistic assignment; Agee was instructed to expose, but his raw material moved him to reveal. In his book, the journalistic machinery exists side by side, and perhaps inseparable from, the poetic apotheosis. Other writers begin with the imaginative impulse and end with higher journalism. In American writers these impulses are not conflictive alone, but also complementary. Though the products of proletarian literature were called novels, plays, poems, most of them should not be judged in our time primarily by aesthetic standards—that is an easy task, resulting in dismissal—but as journalism uplifted. To read them on their own terms is instructive; beyond that, there are subtler possibilities for bringing to this literature a certain imaginative readiness to perceive the expressively ambiguous, ironic, paradoxical implications. Recently, certain writers and critics have urged the creative transformation of nonfictive modes, and a few have predicted the gradual abandonment of the novel as an exhausted medium. But even the spontaneous, authentic outpouring of individual psyches is a kind of psychological journalism: "This is the way I feel" and "this is the way it was" are manifestations of a similar impulse. It is the intensity of Conroy's conscious feeling for the life he depicts that survives the ruins of the Depression, though art, which must balance the subjective and the objective, fails to hold the center.

Daniel Fuchs is one of the lesser-known of those writers of the Thirties who wrote out of a private vision rather than a social consciousness, and thus achieved art. The raw material of his trilogy *Summer in Williamsburg* (1934), *Homage to Blenholt* (1936), *Low Company* (1937), reprinted by Berkley in 1965, suggests that Fuchs could have become an avowed proletarian novelist instead of a mass media functionary in Hollywood. The novelistic conception pervading the trilogy, says Irving Howe in his laudatory essay, is "the power of environment, the tyranny of conditions," and how they "take over a segment of human life to become an overwhelming presence." In novels "dominated by a sense of place," his "entire creative effort was" to "come to terms with his memories," an effort similar to Gold's in *Jews Without Money*. Through his intense subjectivity, we experience, untutored by ideological angling, the environment that produced the more publicly committed novelists who approached their material from an external, abstract doctrine. Albert Halper, a distinctly proletarian novelist, said of Fuchs: "He is a man with a burden. I do not envy him . . . he is a child of sorrow."

Dalton Trumbo, most famous of the Hollywood Ten victimized by McCarthy, is a screenwriter whose early novels were explicitly radical. The personal involvement that characterizes several of these essays is forcibly evident in Leonard Kriegel's approach to Trumbo's *Johnny Got*

His Gun (1939), reissued by Bantam in 1967. For him it is not simply a *tour de force* about a basket case, flippantly dismissed today by its creator, nor a caricature, but a parable of today's pacifist movement, in which Kriegel invests his own emotions. He looks behind the myth that it was "a novel put together as a kind of contemporary *exemplum* to be used by the American Communist Party in the days of the Hitler-Stalin Pact." It "still lives," a unique novel "created around a thing, a consciousness endowed with a humanness which we see as being so revolting that it tests our humanity." Though the sentimentality latent in much of proletarian and tough fiction emerges in this novel, and though its rigged rhetoric fails as Marxist propaganda, the reader experiences Johnny Bonham's disembodied anguish as a living "pacifist plea, perhaps as relevant today as when it was written."

Following the focus section comes a long essay devoted to all the works of a single novelist. Few books on American literature mention B. Traven, nor do Rideout and Aaron. An authority on B. Traven, Charles Miller, who has the mysterious author's confidence, attributes part of the confusion over Traven's image as writer and man to "our slowness to recognize him as a pure proletarian" novelist. A proletarian "indistinguishable," as Traven himself has said, from "the others," he was "born of, worked with, fought for, and continues to stand for, the proletariat"; "a political proletarian writer of the Americas," he is "an international revolutionist and a philosophical anarchist." A "liberated proletarian," Traven writes of those who remain in economic bondage, though often free in spirit. His are novels of work-quest; the son of immigrants, he rejected the American promise, became an international migrant worker, and finally settled in Mexico, the dark subconscious of the American dream. As Traven continues to write, "we are a decade behind in reading him," though Hill and Wang is reprinting much of his canon of more than 15 works. And Miller, while giving us a cogent survey of all Traven's books—their themes, characters, techniques, raw materials—makes no attempt to conceal his impatience: 'What a shame it is to talk about important books rather than read them!" Miller himself exhibits some of the evangelical fervor that animated the novels of the Thirties. Some readers may flinch at critical responses that remain so close to personal involvement—even while Miller's enthusiasm sends them to the books themselves.

Originally, Traven was listed, rather tentatively, on the prospectus for the tough guy volume, but Miller saw that Traven's novels transcended that genre. Josephine Herbst feels that *neither* way of looking at a writer is crucial: "I don't care if writing is 'tough'—but what do the writers do with it? I don't care whom they influence—what does the guy do with the stuff once he gets it? The tough stuff has leaked off into the new pornography, the dullest stuff going. Why do Americans always or nearly always (lots of exceptions) try to box things off?" But like several critics in this volume and elsewhere, she does see that "there's a kind of invisible connection between the two categories" proletarian and tough guy. Both types were in "revolt against the old gentility." "I am not so much opposed to the categories as I am to simplifications." Indeed (like Traven) Cain, Hammett, Chandler, and Horace McCoy exemplified in their life or work, or both, a strong social consciousness, though the tough guy hero himself was a man with fists and a gun, but no creed, while the proletarian hero was a man with a manifesto, who sometimes resorted to fists and guns. A more important influence than Hemingway upon the tough novel, Herbert J. Muller felt, was "the proletarian writers, who have given the whole tendency toward the hard-boiled manner not only a new impetus but a new direction. This tendency is in fact interesting chiefly because of its sources. It is in part an extension of naturalism, which from the beginning subordinated style to matter. It is in part, too, an expression of the post-war mood, with its distrust of rhetoric." But he believed that the simple style was "another sign of distintegration," for it reduced the complexities of life to its simplest elements. "Hence it is attractive both to sophisticates attempting to flee the confusion of their society," in tough fiction, for instance, and "to earnest advocates of some principle of solidarity" (*Modern Fiction*, 1937).

This volume grew indirectly out of *Tough Guy Writers of the Thirties*. The list of possible subjects which I sent around to prospective contributors proposed an essay on the relation between proletarian and tough guy fiction. I did not expect it to arouse much interest. But about half the critics contacted were eager to write on the subject. This indicated a need for a separate volume reassessing proletarian literature and its contribution to the American imagination.

After a close examination of one novelist, we return to a more general approach with two essays. Touching on numerous novels, Marcus Klein examines the conflict between the literature of revolt and literary modernism, a literary revolution that had reached its fullest expression by the end of the Twenties but still vigorously exerted its influence in the Thirties. The Thirties was a time of literary displacement as well as social; more children of immigrants than native Americans responded to *both* situations. The social impulse behind radical writing was "generally not so abstract nor so dogmatic a matter as has been often supposed." Few of the writers were confirmed Marxists, fewer still were communists, and they shared with nonproletarians many techniques, subjects, themes, and attitudes. Klein also deals with problems of aesthetics which arose in this situation. Then, Chester Eisinger "deals with various literary strategies used in the treatment of the individual or the self by authors writing during the Thirties and early Forties in the general ambience of Marxism." Thus he too looks at writers programmatically committed and those who unconsciously augmented the impact of the radical point of view. Eisinger's *Fiction of the Forties* (1963) examines the writers of the ensuing decade who, dissatisfied with the ideologies of the Thirties and the fictional depiction of the collective experience, explored the inner self. But, he feels, even the search for self reflects social history. In his essay, also, he examines some of the novels that thrust the radical imagination into the Forties: Albert Maltz's *The Underground Stream*, Richard Wright's *Native Son*, and Ira Wolfert's *Tucker's People*. He contends that it was their failure to read Marx deeply enough that caused most of the writers to explore and define individual character inadequately.

Frederick J. Hoffman focusses more sharply than either Klein or Eisinger on "the aesthetics of the proletarian novel." It has been our answers to questions of aesthetics that have accounted for the general refusal to accept proletarian novels as enduring literature. Aesthetics doesn't satisfy the urgent needs of the moment; it is peripheral to the waging of a revolution; but it is the life of art that survives the death of events and causes. Hoffman elaborates upon some of the definitions of the proletarian novel and upon the four basic categories presented in Rideout's book: strike novels, bottom-dog novels, novels of middle-class decay, and conversion novels. He stresses, as do several other contributors, the mysterious springs of many of these novels, for they "resist the confinement of an ideological source and explanation."

Proletarian literature—imaginative, journalistic, critical—is instructive more for the paradoxes between the lines than for its obvious intentions. While it does reproach us for having failed, beyond the false and misleading solution of war prosperity, to solve the problems left unfinished in the Thirties, it also raises questions about the nature of art. Proletarian literature is a colossal demonstration of the subject matter fallacy. Submissive to the tyranny of fascinating, significant, and immediately relevant raw material, one can only record, and if, as in the case of proletarian literature, one interprets, one can do so only in terms of a ready-made formula. Ironically, the subjects themselves, the workers, didn't read these books; and few workers wrote about other workers. Is it only intellectuals who love to read about themselves (*Herzog*), while readers in general are more interested in stereotypical projections of wishful images of themselves? Caught in an economic crisis, did the American worker think of his status as anything but temporary? Did he conceive of his identity in terms such as "exploited worker"? Didn't he think that in the American realm of the possible he would soon advance? Dos Passos went beyond this subject matter fallacy; *U.S.A.* is an aesthetic achievement because a conceptual organization focusses his raw material and his narrative and technical virtuosity. But while my own interest in literature, as a writer and a critic, is aesthetically biased, I am, for historical, social, and special aesthetic reasons, interested in and fascinated by the phenomenon of proletarian literature.

Following the general approaches of Klein, Eisinger, and Hoffman, two essays focus on Marxist critics. Thus far, most of the essays refer, at least, to Michael Gold as a critic and as author of an autobiographical quasi-novel, *Jews Without Money*. Neither Rideout nor any of the contributors to this volume besides Lee Baxandall mentions Louis Fraina (Lewis Corey); Aaron refers to him in passing. Baxandall, then, introduces Fraina to his own generation as one of the earliest and best of the Marxist theorists of the arts. Going back to Fraina's early essays in 1910, Baxandall offers a broad historical perspective as he reviews Fraina's aesthetic thought, "noticing in particular what it reveals about our 'proletarian' literature and criticism in the Thirties, which he held in low esteem." He notes Fraina's "capacity for historical and balanced perspective on the creative, erratic process whereby a society produces the emotions and theories it needs to develop." As a young leftist of the present generation, Baxandall discovers that Fraina's "method and values transcend their period of origin and still are of great pertinence and interest today"; but his is a balanced estimation, for he sees faults in Fraina's later perspective on liberalism in America. Not a great deal has been written on Michael Gold either. An authority on Gold, Michael Folsom is another young leftist who is evaluating the past as it lives on in himself. "The Education of Michael Gold" is an account, in a sense, of Folsom's own education, for he is still struggling to come to grips with this man, what he represented and continues to mean to us. Folsom, who closes with words from Stokely Carmichael, relates Gold to the present-day radical movement.

"No account of writing in the thirties," says Josephine Herbst, "should be without" the poets in the movement. Allen Guttmann begins a necessary process of reassessment in his essay "The Brief Embattled Course of Proletarian Poetry" by looking at Edwin Rolfe, Alfred Hayes, Isador Schneider, Kenneth Patchen, Kenneth Fearing, Joseph Kalar, Horace Gregory, Muriel Rukeyser, Joy Davidman, Herman Spector, and Sol Funaroff. Though his own investigation reveals that these poets failed to revolutionize poetic form and "the consciousness of their generation," there are enough "moments of authentic poetic" vision to justify a revival of interest.

We have been able to explore only a few of the possibilities posed by this area of study. Aside from Rideout's perceptive but brief commentaries, no recent work has been done on such writers as Edward Newhouse, *You Can't Sleep Here*; Grace Lumpkin, *To Make My Bread*; Tom Kroner, *Waiting for Nothing*; Maxwell Bodenheim, the bohemian socialist, *Run, Sheep, Run*; Agnes Smedley, *Daughters of Earth*; Thomas Bell, *All Brides Are Beautiful*; Fielding Burke, *A Stone Came Rolling*; Langston Hughes, *Not Without Laughter*; Myra Page, *The Gathering Storm*; Wellington Roe, *The Tree Falls South*; Arnold B. Armstrong, *Parched Earth*; Catherine Brody, *Nobody Starves*, as well as others alluded to in this volume. In "The Boys in the Back Room," Edmund Wilson suggests that Hans Otto Storm (*Made in USA*, *Pity the Tyrant*) is a radical writer worthy of study. Miss Herbst herself was tempted to write about *Morning, Noon and Night*, *Out of the Dust*, and *Hoax*, a trilogy by Philip Stevenson (Lars Lawrence).

In addition to the important books and essays on proletarian literature mentioned in this volume and in Rideout's, Aaron's, and Swados' books, the following should be noted (they, also, offer valuable bibliographies).

Leo Gurko, *The Angry Decade* (Dodd, Mead, 1947).

Henry Morton Robinson, *Fantastic Interim* (Harcourt, Brace, 1943).

Frederick Lewis Allen, *Since Yesterday* (Bantam, 1965).

Frank Brookhouser, ed., *These Were Our Years* (Doubleday, 1959). A different view of both Twenties and
Thirties, a kind of *Since Yesterday* by many hands, few
of whom have the slightest tinge of red.

Herbert J. Muller, *Modern Fiction: A Study of Values*
(McGraw-Hill, 1937). Chapter xii, "Naturalism in
America: Dreiser; Proletarian Fiction."

Halford E. Luccock, *American Mirror: Social, Ethical and
Religious Aspects of American Literature, 1930–40* (Mac-
millan, 1941). Excellent commentaries on novels, plays,
poems, movies, and popular literature of the time.

Leon Howard, *Literature and the American Tradition*
(Doubleday, 1960). Chapter x, "Power and the Past,"
surveys novels, plays, poetry.

John M. Bradbury, *Renaissance in the South: A Critical
History of the Literature, 1920–1960* (University of
North Carolina, 1963). Chapter 4, "New Social Real-
ism."

Warren French, ed., *The Thirties: Fiction, Poetry, Drama*
(Everett Edwards, 1967).

Recently, memoirs, reflections, autobiographies dealing
with the Thirties have appeared: Alfred Kazin, *Starting
Out in the Thirties*; Granville Hicks, *Part of the Truth*;
Irving Howe, *Steady Work*. Part of Josephine Herbst's
memoirs will appear in *North American Review*; part of
Malcolm Cowley's reflections appeared in *The Kenyon
Review*; Jack Conroy has returned to his hometown, Mo-
berly, Missouri, to write his autobiography.

A "seeing is believing" motif pervades several books
which offered a photo-text approach to the life of the
Thirties: *You Have Seen Their Faces* by Margaret Bourke
White and her husband Erskine Caldwell; *An American
Exodus* by Dorothea Lange and Paul L. Taylor; *Let Us
Now Praise Famous Men* by Walker Evans and James
Agee; *Hello, Towns* and *Home Town* by Sherwood An-
derson; *The Inhabitants* by Wright Morris. James D.
Horan's *The Desperate Years* (Crown, 1962) is worth
looking at, too. There were notable attempts to present
the authentic voices of the people, also: *These Are Our
Lives*: "As told by the people and written by members of

the Federal Writers' Project of the Works Progress Administration in North Carolina, Tennessee, and Georgia" (University of North Carolina Press, 1939).

Many movies depicted the troubles of the middle class, somewhat sentimentally, and the plight of workers during the Depression. See John Howard Lawson's *Film: The Creative Process* (Hill and Wang, 1964); Lewis Jacobs' *Rise of the American Film* (Harcourt, Brace, 1939); and Richard Dyer MacCann's *Film and Society* (Scribners', 1964). The following documentary movies are recommended: Pare Lorenz's *The River* (1937) and *The Plow That Broke the Plains* (1936), Robert Flaherty's *The Land* (1942), Joris Ivens' *Power and the Land* (1940), John Ferno's *And So They Live* (1940), and Willard Van Dyke's *Valley Town* (1940).

Though O'Neill's plays dealt with the past, several other plays reflected the times: Elmer Rice's *Judgment Day* and *We, The People*; Sidney Kingsley's *Dead End* and *Ten Million Ghosts*; Maxwell Anderson's *Winterset*; Robert Sherwood's *The Petrified Forest*; Clifford Odets' *Waiting for Lefty*; Lillian Hellman's *Days to Come*; Irwin Shaw's *Bury the Dead*; S. N. Behrman's *End of Summer* and *No Time for Comedy*; Marc Blitzstein's musical *The Cradle Will Rock* and the International Ladies' Garment Workers' production of *Pins and Needles*. The programs of the Group Theater and of the Theater Union, as well as the Federal Theater's "living newspaper" productions, were exciting. For a discussion of the plays of the Thirties see Eleanor Flexnor's *The American Playwright, 1928–1938* (Simon and Schuster, 1938) and Gerald Weales' "Popular Theatre of the Thirties" (*Tulane Drama Review*, Summer, 1967).

One hesitates only briefly to suggest that we look at the realistic paintings of Reginald Marsh, John Sloan, Edward Hopper, Thomas Hart Benton, Grant Wood, John Stuart Curry, and one hesitates a little longer to suggest that we listen to the popular music of the Thirties to discern parallels to the sentiments of proletarian literature.

"Art is a weapon," Conroy said recently, looking back-

ward, "and the leftist writers of the 30's knew who their
enemy was—Capitalism." Though he now thinks this attitude is ludicrous, he feels that the writers of the Sixties fail
to measure up to those in the Thirties. "Where are the
heroes now? Who, what and where are the enemy?"
While heroes may be lacking today, enemies are numerous enough. We are experiencing protest marches, sit ins,
boycotts, demonstrations, teach ins, read ins, on campuses
and in the streets, *for* civil rights and *against* the Vietnam
war and capital punishment—without the impetus of a
major economic collapse or the cohesion of an ideology as
specific as Marxism in the Thirties. Many Negro plays, a
few political satires, such as *MacBird*, and a few social
satires off-off-Broadway, a few movies, but not many novels, exhibit a new radicalism. The novel isn't needed; mass
media news coverage is too accessible. Protest is copy.
Radicals were wrong in the Thirties about the power of
the novel to move men to action. Today all artistic forms
can be used freely; but through them, now as then, the
vocal, literate minority does not reach far beyond the
circle of the already convinced.

When the New Deal came in, Conroy saw no necessity
for violent revolution and dropped out of the leftist movement. But radical youth today doesn't believe in New
Deals, New Frontiers, Great Societies—only in visible and
loud collective dissent. If the proletarian novels of the
Thirties failed, as Eisinger points out, to develop character
in depth, many in the protest movement today seem even
less interested in individual character. And again, it is not
lower-class but middle-class youth who are involved, children of those who survived the Depression and prospered
through the war. It is they who keep alive the past on
more superficial levels also—in folk and protest songs of
the Thirties, pop art, camp revivals of movies, even radio.
They have the basic necessities, the fundamental dignity
of work and much more, and they want others to have it,
and beyond that a more profound dignity. "I would be
subversive today if I knew how," says Josephine Herbst,
"only not along the same lines, of course. I think basic

flaws are at stake today and can't just be patched up, and it does me good to read what some of the college kids are saying. They see it very clearly."

The radical movement today appears even more complex than it was in the Thirties. Now, as then, intellectuals associate themselves more with fashionable, sensational causes, less with those which don't make hot headlines. *Then*, the "mystique of the proletariat and a perfect Soviet state," as Swados observes in his splendid introduction, awed writers. And now, as then, there exists a kind of moral and psychological blackmail. All one's artistic and intellectual friends in various publications and one's colleagues in universities conform to the liberal line, so one moves along, just a little more committed than one genuinely is. Aren't writers just naturally drawn to a raw material that dramatically, daily, calls attention to itself? To some extent art, on whatever level, is the result of a pure impulse to imitate; thus, writers wrote about the working class not just out of conviction but simply because it was there; that even Conroy had literary aspirations apart from his earned convictions is seen in the pseudo-literary style that Larsen observes in *The Disinherited*. And, as Swados points out, the hack mentality as well was drawn to the dramatic subject matter and, even while working in Hollywood, some of these men persisted in their allegiance long after other, more serious writers had broken with the party. While many poets today deeply believe in the causes to which they lend their support, some also merely gravitate, respond to a kind of magnetic force; having read their poetry aloud to groups on campuses, they now see in the protest movement a chance to be visible and vocal in a massive way; the temptation is in some part nonpolitical, the response opportunistic. The complexity of motivations staggers the imagination. Perhaps a closer look at the Thirties, that seemingly simpler era, will steady the imagination in its task.

It is hoped that the student of proletarian literature will find in these fifteen essays a variety of fresh perspectives on familiar material. If this volume stimulates a desire to re-experience this literature, it will have served another of its purposes. The essay collection approach enables the reader to place his own intelligence and sensibilities at the center and to shape his own vision. For men and women of the present generation, this book makes possible an act of discovery. By seeing their points of similarity (which will prove to be many) with the generation of the Thirties, they may perhaps feel robbed of that sense of uniqueness every generation craves, but they may at the same time feel that sense of continuity in the American experience which it is always our obligation, and perhaps our privilege, to discover.

For financial assistance in the preparation of this book and for allowing me time to work on it, I wish to thank Edgar Whan and Arvin Wells of Ohio University and Robert Daniel and Bruce Haywood of Kenyon College. My wife Robbie, Margaret Myers, and Lorraine Howard lightened my burdens in the preparation of the manuscript. For their encouragement, suggestions, advice, I wish to thank George Lanning, Robie Macauley, Harvey Swados, Richard Kostelanetz, Robert F. Hough, James Gilbert, Harvey Curtis Webster, Norman Springer, Paul Romaine, Michael Weaver, Kenneth W. Porter, John S. Bowman, Edwin Bruell, Daniel Aaron, Walter B. Rideout, Alfred Kazin, Russell Ames, Jack Conroy, William Arnold, Jonathan Baumbach, Gerald Weales, Mark Schorer, Wayne C. Booth, Frederick I. Carpenter, Maurice Beebe, Malcolm Cowley, Frank L. Hoskins, James Korges, Granville Hicks, Frederick R. Karl, Harry Levin, Harvey Swados, Norman Mailer, and especially Josephine Herbst. I wish to thank Gerald Green and *The Kenyon Review* for permission to reprint "Back to Bigger;" Indiana University Press for selections from Kenneth Fearing's poems in *New and Selected Poems*; International Publishers, Inc. for lines from *The Spider and the Clock* and *Proletarian Literature in the U. S.*; Mary Rolfe for selections from "Asbestos" in *We Gather Strength*, "Credo" and "To My Contemporaries" in *To My Contemporaries*, "City of Anguish," "Survival is the Essence," "Elegia," and "First Love" in *First Love & Other Poems*; for lines from Kenneth Patchen's *First Will and Testament*, copyright 1939 by New Directions, reprinted by permission of New Directions Publishing Corporation; and Monica Mc-Call, Inc. for selections from "City of Monuments" in *Theory of Flight* © 1955 Muriel Rukeyser.

Athens, Ohio   DAVID MADDEN
April 17, 1967

Proletarian Writers of the Thirties

The Two Memories

Reflections on Writers and Writing in the Thirties

LESLIE   FIEDLER

TO THINK ABOUT the Thirties in the second half of the Sixties seems not a luxury but a necessity: not one of those acts of reminiscence and nostalgia which are optional, the self-indulgence of a baffled critic, looking, perhaps, for his own lapsed youth (though surely there is something of that in me), but the kind of return to roots and sources so often required for cultural renewal; the re-examination of a past never quite understood — out of an awareness that unless we understand it now we will not understand the present or our own surviving selves. We have barely left behind a decade or so spent in re-evoking and re-evaluating the Twenties, reaching back to the years just after World War I in search of a clue to our identity in the post-World War II years; and our own times have been altered as well as illuminated by that search. We have exhumed the Charleston, as well as certain dress styles and hairdos; we have redeemed the fading figure of F. Scott Fitzgerald and revived for a little while memories of Leopold and Loeb; we have even created a magnificent pastiche of the period (its legendary slayings and weary old jokes) in *Some Like It Hot*. And it is the myth of that period, if not the actual fact, which helped make possible a New Jazz Age, a revival of Bohemian Life, complete with Pop Art and what we have agreed recently to call

Camp, plus a new sort of Romanticism, utterly without side or solemnity, despite its celebration of feeling over form, and pleasure over piety.

But our hunger for the Twenties seems satiated for the moment, as the old-fashioned Beat become the newfangled Hip, and our fantasies demand to be fed with myths of quite another past, for which we ransack the Thirties—surrendering nothing, let it be said quickly, of what we have redeemed from the Twenties, only seeking to add something other, something more. The way in has been primarily literary so far: a series of studies and reminiscences to begin with—ranging from academic examinations of the past as something dead and therefore fair game for Ph.D. dissertations (Walter Rideout's *The Radical Novel*, for instance, and Daniel Aaron's *Writers on the Left*, as well as Allen Guttmann's *The Wound in the Heart*) to more journalistic accounts like Murray Kempton's *Part of Our Time*, or personal memoirs like those of Mary McCarthy and Dwight MacDonald and, most recently, Alfred Kazin's account of "making it" in those bleak years. When the New Establishment remembers its origins (and to become established has always meant to feel obliged to remember) it recalls the Thirties.

Even more striking have been the revivals and reprintings of the books which those Establishment figures enjoyed as underground literature in their youth—*not*, be it noticed, those writers whom the official taste of the period itself preferred, Dos Passos, say, or James T. Farrell or even John Steinbeck, despite his almost posthumous Nobel Prize. We tend to agree with the Twenties in their adulation of Fitzgerald—grant, in effect, that they understood themselves, or at least chose to celebrate in themselves what we can share; but we correct the Thirties even as we revive them—instruct them retrospectively about their own meaning. And we are embarrassed to find European opinion, as expressed by the Nobel Prize Committee, trapped still in the established taste of that much-confused era.

No, it is certain relatively neglected writers of the

Depression decade who appeal to us, constitute our mythical Thirties—judging at least by what the critics of our age have bullied the paperback publishers into making available once more: Henry Roth's belated best seller, *Call It Sleep*; the three comic novels of Daniel Fuchs, *Summer in Williamsburg*, *Homage to Blenholt*, and *Low Company*; James Agee's *Let Us Now Praise Famous Men*; and especially, of course, the almost lost novels of Nathanael West, *Miss Lonelyhearts* and *Day of the Locust*, in particular, but even his first half-botched piece of Surrealism, *The Dream Life of Balso Snell*—and, *especially* for the cognoscenti, those real hungerers for the Thirties, *A Cool Million: or the Dismantling of Lemuel Pitkin*. Latterly, even such indifferent efforts as Tess Slesinger's *The Unpossessed* have been put back into print, and even such egregiously though typically bad prose of the period as Mike Gold's *Jews Without Money* or such correspondingly atrocious poetry as Eli Siegel's "Hot Afternoons Have Been in Montana." Surely there is a certain amount of campy condescension involved in the final two revivals, as well as a certain amount of canniness on the part of publishers to whom it has come through at last: the Thirties are in! But there is a kind of vague sense, too, like that which drives the sick dog to consume whatever weeds are nearest by, that the literature of the Thirties is good for what ails us.

All the books I have mentioned so far have been American books by urban Jewish Leftists and their fellow travelers, radicals at least of one or another persuasion; but even the works of Southern Agrarians begin to make it onto the supermarket and airport shelves (John Peale Bishop's *Act of Darkness* is about to be republished); and the books of certain European novelists who moved the Depression generation begin to appear again in the hands of the young. Not so long ago, a second edition (revised as Thirties books tend to be revised when they are reborn) of Silone's *Fontamara* was issued, and though it has, I fear, won few hearts it had not already won twenty-five years before, the retranslation of Céline's *Death on the Install-*

ment Plan which followed it seems to be moving our younger readers, as the original has already moved a new generation of readers in France.

Besides these revivals on the level of High Style, there have been humbler, more popular rediscoveries, too: sometimes in the form of adaptation, like the Clifford Odets' *Golden Boy*—in blackface, with Sammy Davis, Jr. in the title role, straddling the political pieties of two ages; sometimes in the form of remakes, like the long-promised new movie version of *Winterset*; but most often in the form simply of reruns, those twin bills (the very notion of the Double Feature itself a nostalgic revival) which bring back to the local theatre, say, Clark Gable and Greta Garbo, or W. C. Fields and Mae West; after which the real addicts can stagger on home to the Late, Late Show and watch *Grapes of Wrath* or *I Was a Fugitive from a Chain Gang*. One movie face in particular, however, has emerged from the scores called up out of the past, coming to represent the very essence of the period as we redream it: not, oddly enough, Paul Muni or John Garfield who belong to the age completely, but Humphrey Bogart who survived it into the Forties and Fifties, to the verge of our own era—keeping alive (we are now able to realize) the unshaven cheek and the stiff upper lip of the Depression face through a time when we thought we had forgotten it forever. But there it was all the while, awaiting the moment when we would be able really to see it again, whether worn by Sam Spade in Dashiell Hammett's *The Maltese Falcon*, or the last surviving prospector in *The Treasure of the Sierra Madre*, or Harry Morgan in Hemingway's sole true Thirties novel, *To Have and Have Not*—in which, for once, the quite un-Thirties face of Gary Cooper simply would not do for a Hemingway hero.

And with what astonishment we have lived to discover that face, grown magically young, to be sure, sported again in the Sixties by Jean-Paul Belmondo; with what delight learned that we, through Bogey, had been there first. But so, too, were we there first politically; and it is with similar astonishment and delight that we observe the young, on campuses and off, forging once more a Radical Youth Movement, which may be only an analogue of what went on in the Thirties rather than a belated offshoot. It hardly matters, however, since, whatever its roots, such a Movement makes possible the kind of dialogue with the past unavailable to those under twenty-five in the Forties and Fifties. To be sure, there are fundamental differences between their Movement and ours, but precisely this gives us something to talk about, since we are both aware of what divides us as well as of what we have in common—though they, perhaps, tend to be more conscious of the former, and we of the latter.

The Radicalism of the Sixties, like that of the Thirties, is influenced by the Bohemia which preceded it, and with which it remains uncomfortably entangled; and it differs from its earlier counterpart precisely as the one Bohemia differs from the other. The young radicals of the Thirties came out of a world of bootleg and bathtub gin, and the tail end of the first Freudian-Laurentian sexual revolution; the young radicals of the Sixties have emerged from the post-1955 world of "pot" and other hallucinogens, and that homosexual revolution so inextricably intertwined with the struggle for Civil Rights as well as the quest for "cool." Even in moments of violence, in those demonstrations so satisfactory to the young in any age (and not the young alone), those climaxes of mass action in which the students of the Sixties seem to be trying once more—though without full consciousness of the past—to achieve the delusory power felt by the half-million protestors against war on the campuses of the mid-Thirties, a new note of almost feminine passivity has entered. Everywhere the desire to *suffer* violence rather than to inflict it seems to possess a generation untouched by the dream of "hard Bolshevism" proper to a world that had not yet learned to detest Stalin and endure Khrushchev—the aspiration to remain innocent even in conflict by playing the role of the raped rather than the rapist, the Jew as opposed to the Cossack.

And more than this, the New Leftist seems oddly, per-

haps cripplingly, to *know* that he is indulging in a limited
and privileged kind of activity, like joining a fraternity or
playing on a team; that after four years or five, or six, he
will accommodate to the life around him, run for office, or
get a job, in any case, become more like his father than he
can really bear quite to acknowledge—unless he leaves
politics for drugs, abandons the SDS for LSD; but the real
politico cannot abide this way either. But whence, we are
driven to ask at this point, the odd passivity and the
strange (not cynical but ironic) self-knowledge? And part
of the answer lies surely in the Thirties and what they
have come to mean right now: in the particular way in
which the Thirties have survived for the activist young,
which is to say, in their vicarious memory of that period.

The young have a longer memory than their elders—or
even they themselves—are prepared to grant, a memory as
long as the imagined lives lived in the books they read; not
histories and memoirs and analyses by political scientists,
for these seem only dead records of the dead, but fiction
and poetry. And the books which have made the mind of
this generation turn out to be in large part the sort of
Thirties book I referred to earlier, the underground literature loved in their youth by that intermediate generation
of Saul Bellow, Norman Mailer, and James Baldwin, who
have also influenced them, since the time of growing up
which that intermediate generation remembers is indistinguishable from the nightmare visions of Nathanael West.
West is finally the key figure, at work still as a living
influence in the fiction of writers as young as Jeremy
Larner, whose Dell Prize novel, *Drive, He Said*, may have
a title derived from the poetry of Robert Creeley, but
whose vision comes from *Miss Lonelyhearts* and *Day of
the Locust*. But the world of West, we must never forget
for a moment, that "peculiar half-world," as he called it
himself, escaped all the clichés of politics, even of the
left-wing orthodoxy to which he himself subscribed.
Apocalyptics was his special province; and for the sake of a
vision of the End of Things, he was willing to sacrifice
what his Communist mentors had taught him was a true

picture of society. Once out of his books, he felt obliged to apologize for his vision (writing to Jack Conroy, for instance, "If I put into *The Day of the Locust* any of the sincere, honest people who work here and are making such a great, progressive fight . . . [he is talking about Hollywood] the whole fabric of the peculiar half-world which I attempted to create would be badly torn by them"); but once inside them, he remained utterly faithful to that vision, however alien it might be to the Stalinist's theoretical America.

No wonder it is even more alien to the version of the Thirties preserved in official histories, or tenderly recollected by the majority of those now over forty whose proudest boast is that they voted for Franklin Delano Roosevelt three times, or argued over with endless recriminations and counter-recriminations by the survivors of the New Deal. There are, mythologically speaking (and we are in the realm of myth whenever we talk about what survives not in the archives but in the heads of the young), *two* Thirties at least—two memories of that legendary era, not merely different but competing. And those who walk about possessed by one such set of memories find it difficult, almost impossible to communicate with those haunted by the other, or committed, for official reasons, to evoking and preserving it. I listened recently— at a ceremonial occasion presided over by political scientists—to the movie actor Edward G. Robinson (himself a survivor of the Thirties) not this time playing a gangster role, but reading the documents of *his* Thirties: F. D. R.'s First Inaugural Address, topical comments by Will Rogers, etc., etc. And what, I kept asking myself— feeling quite like Saint Augustine crying out, "What has Athens to do with Jerusalem!"—had any of this to do with *my* Thirties?

Yet Mr. Robinson's documents illustrated admirably a view of the Depression decade officially sponsored in the golden time of John F. Kennedy, by such court historians as Arthur Schlesinger, Jr.: a view which sees the Thirties as a period in which we moved from defeat to triumph—

conquering fear and poverty as well as preparing for a victory over the Nazis and Japanese—a time during which Labor came into its own, and the first decisive steps were taken toward the truly Good Society, i.e., the Welfare State. F. D. R. is the hero of this euphoric vision of our not-so-remote past, the crippled and charismatic Happy Warrior, flanked, perhaps, by Eleanor Roosevelt or Henry Wallace, or some favorite ghost writer, brain truster, trust buster, or whatever. But this vision is embodied in no distinguished work in prose or verse—only in the feeblest sort of pious-commercial plays, the sound tracks of propaganda films prepared by the Department of Agriculture, and the final panels of those wartime comic books showing Roosevelt grasping by the hand Captain America or Superman. Even the elegiac verse occasioned by his death has mercifully faded from the mind.

No, the truly distinguished literature of the time of F. D. R., the books of the period that are preserved in libraries, taught in classes, or—best of all—still passed from hand to hand, scarcely confesses the existence of the New Deal at all; and the figure of Roosevelt, when untypically evoked, signifies irrelevance or impotence, the meaningless world of somewhere else. We can find, if we look hard, an ironical reference or two to his ineffectual legislation in some of the proletarian novels so admired during the period itself: in Clara Weatherwax's *Marching! Marching!*, for instance, first and last winner of the *New Masses* prize for fiction, or in the sort of satirical verse published in that same magazine. Though occasionally, and especially during the early years of his first administration, the Left managed to whip up some public indignation toward Roosevelt, he did not even exist for them as he did for the contemporary extreme Right—as the mythological object of rabid hatred and fear, but only as a subject for condescension and offhand contempt.

Characteristically, *Americana* (an independent left-wing review with which Nathanael West was briefly associated) could manage to say in 1932 only: "As for Mr. Roosevelt personally, we consider him a weak and vacillating politician who will be an apt tool in the hands of his powerful backers." Years later, to be sure, Whittaker Chambers, a literary witness of the era (at least, the period itself had considered him "literary," since certain leading Soviet critics had said kind things about his three published stories; and his play *Can You Hear Their Voices?* produced and directed at Vassar by Hallie Flanagan, had shaken the whole Ivy League) had attributed a somewhat more virulent attitude to his *alter ego* Alger Hiss, reporting of the latter that "the same strange savagery cropped out in a conversation about Franklin Roosevelt." This comment he hastened to explain at some length, in terms oddly reminiscent of D. H. Lawrence's *Lady Chatterley's Lover*: "Hiss's contempt for Franklin Roosevelt as a dabbler in revolution who understood neither revolution or history was profound. It was the common view of Roosevelt among the Communists, which I shared with the rest. But Alger expressed it not only in political terms. He startled me, and deeply shocked my wife, by the obvious pleasure he took in the most simple and brutal references to the President's physical condition as a symbol of the middle-class breakdown." The implicit metaphor is clear enough: F. D. R. as Lady Chatterley's impotent husband, the C. P. as her prepotent lover, and the American working class as Constance herself.

Whether this was, in fact, Hiss's opinion scarcely matters (it is a question for the courts and the kind of journalist who loves correcting the courts, not for literary or social critics); it was, beyond doubt, a prevailing one in the Thirties among the Communists and those writers influenced by them. But this means among *most* writers of first-rate talent then functioning in the United States, including certain survivors of the Twenties, as well as young men just then rising to prominence, and even younger ones who would have to wait for the Forties and Fifties for recognition. The only considerable group of gifted artists who then operated completely outside the Communist sphere of influence, were the Southern Agrarians—who numbered in their ranks poets like John

Crowe Ransom and Allen Tate, novelists like Robert
Penn Warren, and who had issued at the very beginning
of the Thirties their own manifesto, *I'll Take My Stand*,
in which they had attempted to define a mythologically
resonant and intellectually respectable politics of the
Right. But F. D. R. in his anti-mythological Middle
seemed as alien to them as to the writers of the Left: an
irrelevant, faintly distasteful representative of the hated
and feared urban Northeast, who, after T.V.A., was revealed as the Enemy.

I have spoken of the poetic invisibility of Roosevelt so
far as if it were merely a historical datum to be researched
and recorded; but his mythological irrelevance, in fact,
belongs to a literary past with which our present is continuous, to which we still respond. The two most influential
literary journals of the Forties and Fifties, the training
ground of the writers who most move us now, or have, at
least, until only yesterday (all the way from Saul Bellow
to Marshall McLuhan, Karl Shapiro to John Berryman),
were *The Kenyon Review*, heir to *The Southern Review*,
and *The Partisan Review*. But *The Southern Review*
came into existence under the doubtful auspices of Huey
Long, redneck rabble rouser and fascist; while *The Partisan Review* was the by-product of the Communist-
sponsored John Reed Club in New York, and the imported notions of *agitprop* it had presumably been formed
to espouse. To be sure, by the time *The Kenyon Review*
itself was being published, the disillusion of the respectable Southern Right with their peasant allies
(fictionally recorded in Robert Penn Warren's *All the
King's Men*) had already occurred; and *The Partisan Review* moved quickly from Stalinist orthodoxy to Trotskyism and Cold War Liberalism. Eventually, in fact, the
two movements coalesced in academic amity, uniting to
form the School of Letters, in which another generation of
writers and intellectuals were trained. But in their most
effective years, both journals reflected the traditions of
radical dissent, Right and Left, out of which they had
been born.

There has been much idle discussion, pro and con, of

late about how "Red" the "Red Decade" really was; but as far as serious writers are concerned, there seems little doubt. In 1932, at any rate, more than fifty writers, among them the best known and most respected of their time, issued a statement called *Culture in Crisis*, in which they expressed their joint despair over the prospects of our society surviving its economic collapse, and pledged their support for the Communist presidential and vice-presidential candidates, Foster and Ford. Among the signers were Edmund Wilson, Sherwood Anderson, Lincoln Steffens, Langston Hughes, Erskine Caldwell, and John Dos Passos, who were later joined—in the American Writers' Congress, an organization which institutionalized the attitudes and positions of that first manifesto—by Edward Dahlberg, Katherine Anne Porter, Kenneth Burke, James T. Farrell, Dashiell Hammett, Richard Wright, Theodore Dreiser, and Ernest Hemingway. If we add to their number Henry Roth and Nathanael West, who were deep in the Movement from the start and needed no large public appeal to recruit them, it seems hard to think of anyone (with the exception always of the unreconstructed Southerners) not on the list whom one would expect to find included in a current college course on the literature of the Thirties. And we remember, finally, that a poll of a sample selected from the American Writers' Congress membership in 1936 showed still 36 voting for Earl Browder, six for Norman Thomas, only two for Franklin Roosevelt. How oddly skewed a result as compared with the voting behavior of the total electorate!

But what had moved the writers on the Left to make a commitment which cut them off from the mainstream of American life in so spectacular a way, pledging them at one and the same time to social action and disaffection from the strategies and techniques of action chosen by the overwhelming majority of their fellow citizens? If we look at the 1932 manifesto itself, we will find two quite distinct, though linked, motivations, both operative from the very beginning. The first is a particular brand of self-righteousness, an almost pharisaical smugness in being among the excluded, which seems an inevitable concomi-

tant of all American radicalism and the isolation such
radicalism implies in the United States: "Very well, we
strike hands with our true comrades. We claim our own
and we reject the disorder, the lunacy spawned by the
grabbers."

The second is a vision of disaster and a pleasuring in
it—a masochistic wish-fear that welcomes the End of
Days, the Pangs of the Messiah, the long-awaited Signs of
Doom precisely because they herald terror and annihilation. The writers of *Culture in Crisis* see the world
around them as "a house rotting away; the roof leaks, the
sills and rafters are crumbling"; but they thrill not to a
promise of renovation and renewal, rather to the hope of
pulling it down around them, of themselves disappearing
under the rubble. How ironically the Rooseveltian phrase
about having nothing to fear but fear itself rings in this
context, where fear seems the last passion; and how oddly
the appeal for hope built into F. D. R.'s speeches by
anti-apocalyptic ghost writers contrasts with the cher-
ishing of despair dear to the hearts of the doomsters. For
the American writer who signs his own name, terror has
been the staple of prose and verse ever since (if, indeed, it
was ever anything else, in this land where dissent has
always meant the rejection of all official optimisms), and
the one thing to fear above all else the failure of fear itself.

And what is present in the manifesto only by implication and nuance is spelled out, fleshed out in the explicit
images and fables of a hundred books that followed.
Straight autobiographical accounts of what it was like to
be alive and responding in this way to the America of the
Thirties are to be found in works like Malcolm Cowley's
Exile's Return and Edmund Wilson's *American Jit-
ters*—out of which not the outmoded rhetoric, but a single
realized image stays in my mind, Wilson's picture of the
just-opened Empire State Building in 1931, the tallest
American house of them all, and one born rotting away,

> the pile of stone, brick, nickel and steel, the shell of offices,
> shafts, windows and steps, that outmultiplies and outstacks
> them all—that, most purposeless and superfluous of all, is
> being advertised as a triumph in the hour when the planless

competitive society, the dehumanized urban community, of which it represents the culmination, is bankrupt. The big loft is absolutely empty, there is nothing to look at in it—with the exception of one decoration: . . . A large male figure is seen standing upright and fornicating, *Venere aversa*, with a stooping female figure, who has no arms but pendulous breasts. The man is exclaiming, "O, man!" Further along is a gigantic vagina with its name in four large letters under it.

And these books are still in print; *again* in print says it more precisely; yet the reader must be careful, for he will find them disconcertingly altered, bowdlerized, as it were, in Wilson's *American Earthquake* or Cowley's revised edition of *Exile's Return*. The author who survives an apocalypse that never comes, can scarcely believe he waited so breathlessly, so hopefully for the End—and tries to keep us from believing it three decades later.

Another kind of record is to be found in the so-called proletarian novels of the period, with their obsessive accounts of strike after strike defeated, defeated, *defeated* (it was Walter Rideout who first observed their distaste for victory in his acute study, *The Radical Novel in America*). If the events at Gastonia provide the plot for at least six novels of the era, beginning with Sherwood Anderson's *Beyond Desire* and culminating in poor Miss Weatherwax's *Marching! Marching!*, it is surely because their outcome was satisfactorily disastrous for labor—though the imagination of the time could tailor fact to suit its own needs, as in the case of the strike at Aberdeen, Washington, which actually ended in a triumph for the unions, but in each fictional case was revised into a defeat. It is one more instance of the discrepancies of the Two Memories: the history books assuring us that the Thirties were a period of immense gains for organized labor, the era of the Wagner Act and the creation of the C.I.O.; and the more poetic accounts seeing only bloody struggle inevitably debouching in defeat, failure, destruction, utter annihilation—this time in contempt of fact, though perhaps not of deeper truth.

Still, the manifestly proletarian books of the Depression

era are its least satisfactory achievements, perhaps in part because of our nagging sense that this is not *really* how things went, our realization that the trade unions succeeded, after all, and that (for us still who are children of that age, as well as for the age itself) nothing fails like success. Certainly, the great causes which moved the Thirties were *lost* causes: local miscarriages of justice, small or large, beginning with Sacco and Vanzetti and going on and on to a kind of climax in the Scottsboro boys. And what a shabby history of the exploitation of quite genuine misery for specious political ends it all seems from the vantage point of the present—compounded by our recent knowledge that the victims further victimized by their protectors may not even have been innocent to begin with—not even Sacco, not even Vanzetti. But mere facts matter little in such symbolic cases, tending finally to obscure their mythic significance.

So, too, with the war in Spain, that deep "wound in the heart" (the phrase is Camus', borrowed by Allen Guttmann for the title of a book about the literature created to express the pain born of the Loyalists' defeat): the war, which to those with memories like my own, made World War II seem when it came second-best, too-late, hopelessly impure. It was a war in which the New Deal, the pious Middle, refused—despite much soul searching—to become officially involved; the war in which Roosevelt forbade shipments of supplies to the forces fighting Hitler and Mussolini, but to which thousands of Americans (mostly Communists, largely Jews) went anyhow as volunteers, disowning both reality and their own country as they crossed the borders. But it was especially a war which captured the imagination of writers everywhere, a war which prompted even Hemingway to write four stories (chiefly bad), a play (utterly awful), and an ambitious novel (not quite good enough); and to make what must be the only public speech of his entire career.

Even more incredibly, it brought William Faulkner's signature to a petition, and—working at the deep level of his imagination where his old characters were being continually recast and furnished with new adventures, persuaded him to ship Linda Snopes off to drive an ambulance for the Loyalists. Yet what was for our best writers the chief event of the age—confirming their prescience of Doom—a cause incredibly pure (at least as mythicized) overwhelmed by the Fascists from without, and compromised hopelessly, even before the military defeat, by the maneuverings of the Soviet Union from within: this last, best, lost cause scarcely existed in the world of F. D. R. In James MacGregor Burns' thick and fascinating study of his character, *The Lion and the Fox,* for instance, the whole matter is given apologetic short shrift in three or four pages out of over five hundred: "Roosevelt from the start had favored the Loyalist cause. . . . Publicly, however, the President was adamantly neutral. . . . As the months passed Roosevelt felt increasingly distressed. . . . . There were arguments and forces on the other side. . . . But nothing happened. . . . To raise the embargo would mean the loss of every Catholic vote in the coming fall election, Roosevelt said." And anyhow he had other fish to fry, other causes closer to his heart. It was left to the poets to celebrate disaster, and if they sputtered away into sentimentalities over bombed children, who then had the *chutspah* to criticize, or the insight to point out that such images of desolation and impotence were precisely what the age demanded? Instead, they listened as Harold Rosenberg sang

> . . . All he knew of life was laughing and growing
> Till the iron dropped on him out of the sky.
> O gaunt horses of Hades
> He has not even one weapon
> With which to defend himself.

and Muriel Rukeyser answered antiphonally,

> Bomb-day's child will always be dumb,
> Cannon-day's child can never quite come,
> but the child that's born on Battle-day
> is blithe and bonny and rotted away.

And though they wept publicly, they thrilled a little, in private, too, at the notion of the rotting child. They did not know it was a Marquis de Sade they were all the time demanding, though they had one of their very own close at hand—since every revolution, failing inevitably at all of its ends but terror, produces a laureate of terror: the original Divine Marquis in 1789, Nathanael West in 1935.

West, too, is an expert in the indignities of children. Think, for instance, of the letter from "Desperate" to "Miss Lonelyhearts": "When I was a little girl it was not so bad because I got used to the kids on the block making fun of me, but now I would like to have boy friends like the other girls . . . but no boy will take me out because I was born without a nose—although I am a good dancer and have a nice shape . . . I have a big hole in the middle of my face that scares people even myself so I can't blame the boys." But West is not content with pathos, even when sanctified by a political cause; it is ultimate horror he is after, a kind of final terror which he attains not only in such full-fledged evocations of apocalypse as the often quoted ending of *Day of the Locust,* but more modestly and slyly, as in the "dismantling" scene of *A Cool Million,* rendered in cool idiot English imitating the style of Horatio Alger:

> At this both actors turned on Lem and beat him violently over the head and body with their rolled-up newspapers. Their object was to knock off his toupee or to knock out his teeth and eye. When they had accomplished one or all of these goals, they stopped clubbing him. Then Lem, whose part it was not to move while he was being hit, bent over and with sober dignity took from the box at his feet . . . whatever he needed to replace the things that had been knocked off or out.
>
> . . . For a final curtain, they brought out an enormous wooden mallet labeled "The Works" and with it completely demolished our hero. His toupee flew off, his eye and teeth popped out, and his wooden leg was knocked into the audience.
>
> At the sight of the wooden leg, the presence of which they had not even suspected, the spectators were convulsed

with joy. They laughed heartily until the curtain came down and for some time afterwards.

But West is a virtuoso of the macabre, after all, from whom we come to expect such effects as his stock-in-trade. What truly astonishes us is to find a sober-minded apologist for sweet reason and the status quo betrayed by the mood of the time into precisely such grotesque evocations of terror. Certainly, nobody on the Left in the Thirties thought of James Gould Cozzens as an ally, and surely no one now associates him (after a series of books pledged to redeeming himself from his temporary lapse) with deep despair, that ultimate *Angst* before the failed possibilities of our civilization—for which Communism once seemed to provide a handy set of formulations, if not a solution. Yet he wrote in the midst of the Depression a little book called *Castaway*, which caught perhaps better than any other single work (being untroubled by ideology) the mood of the times.

Cozzens' book is a modern Gothic novel set in a department store in a large American city, New York perhaps though we cannot be certain. Mr. Lecky, who is the sole character, remains as unsure as we throughout whether he is in Macy's or Gimbels or the May Company or Hell. It is functionally an island, at any rate, the place on which he wakes to find himself cast away, and he becomes, therefore, a new Robinson Crusoe—even discovering at one point the print of a bare foot in an aisle between two display counters. But Mr. Lecky is a Crusoe at the end rather than the beginning of the era of bourgeois free enterprise, a survivor rather than a founder of the Age of Individualism—a Crusoe lost and starving not in an unexplored desert, but in the very midst of a world of Things which he can no longer manipulate or control in his own interest. And when he finally finds (and kills!) the Man Friday, whose footprint has temporarily lifted up his heart, and whom he has pursued as much in fear as in hope, it turns out to be only himself, his own terrifying reflection in the glass.

Mr. Lecky beheld its familiar strangeness—not like a stranger's face, and yet it was no friend's face, nor the face of anyone he had ever met. What this could mean held him, he bent closer, questioning in the gloom; and suddenly his hand let go the watch, for Mr. Lecky knew why he had never seen a man with this face. He knew who had been pursued and cruelly killed, who was now dead and would never climb more stairs. He knew why Mr. Lecky could never have for his own the stock of this great store.

But Mr. Lecky—which is to say those of us who came to consciousness in the Thirties—lived on, saved, perhaps, by that very same Roosevelt in whom we never succeeded in believing. Preserving capitalism, the New Deal also preserved us who had been predicting its death and our own. And the doom which befell us, quite as dark in its own way as our blackest vision, turned out to be the opposite of what we had foreseen. We have moved into the Affluent, the Great Society (so we are told, and so—in some sense—we cannot deny); and are assured daily that, Cozzens and the other melancholy writers of the Thirties notwithstanding, we can indeed have for our own "the stock of this great store." And though we may protest that, alas, we still do not know how to manipulate or control the things we inherit, we have been taught at least how to want and waste them; which means, in effect, that the End for which so many of us so passionately waited has not come, either with a bang or a whimper.

Perhaps this is why some of the writers most profoundly possessed by the mood of the period stuttered to silence when new possibilities demanded new responses for which they were not prepared. Henry Roth is the most striking example—the victim surely of personal problems we cannot pretend to know, but in part too, a casualty of the failed apocalypse. The rediscovery of the Thirties has apparently convinced him that he as well as his masterpiece might be reborn; and newspaper stories tell us that he has emerged from hiding and is off in Spain contemplating a second novel, about the fifteenth-century persecution of the Jews and Indians. And maybe he will find a new voice for the new age; though the examples of Dos Passos and Farrell, ghosts haunting their own bodies and their own later books, should give him pause.

Younger men than he, writers whose first efforts never quite appeared in the Thirties, have managed to be re-born—like Saul Bellow, for instance, with an abortive Thirties-type manuscript stored away for his biographers, or destroyed; and even Nelson Algren, who apparently rewrote his in the form of *A Walk on the Wild Side*. Others, like them approaching their fiftieth year or just leaving it behind, have more disconcertingly produced in the late Forties and Fifties crypto-Thirties works of art, of varying degrees of merit, Bernard Malamud's *The Assistant*, for example, and Arthur Miller's *Death of a Salesman*—in which a kind of secret nostalgia for the Depression underlies all more overt meanings.

Yet with what assurance and authority they move among us, these twice-born younger sons of the Thirties: successful authors now welcomed to the pages of *The New Yorker* or *Esquire* or *Playboy*, though at home still in the *Partisan Review*, where they began, and which has become quite as established as they; or, alternatively, successful professors of sociology or political science or American literature, their commitment to poetry and fiction abandoned with other childish things. And what would our universities, much less our magazines, be without them, these astonishing over-achievers, blessed with an extra quantum of energy, a demon-on-call left unemployed for awhile after the collapse of the politics of the Thirties?

But we at least among the twice-born who are writers still—or critics or teachers of writing—though we thrive in post-Depression America, and, in a certain sense, love our success, cannot love it wholeheartedly. We are still too deeply involved with the persistent memories and defeated expectations I have been trying thus far to define; and like first-century Christians after the failure of the Second Coming, are at our deepest core dead to this world—or convinced anyhow that it is dead to us. It is a hoax, *must* be a hoax (we tell ourselves just before falling asleep, or just after waking up), this depressingly ongoing world with its depressingly immense Gross National Product—all, all illusion. And even at broad noon, we feel ourselves in a kind of interior exile—a comfortable, invisible, but quite real sequestration in the midst of our fellows: profoundly disaffected from everything which our contemporaries with the Other Memory (it scarcely matters whether they be Republicans or Democrats, whether they bless F. D. R. or curse him) consider politics and social action.

For a little while, a vain faith in that eternal loser, Adlai Stevenson, seemed to take us back into the common political arena; and then John F. Kennedy (another loser from the start, though we did not know at first that we knew it) won the allegiance of many of us who had resisted the blandishments of the New Deal—perhaps largely because he created the illusion that if not he, at least his wife, or his wife's sister, read fiction and verse, *our* fiction and verse. But his death produced poetry quite as bad as that which mourned the Happy Warrior before him. And the exacerbation of the situation in Vietnam has completed the process which the intervention in Cuba began (I shall never forget the hippy pickets on that occasion carrying signs which read: *JACQUELINE, VOUS AVEZ PERDU VOS ARTISTES*). The Kennedy *détente* is over; and with what relief we artists and intellectuals—not only veterans of the Thirties but our successors as well—have relearned detachment from the great consensus, with what satisfaction settled down to hating L. B. J.

No one as yet has written a great anti-Vietnam poem (as no one, we recall sadly, ever wrote a great anti-Franco one), but those we have are considerably better at least than elegies to middle-of-the-road Presidents—for they draw on *our* memory of the Thirties, on a reserve of terror and hopeless protest transmitted via certain poems and books into the creative self-consciousness of the youngest poets and rebels amongst us. There have been a whole series of transitional figures who have tried to straddle the gap between the Thirties and the Sixties—Norman Mailer, for instance, whose belated flirtation with Trotskyism is recorded in his fascinating if unsuccessful novel, *Barbary Shore*.

Allen Ginsberg, however, is the figure who pre-eminently represents the link between right now and back then; and in a single remarkable poem called, of course, "America," becomes the living memory of our dying memory of the mythological Thirties. He included the poem in his first slim collection, *Howl*, a little book which raised a lot of hell, out of which there emerged finally a new life-style and a new metapolitics that has remained at the center of the cultural scene ever since. There is much that is quite new in "America," testimonies to drugs and fraternal greetings to Jack Kerouac, William Burroughs, and Neal Cassady, names just then beginning to be heard—but there are other names that need footnotes now, which one is tempted to weep composing: Scott Nearing (still alive and very old, an organic food nut these days, somewhere in New England), Israel Amter (does the *Freiheit* still go on, are there survivors still who read *Yiddish* and long for those pristine days?), Mother Bloor (dead, long dead—that wrinkled WASP who used to tie red bandanas around the necks of little Jewish Young Pioneers).

Almost from the start of the poem, we are aware that we are back with our unforgotten past, as the cry, "America when will you be angelic" becomes "When will you be worthy of your million Trotskyites?"; and suddenly the identification is made between "pot" now and Marx then,

America I feel sentimental about the Wobblies.
America I used to be a communist when I was a kid I'm not
  sorry.
I smoke marijuana every chance I get.
I sit in my house for days on end and stare at the roses in the
  closet.
When I go to Chinatown I get drunk and never get laid.

My mind is made up there is going to be trouble.
You should have seen me reading Marx. . . .

But we are not quite prepared, however, when the old ghosts of those endless protests and defeats begin to arise, the wraith of Ginsberg's mother at the very center of them all,

America free Tom Mooney
America save the Spanish Loyalists
America Sacco & Vanzetti must not die
America I am the Scottsboro boys.
America when I was seven momma took me to Communist Cell
    meetings they sold us garbanzos a handful per ticket
    a ticket costs a nickel and the speeches were free
    everybody was angelic and sentimental about the workers
    it was all so sincere you have no idea what a good thing
    the party was in 1835 Scott Nearing was a grand old man
    a real mensch Mother Bloor made me cry I once saw
    Israel Amter plain. Everybody must have been a spy.

Irony, of course, plays everywhere in the passage—irony directed not only outward at the smug vilifiers of the Movement, but inward at its own pretensions (the last lovely touch being that almost inadvertent "1835"); but there is pathos, too.

And the source of that pathos is more fully revealed in the title of Ginsberg's next volume, *Kaddish*, which is to say, the Mourner's Prayer of the Jews: the prayer of a surviving queer son for his dead mother and all she represented to him, Newark, Paterson, lost strikes, Communism, madness—that paranoia which is only the apocalyptic vision, the prescience of defeat lived in the darkness of a lonely head, rather than evoked on a printed page. But here is his litany:

O mother
farewell
with a long black shoe
farewell
with Communist Party and a broken stocking

*

with your sagging belly
with your fear of Hitler

*

with your belly of strikes and smokestacks
with your chin of Trotsky and the Spanish War
with your voice singing for the decaying overbroken workers
with your nose of bad lay with your nose of the smell
                        of the pickles of Newark
with your eyes
with your eyes of Russia

What, after all, could the (after all) good Jews who stood at the center of things in the Thirties have asked better than being thus remembered by their children, with pity and fear equal to their own, being thus turned into poems? To be sure, we had thought of ourselves in our blither moments as the fathers of a new society, in our darker ones as the last sons of the world. That we are remembered as Somebody's Mother is a final irony, but somehow a not unattractive one.

Back to Bigger

GERALD GREEN

BIGGER THOMAS has been haunting me lately. Every time the traditional novel gets podhoretzed or suffers another sontagging, old Bigger looms up. How clearly I see him—black, ugly, murderous, as vivid as he was a quarter of a century ago when Richard Wright created him. And he still has the power to scare me silly. Perhaps it is middle age, but the plain fact is that James Baldwin has never frightened me the slightest. When I read him I am moved by one fellow's special problems. When I read *Native Son*, the whole raging storm of black hate and white stupidity roars at me. I flinch, shiver, and sweat—and I *learn*. Moreover, I am marvelously entertained, which I still hold to be a function of the novel.

Recently I returned to *Native Son* and other social novels of the Thirties and Forties. Were they really any good? Are they worth reading today? Did the rush of history endow them with literary merits that were only temporary? Were they mere exercises in reporting or in amateur sociology? The question seemed worth answering, for we are told regularly that the traditional realistic novel is kaput. Two main lines of argument are advanced.

1] Novels have no right to be concerned with *meaning*. They should not interpret anything. The real world, real people, real problems are out. We must seek only *style*, preferably an exquisite style that stimulates our gonads, arouses the erotic. This is extra good when the concern is homosexual. One fairy is worth two union organizers,

three migrant workers, and a Negro radical. Descriptions
of furniture are okay also, if you're French.

2] The novel is a gone goose because high-type essay
journalism and even a lot of daily stuff (like television
documentaries) report the actual world far more accurately than the novelist can. In fact, a lot of modern
sociology also does the job better.

There are variations on these themes, and sometimes
they blur at the edges. There are advocates of despair and
chaos (heck, isn't that what life is, anyway?), ex-
Communists in headlong retreat from agents of Satan like
Medicare and the SEC; racial fakes who threaten to kill us
all; and the deep thinker who pronounces: *The concentration camps have made it impossible to write meaningful fiction any more.*

A failure of nerve? Not just of nerve, I think, but of
sense, intelligence, honesty, and whatever marginal obliga-
tions a writer has, apart from becoming rich, famous, and
a freeloader at George Plimpton's house.

Of argument one there isn't much to say except: How
about you folks going to your church and letting us go to
ours? These people are the John Birchers of American
letters. I can get more elasticity from my right-wing neighbors in Connecticut, the people who call FDR "Mad King
Franklin," than I can out of the Okay Critics. What
makes them think their erotic fantasies are so special?
We've all got our private lunacies, but why turn them into
public needs? Wasn't it a character in a Clifford Odets
play (or maybe in S. J. Perelman's parody of Odets) who
kept asking "What's so special in bed"?

The furniture-describers, who, I am told, "closely
argue" their cases, are something else again. I enjoyed a
recent issue of the *Paris Review* that devoted twenty pages
to detailed descriptions of the left-over food and assorted
junk on a writer's table, with line drawings. Pretty wild
stuff, but it suffered by comparison with a Sears Roebuck
catalogue. The catalogue has a more "plastic" style and
more "tactile" illustrations, to use a couple of Okay Ad-
jectives.

But is it true, as argument two contends, that high-level reporting, "in-depth" journalism—and maybe sociology—have robbed the novel of its function? I can only respond that nothing I have ever read on race has made me understand Negroes the way *Native Son* did in 1940, and the way it still does today. Babbitt told us more about the American middle class than David Riesman; Studs Lonigan more about the urban Irish than Glazer and Moynihan; Michael Gold more about poor Jews than the collected bound volumes of *Commentary*.

The journalists and sociologists are fine. They are chock-full of nourishing information. They can inform and educate us. But only rarely can they involve us emotionally, light up the dark corners, open our hearts and change our minds, offer us the living experience, the odors and tastes and sensations of—in the case of *Native Son*—being black. Nothing that happens in Watts or Harlem can ever be incomprehensible to us once we know Bigger Thomas.

Wright was not alone, although he was a pioneer in the field of race. The same year that *Native Son* was published, Meyer Levin's novel *Citizens* appeared. This fictionalized account of the Memorial Day massacre of steel strikers in Chicago is probably one of the most underrated and neglected of our social novels. Even in this age of Jimmy Hoffa and Bert Powers, it isn't at all dated. Levin, a trained reporter, approached his subject like a journalist. The book suffers somewhat from its flat, run-on style, and perhaps also from a rather wide-eyed belief in the innate goodness of working stiffs, but it remains a true and noble work. In dramatic form it lets us know—far better than any journalism—what it was to be swept up in the labor strife of the Thirties, what police corruption was like, what shady roles newspapers played, and, most important, what breathing, fallible, confused, put-upon human beings went through to try to make their lives more decent. Where is the nonfiction work on the great strikes of the Thirties that can enlighten readers the way *Citizens* does? The book demands nothing less than one's total involvement.

Let me expand on my case for the realistic novel as a source of information and understanding. Much labor reporting in the United States is of a very high order. A. H. Raskin of the *New York Times* has never written a sentence that I did not find lucid, pertinent, capable of teaching me. When I was associated with the *Today* television program at NBC, I often invited Mr. Raskin in. I was convinced that our mass audience never failed to benefit from exposure to his views. Mr. Raskin, however, is a reporter, not a novelist. He can supply us with one kind of important information, but a book like *Citizens* can give us the emotional richness that most reportage lacks. Why can't both kinds of writing exist side by side? Must we cancel out one because the Okay Critics like the other better?

As a realistic novelist, Levin showed a good deal more tolerance for other kinds of writing when he said, in an afterword to *Citizens,*

> I believe modern writers are impelled to this method by a sense that the inner human truths of motive and compulsion can be found by examining experiences of reality. By using only actual, attested events as materials, the writer reduces the possibility of arriving at false conclusions. It is not pretended that this method can universally serve, or that it is even a preferred literary approach. For the present work, to the present writer, it seemed the best method.

I've heard it argued that, while it was perfectly all right for Levin to write that kind of novel in the Thirties, nobody should bother today. Today, we can see Jimmy Hoffa interviewed by Brinkley, and the classy magazines—one a month it would seem—run articles titled "The Crisis of American Labor" or "Labor at the Crossroads."

But nobody told a young novelist named Alfred Kern—or, if anyone did, Kern ignored him. I have just read his *Made in USA* (1967), and I commend it to the Okay Critics and the Inside Magazines. It is a splendid book. Sharply written, original in plot and characterization, full of the nuances and specifics and argot of the union world, thoroughly entertaining, it is a realistic novel

—a social novel, if you will—in the honored tradition. With all due respect to *Harper's* and *Commentary* and the *Reporter* and the *Atlantic* (don't get me started on TV documentaries—I've written too many), Mr. Kern's tight narrative tells more about labor unions and the people who run them than any of their finely honed articles. What Alfred Kern possesses are the rare gifts of the novelist for dramatization, highlighting, selection, an ordering and arrangements of events and people—gifts forever denied to most journalists.

So uncomfortable were Mr. Kern's publishers with an old-fashioned novel of sense and meaning that they all but copped a plea on the dust jacket: "It is a traditional novel in its insistence on action and its exploration of human motives. But it is entirely contemporary in its setting, its pace and its psychological insight and its resolution." Come off it, Houghton Mifflin. *Made in USA* is a fine book. It is contemporary in the same way that the best writings of Steinbeck and Hemingway are contemporary. It is assuredly not contemporary in the way Beckett or Burroughs is. If Houghton Mifflin keeps up that kind of chatter, Mr. Kern will decide he is a very sensitive, special fellow and write a book full of exquisite, erotic images that go against the grain of his own sex. He might even start describing the bread crumbs on his kitchen table and make the *Paris Review*. I wonder how many Inside Magazines will get around to *Made in USA* and its marvelous steel town Polacks and Italians and Hunkies?

Well, back in the Thirties and Forties a lot of people wrote books on the order of *Made in USA*. Unfortunately, some began to sound alike. (At least three books were written about one strike in Gastonia, North Carolina.) But what I found in my journey back was a refreshing *variety* in the social novels of that era. My reading list ranged all the way from ham-fisted primitives like Jim Tully to polished stylists like Henry Roth; from quick-sketch artists like Michael Gold to painstaking chroniclers like Josephine Herbst. Are they still readable and rewarding? We don't stop reading Chekhov because there is no longer a decadent Russian aristocracy. Why spurn the early Steinbeck because the sons of the Okies are driving Cadillacs?

But perhaps we are growing up. *Jews Without Money* was recently reissued in paperbound. Like the earlier paperbound which I possess, this edition has excised (an error, the publisher says) Michael Gold's revolutionary exhortation at the end. This reads, in part:

> O Workers Revolution, you brought hope to me a
> lonely, suicidal boy. You are the true Messiah.
> You will destroy the East Side when you come, and
> build there a garden of the human spirit.
>
> O Revolution which forced me to think, to struggle
> and to live.
>
> O great Beginning!

Avon books, according to a review in the *Nation*, has apologized to readers for slicing Gold's threnody, and has promised a new edition. It embarrasses me to admit I never missed it. *Jews Without Money* is so forceful, so gripping, so potent in its message that it doesn't need the party line. I'm inclined to side with Michael Harrington, who says that Gold needn't have been a Communist to have written the book. After all, Socialists, some Democrats, a few Republicans, and even nonpolitical people are as capable of outrage as Marxists. The occasional references to the Revealed Faith in *Jews Without Money* are pretty weak alongside the vignettes. Gold's people, to paraphrase McLuhan, are the message. He doesn't need Marx. Here's the description of an impoverished young doctor.

> He was tall and stoop-shouldered. He stared into people's faces absent-mindedly until they were uncomfortable. . . . He popped in and out of places like a ghost, forgetting his umbrella, his hat, his watch. Once he even forgot his shoes. It was a confinement on a hot summer night. He had taken off his shoes while waiting for the labor pains. When the excitement was over he rushed away without his shoes.

Artless, headlong, sketched with lightning strokes, there is not a wrong note in *Jews Without Money*. Gold's people drag us willy-nilly into their lives. Dr. Isidore Solow moves me a good deal more than that schlemiel Herzog, worrying about whether his wife has upstaged him intellectually. Gold's "Gang of Little Yids" are far more exciting than Franny and Zooey. Why don't Salinger's characters stop that dormitory babble and join the Peace Corps?

Like Richard Nixon's Quakerism, Gold's Communism didn't seem to bother him too much—at least in *Jews Without Money*. But how about some others? Did party-lining weaken or strengthen their novels? In most cases, overdoses of Lenin were contraindicated. The works of that period which are today the heaviest going are those most injected with Marxism. Novels like Albert Halper's *Union Square*, or Josephine Johnson's *Jordanstown*, or Clara Weatherwax's *Marching! Marching!* are of this order. They tend to be predictable, over-simplified, and to conjure up images of old *Daily Worker* cartoons and those posters in fly-blown stores that read: COMMUNISM IS TWENTIETH CENTURY AMERICANISM. Moreover, all exhibit the fatal error of the left-wing revolutionary: faith unbounded in the inherent warm heart and good sense of the laboring man. This sort of innocence did old Trotsky in, and it will probably result in the withering away of Communism in Eastern Europe.

The better writers of the Thirties and Forties were not taken in; vagueness of political commitment is often in direct ratio to talent. Jack Conroy's "rediscovered" novel, *The Disinherited*, is singularly appealing in its honest depiction of itinerant laborers. His working stiffs are confused, stupid, jealous, selfish, sometimes brave, always believable. This story of a depression workman bumming from job to job is a minor classic, full of the sense of time and place. One flinches from the blast of the steel furnace, the stench of the rubber plant, the heat of a mid-western street. Daniel Aaron makes the point that the book is not at all characteristic of the so-called "proletarian" school.

(Michael Gold thought he'd found a real live working-class writer in Conroy; he was badly let down when he learned that Conroy had attended the University of Missouri.) Aaron calls the tone of the novel "bemused and wondering" rather than hortatory, and says that Conroy's absorption in his subject often makes him forget ideology. Perhaps that is why the book is so memorable.

A hilarious malfunctioning of the party line turns up in Nelson Algren's depression novel, *Somebody in Boots*. Algren has always had a galloping sense of humor, but in this book what a dirty trick he plays on the *apparat*! Algren uses epigraphs from Marx to head up sections of the novel. At the beginning of the final section, we read:

> In the place of the old bourgeois society, with its classes and class antagonisms, we shall have an association in which the free development of each is the condition for the free development of all.
> —The Communist Manifesto.

I have a feeling that if you asked Algren what this jargon had to do with *Somebody in Boots*, he would respond the way the late Ernie Byfield, patron of Chicago's Pump Room, did when Dave Garroway asked him what effect Byfield's flaming swords had on the steaks skewered on them. Byfield looked over his shoulder and whispered, *"Dave, we figure it don't hurt the meat too much."*

Marx's observations not only don't hurt Algren's brilliant novel too much, they are devoured by it. *Somebody in Boots* offers no balm to seekers of the revolution. It concerns a wandering, weak-willed, shiftless West Texas kid named Cass MacKay. We follow Cass through bouts of boozing, whoring, burglaries, arrests, and mayhem until, at the very end, a glimmer of awareness is about to touch him through a Negro named Dill, who begins to take him to "forums," in Washington Park. But when a glimpse of salvation appears, up turns Cass's old buddy of the road, Nubby O'Neill. O'Neill is surely one of Algren's mighty creations—a glib, brutal bigot, a troglodyte with a quick tongue. Nubby's notion of fun is ramming his

stumpy arm into Cass's mouth, and Cass is terrified of
him. The book ends with Cass deserting his Negro friend
in order to lick Nubby's boots and wallow in his gutter
philosophy: " 'Well, I'm tellin' you now, then, son, an' for
the last time: no real white man ever runs off from another to join up with some nigger. You got somethin' to
live down with me, son, before I can let you hold a gun of
mine again.' " So much for that glorious society in which
the free development of each will mean the free development of all. Nubby wins. Dill loses. Cass is a bum again.
But, then, Algren has always known how thin the ice is.
Not for him the noble workers standing up and yelling
"Strike!" He has known too many O'Neills. And who is to
say that today (in chinos and button-down shirts and
country club memberships) they will not kill us all with
their plea "Give us Joy, Bomb Hanoi"? But where is the
writer to tell us about them?

Algren's bright honesty also characterizes James T. Farrell. A return to the Lonigan books confirmed what I
knew in my youth. Farrell was too honest and too independent to swallow the party line. A *Note on Literary
Criticism* should not have surprised anyone who had met
Studs. And what a creation Studs was! When I was a
small boy in Long Beach, New York, I often wondered
why the aboriginal Irish, leaving church after Sunday
Mass, would shout at us: "Go Back to Hitler!" (To begin
with, it impressed me as illogical. Why should we go back
to Hitler if he wanted to kill us? Would we tell the Irish
to go back to the potato famine?) But I never really
understood why those red-headed, snub-nosed children
were impelled to scream at us. Later, I went through the
Studs Lonigan and the Danny O'Neill books, and I *knew*
why. No journalist could tell me. No sociologist could.
But Farrell did.

If you say to me that fiction has no business supplying
readers with this sort of answers, we can part right now.
But if we agree that the novel—at least, one *kind* of novel,
to be more tolerant than the pushers of pederasty and
inventories—can add to our knowledge, enrich us, endow

us with understanding and perceptions, then we must concede that the Algrens and the Wrights and the Levins have performed nobly.

The fashionable tendency to denigrate Steinbeck has always bothered me. *In Dubious Battle,* for instance, survives splendidly. I have read many good articles about migrant farm workers; I recall Murrow's documentary "Harvest of Shame." But nothing ever took me into the cruel and heartless world of the fruit picker and the deputy sheriff the way Steinbeck did. Here is one of his people describing how vigilantes wrecked the truck of Dakin, a man obsessed with property:

> A little way this side of town they ran over a bunch of nails, stopped to change a tire. Well, then a dozen men with guns jumped out and held them up. Well, six of them stand the guys up while they wreck Dakin's truck, smash the crank-case and set it on fire. Dakin stands there with a gun on him. He turns white and then he turns blue. Then he lets out a howl like a coyote and starts for 'em. They shoot him in the leg but they don't stop him. When he can't run anymore, he crawls for 'em, slavering around the mouth like a mad dog—just nuts, he went nuts. I guess he loved that truck better'n anything in the world. The guy that came back said it was awful, the way he crawled for 'em. Tried to bite 'em. He was snarling—like a mad dog. Dakin bit a cop on the hand and they had to stick a screw-driver back in his teeth to pry 'em loose.

Chaos? Despair? Terror? I cannot think of anything in Genet, Burroughs, or Beckett that fills me with more horror, makes me more aware of how close we are to barbarism. None of Beckett's human slugs can appall me the way Steinbeck can with the screw driver rammed into Dakin's teeth. But, the Okay Critics will say, that isn't the *business of a novel.* You see, what really matters is the generalized, overall, worldwide, eternal despair that is the very essence of our lives. Says who? Philip Toynbee recently addressed himself to this problem.

> I have never been able to understand why it is regarded as more reputable, less sentimental, more truthful to paint

everything in rose-madder. Why are sophisticated modern readers instantly sickened by the lying camouflage of reality's true hideousness, but not by a lying disfigurement of the joy and moral nobility which are found in *real human beings?* [*my italics*]

One of the reasons, Mr. Toynbee, is that most Inside Magazines and Okay Critics and Establishment Writers are frightened. They have neither the intellect nor the will to confront *real human beings*. But they are shrewd publicists. And, having recognized their inherent weaknesses and grown fascinated with their private fantasies, they are intent on foisting them on us as the Word. Joseph Wood Krutch, that venerable source of good sense, commented recently that the psychological aberrations of reputed "unhappy geniuses" merely make them unhappy—not geniuses.

Even a Neanderthaler like Jim Tully can induce a rare and believable terror, open our eyes to a kind of world that surely exists—one that we might never know about if it were not for Tully. Go back and read "Jungle Justice" in the collection *Shadows of Men*. In Tully's gnarled prose, we learn about the murder of a railroad detective named One-Lung Riley, scourge of the bindle stiffs, by a mob led by a certain Nitro Dugan. By the time Riley has been humiliated, shot, stripped, mutilated, and bound to a log for "the carp," we are sweating. Genet's pederasts, Burroughs' junkies, and all the minor scarecrows—Selby, Rechy, Schneck, LeRoi Jones—are schoolboys alongside old Tully. And he at least has the virtue of absolute honesty, of innocence. He is not at all concerned with promoting himself; he wants to tell you a story. He is concerned with *other* people.

Concern *with others*: on reflection, that is probably what distinguishes the good writers of the Thirties and Forties from today's Insiders. What better example than Henry Roth? Enough praise has already—deservedly —been afforded *Call It Sleep*. But I do wish some of the Establishment critics would stress the extent to which the power of the book derives from Roth's attention to specifics—to the noises and smells and sights of the East Side, to what people wore, ate, sounded like. Of course, Roth is not merely giving us photographic reportage. The debt his technique owes to another great observer of other people, Joyce, is unmistakable. At times David Schearl's interior monologues suggest a six-year-old Leopold Bloom:

> —On the windows how I go. Can see and ain't. Can see and ain't. And when I ain't where? In between them if I stopped, where? Ain't nobody. No place. Stand here then. BE nobody. Always. Nobody'd see. Nobody's know. Always. Always No. Carry—yes—carry a looking glass. Teenchy weenchy one, like in a pocket book, Mama's.

Walter Allen is partially correct in saying that Roth's people—unlike Studs—are "dominating figures" existing as "natural forces." Perhaps, as Allen contends, they are not "wholly conditioned by their economic and cultural circumstances." But they are vital because of Roth's complete mastery of his milieu, his attention to detail and nuance, and, above all, his absolute compassion. Unlike the fashionable terrorists, Roth never loses hope, even if salvation speaks to us through cracked lips. For whatever reasons he had, Roth stopped writing. But there is nothing of the quitter in *Call It Sleep*. Nowhere in this beautiful book is there an ounce of self-pity, of false pride, of self-promotion. Roth, in short, like the best of the writers of his time, reached *out*; today, the writer, to "make the scene," must grope inward—and no wonder so many of them are disgusted.

One of the pleasures of settling down with the literature of a time past is the joy of discovery. I had never come across any of Josephine Lawrence's books, and, since it is fashionable in a piece of this sort to make a "find," I claim Miss Lawrence's novel, *If I Have Four Apples*. Josephine Lawrence is a conservative. Her name does not appear in either Daniel Aaron's *Writers on the Left* or in Walter Rideout's *The Radical Novel in the United States*. Politics, social action have almost no place in Miss Lawrence's

work. She is an old-fashioned, no-nonsense American. Her
theme in *If I Have Four Apples* is the bottomless capacity
of the American lower middle class for self-deception. It is
a grand theme. The book is a minor masterpiece.

In many ways, though on a much simpler and more
direct plane, *If I Have Four Apples* anticipates *Death of a
Salesman*. We are introduced to the family of Penter Hoe,
shipping clerk in the town of Maxwell. The time is the
depression. Penter's salary has been cut to $50 a week. He
has three children. But he clings tenaciously to his house,
which costs him $75 a week exclusive of taxes, water, and
heating. Listen to Penter Hoe's litany—the eternal
doomed voice of *lumpen*-America: " 'I don't believe in
renting. A man with a family ought to own his own home.
Not be paying his good money to landlords. Soon as
things get a little better I'll have my pay cuts back and I
can swing it easy.' "

Penter's wife, Rose, refuses to serve cheap cuts of meat.
She has a kitchen full of appliances bought on credit, two
canaries, a pair of lovebirds, some goldfish. She would like
guppies. Her son Dallas, a lazy clod who can barely get
through high school, is determined to go to college and
marry a rich girl. Older daughter Darthula plans to marry
Neal Willis; she promptly blows their savings on a ba-
roque dining-room set. Younger daughter Sythia (those
Menckenesque names!), who has "bad skin, small eyes
and teeth that were out of line," dreams of becoming a
great dancer. Each member feeds on the others' decep-
tions, encourages them to evade reality. (Sometimes they
sound like a group of Establishment Insiders shilling for
one another's books.) Mrs. Hoe, delighted that Sythia has
set her cap for a rich man's son, an honor student, remarks, " 'As soon as Dallas gets to college, I expect he'll
be an honor student too.' " Dallas, at that moment, is in
bed puffing on cigarettes bought with money cadged from
his grandmother to "pay for a tutor."

Failure mounts on failure for the dream-ridden Hoes.
Dallas not only doesn't make college, he flunks high
school. He then decides he will win $10,000 in a name-

the-movie-star contest, and save everyone. He loses. The HOLC turns down Penter's application for a loan. Sythia freezes at her big concert and becomes a laughingstock.

But, finally, a smidgen of enlightenment touches the disaster-prone Hoes. Neal Willis, Darthula's fiancé (he is a treasure among depression characters: resilient, slangy, down-but-never-out), takes all three Hoe children to a union meeting. Dallas listens—apparently learning something—to a young radical who tells him " 'every man who earns wages is entitled to protection.' " Darthula settles back to hear the union organizer speak and wonders whether "maybe Dad had the wrong dope."

But Miss Lawrence, sensible lady, doesn't let her fish off the hook easily. It is by no means certain that the self-deceiving Hoes will learn much, or profit by what they learn. As the speaker talks about the right to organize, Darthula dreams of marrying Neal, who is now earning $46 a week as a milkman. She muses: "There's one thing I'm going to have and that's a baby grand. A piano gives tone to a room and perhaps when I get it paid I can take music lessons."

And the novel ends—a triumph of genre, of shrewdly observed folkways, of wonderfully realized scenes, of pathetic—but never sentimentalized—characters, a tribute to the American dream soured.

The Penter Hoes are still among us, but perhaps instead of material and artistic goals they are now seeking political power. I have seen Penter Hoe visiting an American Opinion Library and attending meetings where Nelson Rockefeller was cursed as an "International Socialist." Where is the young novelist who can record that chilling—and important—direction of American life in the manner in which Josephine Lawrence wrote about the depression?

How curious that none of our leading contemporary writers—most of whom incline leftward—has skirted the renascence of right-wing fanaticism in America. If they think we are dealing with a few cranks and nuts, let them study the amount of money pumped into extremist campaigns by willing millionaires. I suspect our novelists are frightened, burned. Unconsciously, they must reason thus: Stalin murdered Mandelshtam and Babel and lots of other people. And we once supported Stalin, so we are rats. Therefore, no politics at all, no social issues, no realism, nothing except ourselves, a good safe subject. Besides, liberals are poorer-spirited than Communists. One thinks with sadness of that giant of his time, Dos Passos, reduced to writing snide essays about Eleanor Roosevelt. Can he really draw satisfaction from such nonsense? Must he go on forever proving that he never was a liberal? We believe him by now.

Paralleling this massive bug-out is another circumstance that makes it hardly worth a writer's while to tackle race, or unions, or the right wing, or the crisis in medicine, or the American pursuit of pleasure, or the press, or organized religion, or the savagery of our youth, or anything else that is meaningful. To write about these things, a novelist must extend his mind and his heart beyond his own skin. He must do what Steinbeck did in *In Dubious Battle*, what Wright did in *Native Son*, what Josephine Lawrence did in *If I Have Four Apples*. But, alas, all occasions do inform against the writer who tries. The demand today, a demand conditioned by Okay Critics, Inside Magazines, and the Establishment, is for self-promotion, not involvement. Writers are both publicists and celebrities, client and advertising agency, sponsor and star. *They* matter, not anyone else, and certainly not all those people *out there*.

The saddest example of this fall from involvement to self-worship is Norman Mailer. I recently reread *The Naked and the Dead*. It is a monument. It makes other war fiction read like *The Boy Allies*. Walter Rideout correctly includes it in his list of the best novels of the Forties—a radical novel in direct line from Wright and Algren and Farrell. Good God, those people—Croft, Hearn, Goldstein, Polack! Even the best of the war reporters—Hersey, Tregaskis, Sherrod—couldn't make us know that war the way Mailer did. Did any of them dare to depict American GIs as sadists, bigots, cowards, jerks? Recently, Alfred Kazin wrote: "our faces are always turned toward the headlines, the television screens, the monster advertisements, the instant news that brings us simultaneous apprehensions of disaster, assassination, fallout, war. Many writers have put this into fiction only to recognize that they have duplicated the newspapers."

But need they duplicate the newspapers? Is there any war reportage, anywhere, that can rival *The Naked and the Dead*? Is it not conceivable that a writer tackling Vietnam might produce another novel on that high level —if the critics would let him?

There's no point in reviewing Mailer's descent from realistic novelist to publicity saint. The details are well-known, and the sight of this brilliant, talented man reduced to playing low comedy shill for William Buckley can only summon up visions of Grover Cleveland Alexander in Hubert's Museum.

An American Dream was inevitable—a hash of adolescent day-dreaming, a dirty Frank Merriwell. One gets the feeling that the book is Mailer's revenge on the Kennedys for not inviting him to the White House. Styron and Baldwin made it, why not him?

As dreadful as *An American Dream* is, Mailer almost got away with it. A few High Okay Critics, notably in England, where accent and syntax make do for sense, have decided it is a great achievement, a new art form. *Life* magazine discovered that Mailer is "one of us," just folks. He even likes Puerto Ricans. (Luckily, the *Life* Boswell explained that Mailer's Puerto Rican pal was José Torres, light-heavyweight boxing champion of the world. For a moment I was fearful Mailer only cultivated Puerto Ricans who were celebrities like himself.)

But, while we retreat, Bigger Thomas won't stay dead, and neither will Studs or Dr. Isidore Solow. The tradition is with us, and there *are* books being written today that are in that tradition. I would, however, qualify my judgment in this way: the stimulus for most realists of the Thirties and Forties was political, usually Marxist. The stimulus today is more generalized. The good novelists handling contemporary themes are usually men who write from direct experience with those themes, but this is rarely a Marxist-oriented experience. The best example I can think of is a "Catholic" writer like J. F. Powers. *Morte d'Urban* is surely a traditional novel—and a superb one. There is nothing political in it, but it is a revealing social document, telling us more about the problems of the priest in high-pressure America than any essay could. In the same way, Louis Auchincloss can take us into the realm of high finance and inherited wealth. Neither of these writers owes anything to the *radical* tradition, but each is surely in the tradition of the realistic, searching, social novel, the novel dealing with a broad aspect of society. These men know their subjects. They know how to engage our participation. They entertain.

And there are a few—precious few—good writers still willing to tackle the thematic novel. For instance, John Hersey's inquiring mind has produced a rewarding variety of books, ranging from *The Wall* (the Warsaw ghetto) to *The Child Buyer* (the plague of scientism) to *Too Far to Walk* (the surrender of college students). Less well-known, but equally courageous in his willingness to write about topical matters, is David Karp. Karp, a concise, spare writer, is always pertinent, always *engagé*. His novels deal with such themes as inquisitorial societies (*One*), revolt in colonial states (*Day of the Monkey*), stupidity in the suburbs (*Leave Me Alone*), and right-wing cabals (*All Honorable Men*). Karp is invariably overlooked in the Insiders' catalogue of bright young authors; obviously, any man so concerned with the real world is hopeless.

Or take a novel like *The Sand Pebbles*, the late Richard McKenna's work on China in the Twenties. Recently, I had to wade through thirty volumes on China to prepare a documentary script. Not one of them could give me as sharp an insight into why the revolution succeeded, into what spurred the Communists and why they rallied the support of ordinary Chinese as McKenna's novel did. It is a hard, pitiless book. It makes us see clearly why they hate us.

Traditionally, the novel has possessed this power. I

would suggest to anyone who wants to understand the Congo that he read *Heart of Darkness*. Conrad saw more than any journalist of his day could. (He saw a lot more than any of our modern hot-shots have been able to report.) Go back and read about Kurtz dying surrounded by the severed heads of rebellious blacks, and you will understand the massacres of 1965.

Surely, the City is one of the great themes of our time, but no Establishment writer would soil his image by daring to extend his skills beyond himself. In the last few years, however, two non-Establishment writers turned out excellent books on the subject. (Both are working journalists, which may explain why the Inside Magazines ignored them; who can get excited about two fellows who work for a living?) One book is James D. Horan's *The Seat of Power*, a study of high-level corruption in the numbers racket that suggests an earlier work, Ira Wolfert's *Tucker's People*. The other book, a study of the trials of an honest police official, is *The Commissioner* by Richard Daugherty. It is possibly the best American novel on police I have ever come across—authentic, funny, absorbing, and with cops and detectives who have the absolute ring of truth. Again, it is Mr. Daugherty's special knowledge that supplies the raw material, his skills as a writer—selection, dramatization, plotting—that create a work of art.

Two comic novelists—their work is anything but realistic—should be included here because of their talent for using the stuff of history, of actual events, to create memorable works. There is not a little of Algren's nutty humor in one of the men, Thomas Berger. Berger's books—*Crazy in Berlin, Reinhart in Love, Little Big Man*—are wild comedy, but they are not the facile, anything-goes surrealism of the black humorists. Neither are they satires, or polemics, or politically motivated gripes. They are funny in the way *Don Quixote* or Rabelais is funny—the laughter of a wise humanist, experiencing the world in all its absurdity: tolerant, pleased, saddened—and *involved*. The glory of *Little Big Man* lies in the way Berger imposes his comic view of life on a deadly accurate portrait of the Old West. I know from conversations with him that he researched the period as thoroughly as any historian, that his outlandish Cheyennes and their hilarious locutions are based on actual recorded testimony of Indian warriors. It is the truest kind of humor, a humor that derives from real situations and real people. Who can resist Berger's Cheyennes, who refer to themselves haughtily as "The Human Beings"? Or his description of the way an Indian camp smells? Or the Indians' disdain for time, schedules, anything continuous—a trait which causes them to hate the railroad?

John Barth's *The Sot-Weed Factor*, a breathtaking account of "poor beshitten Maryland," could only have been written by a scholar, a student of Colonial America, a man who had dug deeply and lovingly into archives, stacks, old journals, logs, and courthouse records. In short, the writer was required to extend his mind, to work beyond his own skin, to involve himself in the past in a way hardly fashionable now. (It was not until Stanley Edgar Hyman devoted a two-page review to *The Sot-Weed Factor* in *The New Leader* that a few Okay Critics latched onto it. There's still hope.)

There is the ring of truth, of transcendent satire, of bursting Elizabethan energy in the novel—as refreshing as a sea breeze off the Maryland shore. (That the breeze is often soiled is no matter; *The Sot-Weed Factor* is one of the most splendidly scatological works ever written. But it is scatology that is appropriate; it is not arbitrary or mean.) There are more loud laughs on one page of this joyful work than in all of *Candy*, that trick of Establishment promotion that is not dirty enough and not funny at all.

Both *The Sot-Weed Factor* and *Little Big Man*—and I make no apologies for sounding like the ultimate in squaredom—are books that enlarge our vision of the world, that enrich us as they entertain us. The purpose of art, Berenson said, was to enhance life. Not all of us can attain so noble a goal, but it is worth a try. Why are so few writers willing to attempt it? Is this fascination with one's own precious skin all that is left for us? Are the erotic imperatives of Insiders all that matter? Must we forever be told that literature must go the way of the homosexual writer-of-the-week and the French cataloguers? What a tumble from Richard Wright to LeRoi Jones! The difference between the new Insiders and the oldtimers is the difference between Sean O'Casey and Edward Albee. O'Casey had a heart. I have my doubts about Albee.

How brave of our select writers to keep telling the President to clear out of Vietnam! Maybe they are right. Maybe the world is going to hell in a basket, faster than any of us knows. But where were they when the lights went out? Let them look to their own books and their own critics and their magazines. If they have turned their backs on the world in favor of their lovable flesh, maybe the world has a right to turn its back on them.

John Dos Passos' U.S.A.
A 1930's Spectacular

LEO GURKO

THROUGH THE EARLY Thirties the work of Dos Passos and the work of the proletarian writers ran along the same track. They shared certain attitudes: distrust of big business, hostility to the capitalist system, sympathy for the oppressed worker and the "little man," contempt for money values, and a conviction that the individual, by himself, was helpless in the grip of society. Their novels displayed characters as class types and centered on the conflict between those selfishly devoted to their own interests and those dedicated to advancing the interests of others. Their morality leaned toward the simple ascription of wickedness to the haves and virtue to the have-nots. The principal dilemma of their novels was whether a particular figure would "sell out" to the interests or continue, at great sacrifice, to struggle for the better world.

The differences, however, were equally striking and became, by the end of the decade, overriding. Dos Passos was a pessimist. He had had his love affair with Soviet Russia and become disillusioned even before the depression began. He had begun *The 42nd Parallel*, volume one of *U.S.A.* (published in 1930), in 1927, and worked on a number of chapters while visiting Russia in the summer of 1928. Stalin's ice age, as he called it, had not yet set in, but the signs of it were already evident. "Writers of the world, unite! You have nothing to lose but your brains!" was the acrid slogan he subscribed upon returning. He was still attracted to Marxism, but was disturbed by the advancing menace of the dominant Stalinist variety. *The 42nd Parallel* was therefore saturated with a sense of hopelessness about the better world. If it came at all, it was not going to come about neatly through a simple uprising of the workers. This mood grew stronger in *Nineteen-Nineteen*, volume two of the trilogy, which appeared in 1932, and rose to a climax in volume three, *The Big Money* (1936).

The proletarian novelists were younger than Dos Passos. Few of them had had any firsthand view of Bolshevik society. They were almost entirely molded by the depression at home, and they, together with other sections of liberal-left America, were to have their love affair with Soviet Russia in the Thirties, an affair that came to its formal end with the Nazi-Soviet pact late in 1939. Their view of the future, even the immediate future, was the standard Marxist brand of excited optimism and expectancy, nourished by the general optimistic ambience of the New Deal. Where each of Dos Passos' three novels began at a high emotional pitch and gradually declined, the average proletarian novel ended on a rising note. Even some final disaster, generally a lost strike, was seen as preparing the way for a forthcoming breakthrough.

There was also a difference in aesthetic theory. The proletarians looked upon the novel as a tool for social reform. Jamesian preoccupations with fiction as an art form were so much decadent nonsense. Concern with aesthetics as such was empty, frivolous, or irrelevant. The proletarian writers did not as a rule go to the extreme of Zhdanov or Mao Tse-tung and regard the artist as a soldier of the revolution whose energies and thoughts were entirely at the service of the state, but they moved far enough in that direction to regard art for art's sake or D. H. Lawrence's "art for my sake" as degenerate slogans. Dos Passos, even at the height of his social consciousness, never equated art and propaganda, nor did he ever waver in his conviction that *his* writing should express *his* vision of things, not the state's, the party's, or the revolution's. One therefore finds in him an element singularly absent in the proletarians: a joy in style and technique, even in the display of technical fireworks, that is one of the vibrant aspects of *U.S.A.*

Still a third difference between them was their view of power. To the proletarians power was neither good nor evil; it was simply an instrument to be used for beneficent ends and to be kept away from those who would use it wrongly. Dos Passos regarded it as dangerous in itself. Power was an unavoidable fact of life and could not be eliminated. All the more reason for it to be controlled. The wise society would prevent an excessive concentration in the hands of any group, and would diffuse it instead over as wide a spectrum as possible. No group or class could be trusted with too much. Dos Passos' whole career as a novelist and historian has been devoted to the decentralization of power: to remove it from the hands of Big Business during the first thirty years of the century, from Big Government during the Thirties and Forties, from Big Labor in the Fifties and Sixties, and presumably Big anything else in the future, whether engineers, technocrats, political parties, or potential dictators. Even Dos Passos' involvement with Trotskyism in the Thirties can be read as an assault on Stalin's assumption of absolute power. The proletarian writers, whether they admired Stalin or not, could never accept the idea that unchecked power in the hands of the working class or the oppressed masses could prove corrupting or could lead to anything but a better world.

U.S.A., covering the years 1899–1929, is concerned with the first power group to confront Dos Passos as a writer, the great corporations—what Mr. Dooley called "the interests" and F. D. R. labelled "the economic royalists." But though central to the story, they are subordinate to Dos Passos' larger theme, the life process of the nation to which the title of the trilogy refers. As a work of fiction, *U.S.A.* illustrates the qualities of the country it takes as its theme: energy, ceaseless movement, dazzling techniques, admiration of quantity, and an irresistible tendency to subserve individuals to the social process. The trilogy is a metaphor for its subject. Few works have set up so close an intimacy between their form and substance.

At the outset, Uncle Tim, an apostate Irish Catholic printer in Chicago and a Socialist, announces an essential motif.

> "It ain't your fault and it ain't my fault . . . it's the fault of poverty, and poverty's the fault of the system. It's the fault of the system that don't give a man the fruit of his labor. . . . The only man that gets anything out of capitalism is a crook, an' he gets to be a millionaire in short order. . . . But an honest workin' man like John or muself we can work a hundred years and not leave enough to bury us decent with. And who gets the fruit of our labor, the goddam business men, agents, middlemen who never did a productive piece of work in their life. It's the system, John, it's the goddam lousy system."

Not a word here with which the proletarian writers would disagree. A few pages farther on, in the biographical sketch of Eugene Debs, one of the true saints in the author's American galaxy, Dos Passos introduces his counter-theme.

> Where were Gene Debs' brothers in nineteen eighteen when Woodrow Wilson had him locked up in Atlanta for speaking against war,
> Where were the locomotive firemen and engineers when they hustled him off to Atlanta Penitentiary?

The abandonment and betrayal of Debs by the workers whom he organized links them morally with the exploiting bosses. They are no better than their exploiters; they are only worse off. To be exploited, to be worse off is a lamentable condition, but it does not of itself bespeak a superior virtue. Dos Passos was bitter at the misery imposed on the proletariat and sympathized with the struggle of the I.W.W. to improve its lot. But he never accepted the idea of the superior proletarian soul. He thus freed himself from an a priori dogma which froze the average proletarian novel into a predetermined moral formula.

The first of the fictional characters in the trilogy, Mac, has the most authentic working-class origin. His father is a night watchman in a New Haven factory, and after losing his wife, turns himself and his two children over to Uncle Tim. Mac grows up in Chicago, and at that mid-point in the country begins his picaresque adventures in the lower reaches of the American scene.

The conception and treatment of Mac, at the very start of *U.S.A.*, announce the qualities of the whole work. He descends from Tom Jones, revealing the author's debt to the episodic novelists, Defoe, Fielding, and Smollett, of the eighteenth century. Like Tom, Mac is good-natured, well-intentioned, vaguely idealistic, and incurably sensual. Uncle Tim's admonitions about the evils of capitalism serve him as a hand-me-down philosophy of life. He drifts about the country, going from place to place on the spur of the moment. He helps the amiable charlatan, the Reverend Bingham, sell Bibles and pornography to lonely farmers' wives, bums his way across the continent to California, whoring, drinking, and working at odd jobs, meanders over to Goldfield, Nevada, where he joins in the miners' strike, listens to inspirational words from Big Bill Haywood, and prints inflammatory leaflets for the I.W.W., wanders down to San Diego where he marries an ambitious middle-class girl, has two children, feels suffocated by his wife's longing for money, goes to Mexico to join the Zapata revolution only to wind up as the comfortable owner of a left-wing bookshop in Mexico City and in the arms of a pretty Mexican girl named Carmen.

Like Fielding, Dos Passos uses his protagonist to describe the national milieu in dense detail. We learn what life is like in the slums of Chicago, on isolated farms in Michigan, in shabby cafés in Duluth, in Nevada mining towns patrolled by company guards. We are bombarded with information about strikes, trade union struggles, class warfare, and the travails of the poor. Mac's temperament, like Tom Jones', is essentially passive, so that he never interferes with this exposition of the American experience.

Passivity, descending at last to inertia, characterizes Dos Passos' figures. Mac is the supreme example of involuntary movement. The world happens to him, not he to the world. He shares the cheerful, slothful, directionless passivity of his eighteenth-century ancestor. He enjoys eating, drinking, making love, doing things with his hands and body in mindless passage from moment to moment. He may be a radical, but a radical from family upbringing and economic circumstance rather than compelling personal conviction.

At one point he thinks, "A man's got to work for more than himself and the kids to feel right." An admirable sentiment, but in the end he winds up working for himself. On another occasion he remarks, "I wanta study an' work for things; you know what I mean, not to get to be a goddam slavedriver but for socialism and the revolution an' like that, not work an' go on a bat an' work an' go on a bat." But when last seen, he is on a kind of perpetual "bat." He has just enough self-awareness to realize that "I was just on the point of selling out to the sons of bitches." Yet, as time passes, it is a fear that grows dull and flickers out. The tenuous hold of ideology on Mac is what makes him so convincing a portrait of an American "working stiff." He lives in the flesh, in the passing instant, and under the patina of ideology he is the petit bourgeois to the life, edging his way at last into a secure nook, governed by prudence, comfort, and safety. Looking back upon Mac with the hindsight of the whole trilogy, the reader sees that he did not drift into his last retreat after all, that it expressed instead his deepest self.

The central act of Mac's life, and the lives of the other characters in *U.S.A.*, is travel. Dos Passos is the great roadmaster of American fiction. His figures rack up more mileage than any since Smollett. They are constantly, incessantly on the go. The railroad train is the common carrier, with J. Ward Moorehouse ensconced in a compartment and Mac riding the rails, passengers making the same journey through space. The two may be only a few feet apart, but that narrow distance suggests the class division between them even as it highlights their intimate juxtaposition. They meet briefly in Mexico, just long enough for Mac and his friend Ben to tag Moorehouse with a derisive epithet.

"Jez, Ben, that's a smooth bastard," said Mac after J. Ward Moorehouse had gone.

"Mac," said Ben, "that baby's got a slick cream of millions all over him."

Travel has traditional advantages for the novelist. It freshens his story with a running current of new impressions and sensations. It increases and renders more plausible the chances of his characters' meeting, especially if they grow up in widely separated places: Moorehouse and Mac, because of their differences in background, were not likely to have met in their home cities; their encounter in Mexico is more probable. It supplies a built-in mechanism for dissolving personal entanglements.

But for Dos Passos it has two special uses. First, it enables him to suggest the transience of life in America. Rootlessness is the prime aspect of American civilization. No one settles down anywhere or is attached to anything for long. Moorehouse has no visible connection with his father, a station agent in Wilmington, Delaware, nor with either of his two rich wives. He becomes a public-relations man, unattached to any corporation or product, selling his services and his ideas for "pacifying" or "reconciling" labor to the highest bidder, and moving ceaselessly from one city to another. Joe Williams, an able-bodied seaman, is as unattached as Mac and Moorehouse. He goes from one ship and port to another without thinking beyond the day. He marries, but his marriage comes to a quick end. Thousands of small incidents happen to him without making any special impression, and at the end he is still bobbing aimlessly on a tide of small sensations. Meanwhile he logs as vast a distance on sea as Mac does on land. The transience of life is registered in his case, as with all the others, in the simple but continuous act of moving from place to place.

Second is the striking and dramatic equation of travel and the American mania for quantity, the conviction that reality is established by the heaping up of things. The advancing juggernaut of technology creates vast numbers of goods and services, swamping the individual's power to discriminate among them and tending to reduce him to an object haplessly absorbing the kaleidoscope of new objects constantly assembled and paraded before him. To embrace this idea fictionally, Dos Passos creates in the imaginative consciousness of his characters an equivalent of this hectic process. Through his special kind of compulsive travelogue, his people are exposed to an equivalent barrage of sensations and experiences, so numerous and demanding that they finally reduce the wanderers to recording mechanisms and leave the reader with the overwhelming impression of an endless unreeling of detail that soon seems much the same, reaches a saturation point and yet continues to spin without letup and with increasing acceleration. The result is an overpowering monotony, from which everyone, characters and reader alike, emerges numbed and flattened out. It is this pervasive sense of formless monotony which is one of the manifest triumphs of *U.S.A.*, for it expresses simultaneously the lives of the characters and the larger life of the country of which theirs is now the demonstrated microcosm.

Space and the spatial dimension of travel are suggested by the title of the first volume. The 42nd parallel stretches across the United States like a magnetic line from coast to coast, drawing the characters into incessant pursuit. With America's entry into the First World War they are drawn, as through an immense suction pump, to New York, the eastern end of the parallel, and follow the soldiers across the Atlantic. Here the second volume, *Nineteen-Nineteen*, begins. Most of the figures join the Red Cross, and in Europe resume their peripatetic commutations, this time between Paris and Rome, with side trips to Greece, Switzerland, and Spain. The relatively stationary position of the armies in the front lines only throws into stronger relief the constant roaming-about of Moorehouse, Joe Williams, Eleanor Stoddard, Eveline Hutchins, Richard Savage, and Daughter.

Their experiences produce no psychological growth and create no inner substance. As their external sensations become denser and more rich, the characters grow emptier. Moorehouse had reached his climax as a human being when, as a boy in grade school, he cornered the agate market and made a small fortune renting out marbles to the other pupils; his life subsequently is only a complicated degeneration into an attractive smile and a charming manner. Joe Williams, rough and uneducated but thoroughly masculine and alive, searches in vain for some solid ground to stand upon, whether as husband, ship's officer, or just plain citizen; his life is doomed to be as shifting and unsteady as the sea on which he spends it. Eleanor Stoddard, cut off in childhood from a healthy sensuality by the daily sight of her father coming home bloody from his job in the stockyards, becomes a fashionable interior decorator, trying to make up what was originally destroyed in her by aesthetic bric-à-brac and brittle, meaningless human relationships. Eveline and Daughter are two restless young women whose sexual misfortunes lead them to suicide. And Richard Savage winds up as Moorehouse's assistant, feeling "sour and gone in the middle like a rotten pear." The aimlessness of his career is brilliantly suggested in the moment when he deliberately throws his compass overboard.

After three years, they all trail back to America, and in *The Big Money* are caught up in the boom of the Twenties. Moorehouse, Savage, and Eleanor Stoddard continue to prosper and be influential while running downhill emotionally. They are not producers; they do not make things or contribute anything to the economy. They are simply arrangers, and their arrangements symbolize the hollowness of American capitalism as Dos Passos, anguished over its human emptiness, sees it. Of the short biographies that punctuate *U.S.A.* perhaps the greatest is that of Thorstein Veblen in *The Big Money*. This crotchety student of conspicuous consumption is the sociologist made to order for an America incarnated by J. Ward Moorehouse on the male side and Eleanor Stoddard on the female.

Equally wasteful is the career of Charley Anderson. An itinerant garage mechanic in *The 42nd Parallel*, he had fought as an aviator during the war, and perhaps for that reason had not appeared at all in *Nineteen-Nineteen,* for that novel, like the others, devotes itself less to the doers than to the wasters, hangers-on, influence peddlers, and parasites. After the war Anderson gets into the airplane industry, is an inventor and developer, and seems on the verge of becoming productive when he is seized by stock market fever, plunges on Wall Street all the way to the great crash, and in private life turns into an alcoholic playboy finally killed in an automobile smash-up. His companion during much of this joyride, Margo Dowling, after a raffish beginning in the nether regions of American poverty and mean living, winds up bizarrely in Hollywood as a movie queen. The movies, like the stock market, are another of the illusion-making substitutes for the real thing—a process of displacement that is, in the author's view, all too characteristic of the American scene.

Meanwhile, on the other side of the class struggle, Mary French and Ben Compton are doing what they can to advance the cause of labor. Their efforts are pathetic and relentlessly futile. Every strike to which Mary French attaches herself fails, every cause into which she throws herself—notably the Sacco-Vanzetti case—loses. Her love affairs are with second-rate men and end in frustration or betrayal. There hangs over all her activities an air of shabby heartbreak. Ben Compton is a dedicated Communist, humorless, fanatical, self-important. Nothing he does seems to help either the working class or the Communist party and, like Debs, he winds up in Atlanta for opposing the war. He has managed to commit the two crimes defined in *The Big Money.* The first is public: "Tried to organize the workingclass, that's the worst crime you can commit in this man's country." The second is private: he uses human beings, himself included, as instruments for abstract ends, the same crime being committed by his deadly enemies the capitalists—an ironic similarity that Dos Passos takes pains not to overlook. This also provides the answer to a question posed in a letter to the "I" of the Camera Eye: "Explain why being right the radicals in their private lives are such shits."

The titles of the three volumes suggest, as does the overall name of the trilogy, that Dos Passos is concerned with more than the private destinies of his dozen fictional figures. *The 42nd Parallel* introduces the dimension of space; *Nineteen-Nineteen,* time; *The Big Money,* value, with the adjective "big" referring not simply to the American glorification of money but to its equal glorification of size. The country is far larger than the sum total of its individual characters. To fill the gap and adequately express the larger theme, Dos Passos introduces three other technical devices which, though not strictly new, taken one by one, are new in their assemblage.

The first of these is the Newsreel, a splicing of newspaper headlines interlaced with snatches of popular songs. The typefaces are cunningly arranged to suggest our topsy-turvy judgments of what is important and unimportant at any given time, while the abrupt running of one news item into another suggests the disconnectedness of the historical moment. The Newsreel seizes history in the mass, the events shared in common by everyone, seen by the mass eye through the large end of the telescope. The song hits, with their instant nostalgia and amusing pathos, bring us back at once to the year in question. The device was a magnificent technique for organizing and countering the chaos of history. Dos Passos borrowed it from the German expressionist drama of the Weimar Republic. It flourished later in the plays of Bertolt Brecht, but no more successfully than in *U.S.A.* Dos Passos had written two plays of his own in the late Twenties, though he was less interested in the drama as such than in scene designing. It was the theatre-as-spectacle that attracted him. He remembered loving the circus when at Harvard and thinking that "Boris Godunov" was the greatest theatrical work of the age. The Newsreel was in itself a dramatic spectacular, which Dos Passos, as his own impresario, handled with astonishing dexterity.

Juxtaposed with the Newsreel is the Camera Eye. Here the events are seen through the small eye of the telescope. The viewer is as anonymous as the mass viewer of the

Newsreel, but though never named he is always the same unique, quivering individual. He has an exquisite capacity for suffering. The grass blades he treads on as a small boy seem to wince with pain. After growing up, he associates himself with the victims of every terrible thing done to human beings, experiencing with them, sometimes vicariously, sometimes in fact, the anguish of existence. He seems flayed; without the barrier of skin, there is nothing to interfere with or muffle the piercing impact of a cruel, tormenting universe. This nameless, faceless, almost abstract sensibility, defenseless and totally susceptible, is rendered in a stream-of-consciousness flow. There are no punctuation marks or capitalization, only blank spaces to indicate breaks in thought. Dos Passos absorbed *Ulysses* and *Mrs. Dalloway*, borrowing from them as freely as he did from the expressionist dramas of Wedekind and Georg Kaiser. The Camera Eye thrusts as deeply inside the human consciousness as the Newsreel penetrates into the external stream of events. The reader is brought into intimate and successive contact with pure emotion and impersonal event.

Finally there is the insertion of the short biographies. The country exists in fact as well as in imagination, and the actual historical personages who make their separate appearances are a link between the facts of the Newsreel and the fictions of the invented characters. The subjects of the sketches are real people, yet Dos Passos gives each his particular imaginative shape in the semi-cadenced prose-poetry of his biographical interludes. There are twenty-six in all, falling neatly into three categories: heroes, villains, and those with heroic possibilities who failed to live up to them or allowed themselves to be used. Typical of the first is Fighting Bob La Follette, of the second Minor C. Keith, of the third Steinmetz. Heroism and villainy are always defined in proletarian terms. Heroic figures like La Follette, Haywood, and Debs struggled to improve the lot of the common man or, like Veblen, tried to understand the processes by which men were exploited. Villainous ones like Keith, who founded the United Fruit Company and set up the banana republics of Central America, were the greedy men who squeezed others to enrich themselves. J. P. Morgan was another such. Henry Ford and Andrew Carnegie were in the same class, though the first mitigated his "sins" by genuinely raising the living standards of his workers and the second gave away many of his ill-gotten millions for libraries and peace foundations.

Sometimes the author's anger at the course of history affects his judgment. His scorn of Woodrow Wilson as a mouthpiece for the Morgan interests during the First World War is a gross oversimplification, provoked by Dos Passos' opposition to the war and bitterness toward the President who led the nation into it and jailed Debs for opposing it. Outside the socio-economic sphere, Dos Passos is singularly unsuccessful in pursuing the sources of heroism. His apparent ignorance of architecture, for example, makes his portrait of Frank Lloyd Wright disastrously superficial and empty.

The biographies, whether individually effective or not, represent the author intervening most directly in the book. His slant is most clearly revealed in them. Of all the extra-fictional techniques in U.S.A. the biographical vignettes link Dos Passos most closely with the proletarian novelists. These authors went to great pains to establish their own judgments inside their fictions and to work their ideological value systems into their texts. No one reading *The Underground Stream* could possibly mistake Albert Maltz's attitude toward the Communist party. No reader of *A Sign for Cain* could miss Grace Lumpkin's personal view of the Negro in the South. Leane Zugsmith is equally forthright about the liberal mind in *The Summer Soldier*, Thomas Bell about the pulverizing steel mills in *Out of This Furnace*, and Tess Slesinger about the New England conscience and a dozen other subjects in her feverish potpourri novel *The Unpossessed*. As a rule the proletarian writers relentlessly pumped their messages into their work.

Dos Passos allows himself this luxury only in the biographies, while firmly restraining himself everywhere else. His purely doctrinaire outbursts are widely spaced. One occurs in the sketch of Paxton Hibben, the once well-known liberal diplomat and journalist.

> Something was wrong with the American Republic, was it the Gold Standard, Privilege, The Interests, Wall Street?
> The rich were getting richer, the poor were getting poorer, small farmers were being squeezed out, workingmen were working twelve hours a day for a bare living; profits were for the rich, the law was for the rich, the cops were for the rich.

Another appears in the portrait of Veblen.

> Nobody could understand why a boy of such attainments wouldn't settle down to the business of the day, which was to buttress property and profits with anything usable in the debris of Christian ethics and eighteenth-century economics that cluttered the minds of the college professors, and to reinforce the sacred, already shaky edifice with the new strong girderwork of science Herbert Spencer was throwing up for the benefit of the bosses.

Such straight, quasi-Marxist statements, baldly injected into the narrative flow, was standard proletarian procedure. But on the whole Dos Passos avoids the overt utterance and allows his trilogy to speak for itself.

The overwhelming impression it leaves is an acute disaffection with life in America during the first thirty years of the century, without, however, proposing any specific blueprint for remedy or reform. Dos Passos does not mark out the path to an ideal world, and even doubts that it is possible. He once described his credo as a writer with uncompromising pessimism: "The basic tragedy my work tries to express remains monotonously the same: man's struggle for life against the strangling institutions he himself creates."

Though this struggle is one-sided, it is at the same time unending, and from it Dos Passos drew the narrative energy that sustains his celebrated work. No aspect of the world around him escaped his interest or failed to arouse his close attention. Whatever he may have thought of it on the moral or philosophical side, he was magnetized by it on the dramatic. The fantastic amount of detail he managed to pack into his story, covering every conceivable genre of experience, flowed from this fascination with the life process in its endless proliferation.

What keeps the lives of his characters from being sociological case studies, pinned down to the last small fact, is this fascination with metamorphosis, movement, and change. Moreover, the movement is emotionalized, and the perpetual changes in fortune are minutely accompanied by the analogous changes in feeling. In the scheme of things, these changes, whether of situation or thought, are necessarily small, perhaps even minuscule, but they are recorded with an enthusiasm, a passionate fervor not exceeded in the great panoramic novels of scene, like *War and Peace*, or of the soul, like *Anna Karenina*, where the author believes in vast changes and they do take place. It is this commitment to the larger field of human experience that underlines the claim of *U.S.A.* to being a masterpiece and that frees Dos Passos from the narrower framework of the proletarian school to which he is in some ways allied.

Within this larger field, his energies as a writer are freely released. There is the poet in Dos Passos, and his trilogy is peppered with marvelous moments of sensory evocation. Here is one, a description of Paris during a Zeppelin raid.

> They stood on the porch of the Sacré Coeur and saw the Zeppelins come over. Paris stretched out cold and dead as if all the tiers of roofs and domes were carved out of snow and the shrapnel sparkled frostily overhead and the searchlights were antennae of great insects moving through the milky darkness. At intervals came red snorting flares by the incendiary bombs. Just once they caught sight of two tiny silver cigars overhead. They looked higher than the moon.

There is Dos Passos the image-maker, who can sum up an undergraduate education at Harvard as "four years under the ethercone," refer to Wilson's drive for war against Germany in 1917 as a "crazy steamroller" which six opposition senators tried "to hold back with their bare hands," and metaphorize the mind of one of his characters in a single trenchant statement: "Words, ideas, plans, stockquotations kept unrolling in endless tickertape in his head."

There is Dos Passos the organizer, perhaps his most impressive role. Confronted with a task of colossal magnitude, nothing less than imaginatively rendering and penetrating three decades of American history, he attacks it on all sides with an élan that refuses to shirk or slough off any part of the assignment. Everything must be included, every subject and emotion not simply touched on but explored. "He must run up the gangplanks of all the steamboats," exclaims the young man in the preface, "register in all the hotels, work in the cities, answer the wantads, learn the trades, take up the jobs, live in all the boardinghouses, sleep in all the beds." The refrain of *all* announces the intention and sets the tone.

Aside from his four narrative devices, which keep the multiplicity of the subject within bounds, Dos Passos has a highly developed sense of the concrete, and it is this sense which prevents his many abstractions from remaining simply and remotely abstract. By rooting them in the specific, he makes them quickly intelligible and thereby manageable. Wall Street is an immense and arcane abstraction, like the science of economics in general. Dos Passos' first reference to it is "a column of stockquotations rubbed out and written in by a Western Union boy on a blackboard." The revealing little action of the uniformed boy performing his feverish ritual on a blackboard (with the hungry eyes of anxious speculators upon him) lights up and releases the whole scene. Culture is another of the large abstractions that inevitably turn up. The writer first speaks of it as "a public library full of old newspapers and dogeared history books with protests scrawled on the margins in pencil." Again a subject that threatens to be too formless for definition is neatly caught in an instantly recognizable scrap of familiar experience that yet contains without distortion the large whole of which it is a small part. This remarkable ability effectively to lodge the universal in the particular is what makes *U.S.A.* a true work of the imagination, not what it might easily have been in other hands, history disguised as fiction or an essay posing as a novel.

But for all its skills and ingenuities, for all its author's admirably applied talents, the trilogy is singularly lacking in memorable characters. Mac, Moorehouse, Joe Williams, Charley Anderson are well done but hardly arresting, and in retrospect blur and fade. They exist only within the context of the novel and even there struggle for a secure footing. Though natural and credible, they lack dimensionality and do not generate their own sources of life and power. Dos Passos is no Tolstoy, with his mysterious capacity to convince us that his heroes and heroines are superior creatures. Yet the narrowing of his psychological range is due as much to his theory as to any creative shortcomings. The theory of the individual being strangled by social forces makes it all but impossible to allow him his own independence and latitude. From the start he is doomed to a losing battle. The battle is never wholly lost; it goes on continuously, perpetually. But it is not to be won, nor is the pressure of society to be equably borne. Without hope of victory or even the possibility of a draw, the autonomous existence of the individual is denied; without autonomy, he cannot grow into the fullness of stature, into the richest possibilities of his own nature that alone can make him memorable.

This lack—failure would be too misleading a word—Dos Passos shares with the earlier writers of the naturalist tradition. *Nana, Esther Waters, The Red Badge of Courage, The Octopus* are equally void of distinctive personalities. The external stream of events is more heavily weighted than the internal response. Inevitably Dos Passos addresses his major energies to the social and historical process, to which his characters are slowly subserved. They have a certain freedom of movement as children while still shielded from the full-scale world, after which they proceed to survive rather than grow. Dos Passos whips them into instant shape; they are indeed instant characters, appearing full-blown at the very beginning. By the end of the first paragraph of Eleanor Stoddard's first appearance, the central distortion of her nature is already driven home to us by the terrible dream she has over and over again as a small girl. Nothing that happens to her afterward changes her in any significant way. And so with the others. Dos Passos is as resourceful as ever in finding the right key in which to launch his figures. Thereafter, in terms of inward development, they become peripheral.

Much, though obviously not all, is redeemed by the masterly demonstration of the outside. Yet even this does not hide the irony behind the career of a writer who, though devoted to protecting the individual against the institutions strangling him, should achieve a more vivid portrait of these very institutions than of their human victims. The paradox is shared by the proletarian novelists, who were also dedicated to protecting the exploited people and also emerged from their work with a far less keen perception of these people as individual human beings than of the abstract forces pressing them down.

The triumph of *U.S.A.* is primarily a triumph of organization, but of an organization so complex and ordered as in itself to constitute an original vision of its subject. It has the added virtue of being open-ended. The trilogy begins with a young man walking fast through a night crowd and ends thirteen hundred pages later with the sketch called Vag. Here the young man is whirled along on a last, breathlessly accelerated tour of the country. The final image is a quick view of a crowded highway, stretching "a hundred miles down the road." The anonymity of the young man fuses with the size, speed, technological power, and lonesomeness of his journey to suggest in the brilliant microcosm of this ultimate travelogue the heart of the literary enterprise that Dos Passos has managed with such supreme virtuosity.

Edward Dahlberg, *Early and Late*

JULES CHAMETZKY

IT IS TIME to stop thinking of Edward Dahlberg as a sport in American letters, whose principal achievement would appear to be his unique style. When critics today talk about Dahlberg's style, they are usually referring to his late work; his early work of the Thirties is usually regarded as a stylistic phase that Dahlberg had to outgrow in order to achieve his maturity. The mature style reveals itself to best effect in *Because I Was Flesh* (New Directions, 1964) in a prose a-dazzle with rich metaphor, erudite allusions to religious and pagan mythologies, passionate attention to the rhythms and music of the periods. To his admirers, Allen Tate for instance, Dahlberg's "formal elegance" is a vital part of his achievement (I quote from the dust-jacket); to others, less enchanted, the style can often seem pretentious, arbitrary, freakish—especially when it is in the service of dubious prophecy, as in *Reasons of the Heart* (Horizon Press, 1966), and not, as in *Because I Was Flesh*, the necessary illumination of a vividly concrete center. I want to suggest that Dahlberg's mature style is a strategy for distancing himself from and yet, paradoxically, possessing the myth of his life; and that this purposeful use of an ornate, idiosyncratic style is one characteristic he shares with, say, Walt Whitman, Augie March, and scores of other American writers and Ishmaels. The first task, therefore, is to place Dahlberg securely in the American grain; the second is to assess "the myth of his life" and evaluate its relevance and force as literature.[1] As a beginning, I propose to look more closely than is usual at his first two novels, *Bottom Dogs* and *From Flushing to Calvary*, both as interesting works in themselves and as background for the widely recognized achievement of *Because I Was Flesh*.

Much of the slang in *Bottom Dogs* dates the book ("Those micks were sure-fire slingers, no spiffin"), threatens to trivialize it, but finally can be endured by a sympathetic reader. More significantly, much of the book is written, as Dahlberg says in the new City Lights edition (1961), in a "rough, bleak idiom": "The rocks . . . rested in the diphtheria stream, like some dirty rain-cloud. He went around the pond, an old rotten raft on it, slugging against the mud like wet, floating rats." "The alley clotted with mud, night and the spud cans of grease from Peck's Quick Lunch was spread out like a broken spider web." We can recognize at once that the loathsomeness of the observed world is in the naturalistic tradition everywhere evident in American letters between *Maggie* and *Last Exit to Brooklyn*. The rats, muck, grease, and spiders of the bottom-dog world seem to have been spewn up by that same "explosion in a cesspool" which had so disgusted Paul Elmer More when he contemplated *Manhattan Transfer* a few years earlier. The naturalistic impulse, so strong in the Thirties, was by no means the exclusive possession of that period. Nor was the use of "the rude American vernacular," so much favored by early proletarian realists. Dahlberg notes in his preface that he shared with other writers of the Twenties (he mentions John Hermann and Robert McAlmon) the notion that they "could not write about the midwest, Texas or Montana except in the rude American vernacular." Dahlberg's free use of this vernacular, combined with his predilection for the harsh bottom-dog world of America that he had experienced at first hand, suggests immediately his important position on the eve of the Depression with its subsequent vogue of proletarian realism and naturalism. It is more difficult to assess Dahlberg's influence upon that vogue than it is, say, Mike Gold's, whose influence through the example of *Jews Without Money* (1930) and through his exhortations in the pages of the *New Masses* is manifest. But Dahlberg's language of disgust, his imagery of rot and decay—and most importantly—his pioneering exploration of the bottom-dog milieux of flophouses, hobo jungles, and freight cars certainly places him in the vanguard of that school. In his first two novels Dahlberg charted in original fashion the territory that was to become painfully familiar in so much of the radical literature of the Thirties.

There is no gainsaying this side of Dahlberg's early work—and if that were all, it would merit, at best, a footnote in our literary history. But that is not all: what remains to be seen and demonstrated is the special quality of his voice and concerns.

What may strike a contemporary reader at once is the uncertainty of the narrative voice in *Bottom Dogs*. There is much inconsistency, e.g., in the spelling and use of the slang, and the narrator falls in and out of his bottom-dog idiom rather erratically—a reflection, surely, of the author's uncertainty about his point of view toward the material at hand. And that, of course, is the crucial issue; what is Dahlberg to make of the lives of his chief protagonists, Lorry and Lizzie Lewis?

These lives, so intertwined that we may call it *this* life, is the subject of Dahlberg's early fictions—and of *Because I Was Flesh*, which he calls an autobiography—and this life, even in outline, is an eccentric one. In *Bottom Dogs* we learn that Lizzie Lewis is the proprietor of the Star Ladies Barber Shop in Kansas City during the early years of the century. Lorry is her son. His paternity in doubt, not even a nominal father in sight, he is sent off to an orphanage in Cleveland at the behest of one of his mother's suitors. Lorry subsequently kicks about the country in an aimless way, winding up at the Los Angeles YMCA in the company of the other aimless types. In *From Flushing to Calvary* the story centers on the last days of Lizzie. Lorry has persuaded her to move in with him in New York, where she tries to piece together a life as an eligible "widow," a letter of rooms, a part-time homeopathic abortionist. There are important flashbacks to Lizzie's Kansas

City barbershop days and to Lorry's experiences at the
J.O.A. (we learn that the Cleveland orphanage was the
Jewish Orphan Asylum). Except for these flashbacks, and
Lorry's one brief trip back to the site of the orphanage
(riding the freights, of course), the action converges upon
the moving climax of Lizzie's last operation and her
death.

The elements of the life are bizarre, marginal: a calculated study in alienation and displacement. A lady barber?
A Jewish lady barber in the heartland of America in the
"Teddy Roosevelt Days" (as the first chapter in the saga is
called)? A Jewish illegitimate non-orphan orphan? What
indeed to make of this matter, and how to come to terms
with it? That is Dahlberg's subject in the early days, and if
the voice is occasionally uncertain, we should remember
that the territory he pioneered was only fully claimed in
the Fifties—in the wake of Saul Bellow's Augie March,
that other Jewish illegitimate non-orphan orphan from the
American heartland. A measure of the distance we have
come is that Augie could unself-consciously proclaim his
American identity in his opening words, and what to
Dahlberg must have seemed eccentric would very likely
seem to a contemporary only a walk somewhat on the wild
side, and probably quintessentially American. In Dahlberg's early efforts to come to grips with his subject, it is
too easy to see only despair or, as D. H. Lawrence says,
"the last word in repulsive consciousness" (Introduction
to the 1930 edition). But this is only to see Dahlberg
wearing his mask as the child of sorrows and to overlook
his ambivalence: the sadness *and* the joy in this work, and
the effort made to embrace both aspects in an appropriate
style.[2]

In his introduction to the first edition, Lawrence distinguishes Dahlberg from the true tragedian, who "dramatizes his defeat and is in love with himself in his defeated
role . . . Lorry Lewis is in too deep a state of revulsion to
dramatize himself." As usual, Lawrence offers us an important insight: in this case to the curious passivity of
Lorry Lewis throughout *Bottom Dogs* and to a great
extent in *From Flushing to Calvary*. It is not wholly true,

however, as Lawrence suggests, that this is a condition stemming from mere revulsion. Certainly the rats, mud, and grease imagery, the sordid image of a world of sleazy rooms in which someone's hand is always up a woman's dress, records the deep revulsion of the narrator toward much of Lorry's milieu. Yet much of the book reveals a narrator as elegiac as he is repulsed. The legendary figures of the orphanage to whom he devotes chapters of the book are, one concedes, nobodies, engaged only in petty food pilfering and pathetic quests for identity; hi-jinks at the Y are more locker-room horseplay than epic encounters; and the culmination of the book at Solomon's dance-place, where a young couple is married in a jazz wedding to the tune of "Avalon" (after which "the house howled, and made for the cloakrooms and lavatories"), may seem only the epitome of fatuousness and emptiness. Yet there is a stubborn sense in which none of this is just "the last word in repulsive consciousness." In the first place, much of it is funny in a zany way reminiscent of Maxwell Bodenheim, Henry Miller, some of the beats and black humorists, and other writers inside the whale. More to the point, in the orphanage sections, in the section on Los Angeles, and under the 8th Street viaduct in Kansas City, one is struck by the narrator's effort simply to name, and perhaps thereby to claim, the elements of his experience. By the act of recording, he hopes to invest them with a kind of epic dignity, conscious always of a pathos and continuous irony because of their commonplace and unheroic nature. But the effort to include, legitimize, and even celebrate, these ingredients of what we are now less embarrassed than formerly to call "an American life" seems to me to require recognition. This side of *Bottom Dogs* may best be seen in the characterization of Lizzie—a characterization that is most effective when it is conveyed in her own idiom.

> Well, if God would help her, perhaps she could still sell the shop, take it easier, and become a real-estate agent, do a little speculating. It was no use, you could only make so much with your ten fingers and not one penny more. She

should have seen that long ago and not slaved night and day, without a bit of sunshine, as she did. All her sweet youth blown through the window and for what? It didn't pay; she could by this time have something; but she was afraid to take chances. If she lost, who should help her? You didn't find money in the street. If you had a pocket full of money everybody was your friend, but if you were down and out nobody recognized you. Oh well, she went on, God would help her and everything would come out all right.

Only the first chapters are devoted to Lizzie, but her emotional ambience controls Lorry and the book. When the narrator (and Lorry) is not in anguish over her irregular life, or dwelling upon her self-deluded petty bourgeois values and "wisdom," he is clearly elegiac. Lorry and the narrator are not repulsed: they are in conflict over their heritage. This conflict accounts for the passivity—at times a kind of paralysis—of Lorry. The struggle central to and constant in *Bottom Dogs, From Flushing to Calvary*, and *Because I Was Flesh* is between rejection and acceptance, repulsion and love, of the mother. In *Bottom Dogs* the issue is not as clearly in focus as it will be in the later books: the narrator is so close to an experience that seemed unique, eccentric, and painful, that the best he can achieve is an act of naming.

In *From Flushing to Calvary* Dahlberg closes upon his subject with more assurance. The structure is very much tighter, the action complete, the scene more unified, the problem of mother-son-identity more definitely at the center. Lorry's attraction and repulsion is dramatized in many small ways—by his fascination and despair, e.g., with Lizzie's minor Machiavellian shenanigans—and in the larger plan of the book. Lorry tries some "action" in this book, to the extent that he insists Lizzie give up her barbering and come to live with him in New York, abandons her briefly (in order to make a pilgrimage to the orphanage in a futile effort to resurrect spiritually a deceased surrogate father), and then returns to New York in time for her death.

If the vernacular and the literary tend to jostle one another uneasily in *Bottom Dogs*, they are more clearly defined and separated in *Flushing*. The narrator commits no "errors" in diction and spelling, and he divides the literary and the vernacular worlds between Lorry and Lizzie (there is some mixing: Lizzie reads five pages a day of *Tom Jones*, chiefly to get "tony" words to use in answering matrimonial ads). Lorry is more clearly a word-man and aspiring writer in this book. "In the beginning was the word," he reflects at one point, reminiscing about his time in Los Angeles: "metempsychosis, metamorphosis, transmigration, protagoras, transcendentalism, swedenborgianism, swedenborgian fungi . . . de profundis, out of the depths, dorian dorian the portrait of dorian gray, thêophile gautier, multifarious, asphodel, santa monica, capistrano, monterey, carmel-by-the-sea. . . ."

Flushing is Dahlberg's portrait of the artist as a young man. Unlike Joyce's young man, however, who had been to school to the Jesuits and could soar above the nets of religion, country, and family by committing himself wholly to his mythic father, Dedalus the fabulous artificer, to art, Dahlberg's artist is an auto-didact American, uncertain about even locating his country, family, religion. At the end, he can only commit himself to the road. Lorry's final snatch of a Maccabean stanza, "triumph, triumph crowns our glorious way" is therefore a bitterly ironic commentary on his sense of defeat rather than his exaltation. The road from Flushing—the dreary wasteland of Brooklyn and Long Island flats, his America—to Calvary produces a crucifixion but no apotheosis. The death of his mother follows upon the death of his hopes for a spiritual father, so the artist is completely orphaned.

Opposed to Lorry's life and its crises are the long sections devoted to the rhythm and pattern of Lizzie's days. They are the book's triumph; her voice and the vernacular tradition it embodies are the real strength of *Flushing*. In a language authentically her own—and recognizably the product of an American experience—she reveals herself in all her shabbiness and glory. Her language is full of Sunday supplement and backyard science and sophistication, the jargon and delusions of the petty bourgeois, the unexamined shards of a life lived close to the unliterary bone of American life. A sometime Machiavellian, a petty charlatan of homeopathic nostrums, her strength resides, finally, in her ability to accept the reality of the life she lives. She refuses to see it as irregular or odd: at whatever stage and with whatever oddball materials, the flotsam and jetsam of our urban civilization, she makes her communities. Lizzie's glory is that however much she seems to have an eye out only for money and personal advantage, she is continually undone by her humanity: what she is really after, always, is respect, sympathy, love. Though she is the despair of Lorry Lewis, her death removes a vital force from his life and can only leave him desolate.

So the ambivalent relation to the mother is at the heart of this book. Besides the obvious Oedipal overtones, what I am trying to suggest is the cultural significance of the relationship. Dahlberg's love-hate relationship must perforce include Lizzie Lewis's America. *Flushing* reveals a perfect tension between exorcism and celebration, an achieved dramatization of this problem. It is unjustly neglected as such, and as another document in the long tradition of American writers struggling to accommodate themselves to their complex fate.

Dahlberg has presumably repudiated these works of his suffering youth. A wholly different man appears in the later work—especially those books and essays concerned with "the dialogue with the body"—in a voice that is prophetic when it is not crotchety. Yet the subject of *Because I Was Flesh* is obsessively, it would seem, the same as in the two early works discussed, and in them elements of the new voice are present in one way or another. There are important differences, of course—among them, two are especially noteworthy. First of all, Dahlberg can accommodate without a feeling of strain his acute sense of the observed world and its "rude vernacular" with his vast learning and his penchant for high style, to the enrichment of both. It would seem that after thirty years, in this respect at least, Dahlberg and America may have come of age. That is, despite the rage and thundering of his prophetic works, Dahlberg's pain in accommodating himself to his two worlds has abated: so long, that is, as he removes it from the sphere of action demanded by the novel form, he can come to terms, at least verbally, with his mother's life and his own. The chief difference, and it probably makes all the difference, is Dahlberg's process of mythicizing and so both distancing himself from and possessing his past.

By placing his mother and his America within a context of timeless literature, religion, and mythology, the pain and misery of his own time is transcended, singularity is transformed to universality. The earlier process of exorcism and celebration seems to me the same, but on a new level: "Let the bard from Smyrna catalogue Harma, the ledges and caves of Ithaca, the milk-fed damsels of Achaia, pigeon-flocked Thisbe or the woods of Onchestus, I sing of Oak, Walnut, Chestnut, Maple and Elm Street. . . . Could the strumpets from the stews of Corinth, Ephesus or Tarsus fetch a groan or sigh more quickly than the dimpled thighs of lasses from St. Joseph or Topeka?"

Later in the book he recalls sitting in his mother's room in Kansas City, "filled with a fatherless emptiness" and asks further along "why was it impossible for me to let go of the misery of my boyhood?" There is still no certain father in *Because I Was Flesh*, but for the moment he is able to "let go" the misery of his past by mythicizing it and enveloping it in the incantatory magic of his rhetoric. "Mother and father is one flesh," says Hamlet, and Dahlberg leans on Hamlet's dubious logic (one of his chapter headings, ". . . and so, my mother" comes from this speech by Hamlet) to resolve his quest for a past and an identity. Perhaps in an American context this logic is not so dubious: as Erik H. Ericson in *Childhood and Society* has pointed out, "the post-revolutionary descendants of the Founding Fathers forced their women to be mothers *and* fathers." In any case, Dahlberg's fatherless emptiness is filled in a beautiful and final acceptance of the mother,

her life, and his. "When the image of her comes up on a sudden—just as my bad demons do—and I see again her dyed henna hair, the eyes dwarfed by the electric lights in the Star Lady Barbershop, and the dear, broken wing of her mouth, and when I regard her wild tatters, I know that not even Solomon in his lilied raiment was so glorious as my mother in her rags. *Selah.*" In *Because I Was Flesh* action is over and past, and words take over. *Selah,* and *Shantih.*

Robert Cantwell's *Land of Plenty*

JACK CONROY

HAYS JONES of the *Marine Workers' Voice* offered both an invitation and a threat to the assembled delegates of the first American Writers' Congress, meeting in New York City in 1935, when he said

> For a long time it has been regarded that in the working class there is no life, no interest, just a dead sodden mass that the writer has no need to look to as a source of material. But I say that today the only thing that's alive in capitalist society is the working class. The day in the life of a man who spends nine hours in front of a punch press or on a ship has more reality, more beauty and more harmony than you will find in all of Park Avenue with its boredom, its waste of time and its quest for joy that doesn't exist. Therefore we want to issue an invitation to these writers assembled tonight, to come down among the workers to find life and to create a synthesis for it with their tools as writers. Well, that is a big job. Some of us are a little skeptical about it. If the writers accept our invitation, we will furnish the market for their works and that is what they are looking for.
>
> On the other hand, if they don't take the invitation, we'll give them an ultimatum. They can go on writing about the dead until finally we have to shovel them into the grave and cover them up with dirt.

Some of the delegates were responsive, and for a time a fairly common feature of labor union meetings was the appearance of a writer who asked the brethren to give him advice on some "problem" that had arisen as he attempted to mirror a strike or depict life as it was in the factory from the hired hand's viewpoint.

John Chamberlain, who had just written *Farewell to Reform* and had been infected to some extent by the radical or revolutionary virus then in the atmosphere, was a guest. From the floor he complained that all the proletarian novels he had read within the past two years largely ignored problems of morals—the moral conflict. He cited Joseph Conrad's *Lord Jim* as a great novel in which there is "a terrific internal problem within one man." Instead, he added, proletarian novels "are either a story of a pilgrimage or as in William Rollins' *The Shadow Before*, the struggle of man against man, workers against bosses, the story of a factory struggle."

Two years before, Chamberlain had commented sarcastically in the New York *Times* about how, in *The Great Tradition*, Granville Hicks had "by implication urged the novelist to go out into the shop and the mine, to visit the farm and the railroad yard, to wait in the breadline and to sit with sparrow-bright eyes upon the park bench."

Chamberlain added that this admonition, in his opinion, was misdirected. "It would be rank futility," he continued, "to send Marcel Proust out to observe the embattled farmers of Milo Reno, or to sick a Thomas Mann upon the Edgar Thomson mill of the Carnegie Steel Company. Thornton Wilder on the picket line at Gastonia would not result in good art, but merely in very bad Wilder."

The objection of Chamberlain was also a bit misdirected. His contention that "one's subject material is a matter of fortuitous and slow saturation" had already been disproved by a number of novels whose authors had had a short or fleeting acquaintance with the situation or locale they had chosen, but had possessed the compensating qualities of keen observance and sympathetic understanding. Upton Sinclair's *The Jungle* (1906) might provide an early example.

Robert Cantwell, born in 1908 in the town of Little

Falls (later Vader), Washington, was admirably fitted both by experience and ability to produce an authentic proletarian novel. Not only the minutiae of the workers' life in a factory but the militant traditions of the World War 1 Wobblies became familiar to him early in his life as a veneer clipper operator in a plywood factory. This was in Hoquiam, a small city on Grays Harbor near Aberdeen. The brutal lynching of Wesley Everett, a war hero who had the misfortune to be an active Wobbly, by a mob of ultra-patriotic vigilantes had occurred in nearby Centralia in 1919. Cantwell was graduated from Aberdeen High School, and struggled through a dreary year at the University of Washington. Though he does not seem to have relished the academic discipline, he read widely and had an inquisitive and retentive mind. It would not be many years before he wrote astute (and one might even say erudite) critical articles for *The New Republic*, of which he was for a time a staff member.

In his leisure time and between jobs, of which he held a variety before he headed to New York City in 1931, Cantwell assimilated the prefaces to the novels of Henry James. His publisher claimed he had learned to write novels from this activity. More than one person wondered what the genteel expatriate would have thought of Cantwell's rough-and-ready lumber mill hands. Cantwell explained that, while he admired James' grasp of technique, he often found his novels boring.

James was not the only writer to influence Cantwell. Some critics, in addition to insisting that only working class themes had any contemporary validity, maintained that a thorough knowledge of the theories of Karl Marx was also essential to a clear understanding of the American worker and his concerns. "I find 'beauty' in a pamphlet by Marx, and in Lenin's words, roaring and dancing like an earthquake," wrote Michael Gold, sometimes called the "best loved American revolutionary writer" and "dean of the proletarian school." He was not alone among creative writers who turned earnestly to *Das Kapital* for guidance and illumination. Lenin's pronouncements, too, were diligently scanned for relevance to the current American situation when starvation threatened millions in the richest country the world had ever known. In the ideological battles that ensued, four and seventy jarring sects emerged, each claiming to expound the true Marx and each quoting chapter and verse to fortify their arguments. They resembled zealous Christian disputants wrangling over the exact meaning of passages in the Good Book. As with the Bible quoters, a wide variety of conflicting interpretations was possible.

Cantwell gave considerable attention to Marxism, particularly after he moved east in 1931 and became a friend of Malcolm Cowley. In one letter to Cowley he was irked at what he took to be Cowley's reluctance to assign as much validity to Marxist criticism as had conservative critics like Joseph Wood Krutch, Henry Seidel Canby, and William Troy. Marxists, he held, were fundamentally more serious and more conscientious in their approach to criticism than were the staid traditionalists.

Cantwell was not exactly a literary newcomer when his first novel, *Laugh and Lie Down,* was published in 1931. He had contributed short stories to "little" magazines such as *The Miscellany* and a short story called "Hanging by My Thumbs" was included in the 1929 edition of *The New American Caravan*. His four years in the plywood factory gave him ample grist for the novel.

In *Laugh and Lie Down,* Kenneth and William McCardle are the sons of James McCardle, whose death "extended over a long period of time" and who had spent the last years of his life in "a vain, almost an hysterical attempt to make some financial provision for the future of his family." William, the younger, pondered most over his father's death and failure, "for he considered himself most wronged by it." The plainly autobiographical connotations seen in the following passage are similar to others relating to each of the brothers in the course of the book.

> He started to work in a factory, working from four o'clock in the afternoon until midnight. In this strange place, for he never entirely lost his sense of its strangeness,

in the upside-down world that working at night seemed to create for him, he was reasonably happy; he found his industry rewarded and his awkwardness corrected, his laziness tolerated with a congenial indifference that seemed to indicate a civilization of the highest type. Certainly it seemed to him a more sophisticated, a more vigorous society than he had known in college. He was ambitious; he worked with his mind intent upon some job just over his own, for at this period it was neither hard nor unpleasant for him to imagine himself owning the factory.

Laugh and Lie Down was justifiably labeled as "sensitive." In accentuating the relationship between the two McCardle brothers, Cantwell was adhering to a pattern that established critics found both familiar and acceptable. For some time the Marxists had been advocating a shift from the psychological to the sociological, from the private to the public. Thus, a novel in which a factory or the workers of a factory figured as the protagonist would fill the need for the so-called "collective" novel. Writing in the September–October 1933 issue of *The Anvil*, Granville Hicks observed: "Of late there has been much interest in and some confusion about what's called the collective novel. In ordinary usage a collective novel seems to be any novel the interest of which does not center in a single individual or in a single family or in a complex of closely related individuals. It contrasts not only with the biographical novel so common in English literature but also with the family novel of the Butler-Mann-Galsworthy type and the 'situation' novel such as we find in nineteenth century French literature."

How was the "collective" novelist to present the mass or group as central character without reducing individual people to mere faces in the crowd, vaguely or sketchily developed? Considering the delicate problem of balance, Hicks continued: "On the one hand, the author must fully convey his sense of the group's unity in feeling action and his recognition that it is more important than the individuals who compose it. On the other hand, he must make the reader feel that the group is made up of comprehensible human beings, and he must differentiate individuals insofar as they have separate parts to play. It is a task that can be performed only by a writer who combines insight into the life of the group with an unusual mastery of narrative and structure."

The collective play was not then unknown in Europe, for Ernst Toller and other Expressionists had introduced the idea in the drama. Toller's *Mass Men* had electrified the Berlin stage as early as 1921. Various American authors were to try their hands at the collective novel, usually choosing a strike as the galvanizing or coalescing agent. Especially notable among these was Walter Havighurst's *Pier 17* (1935). None approached Cantwell's *The Land of Plenty* as a fulfillment of Hicks' recommendations. Farrar and Rinehart published it in 1934. Their experience with *Laugh and Lie Down* was not calculated to give much reason for hope in its success. Only 1,000 copies were sold of the first novel, and the rest of the small edition was remaindered. Cantwell wrote me in October, 1932, that he had been lucky enough to get the publishers committed to bringing out a second novel. They had so much invested in him that they felt they must gamble on another one. *The Land of Plenty* finally racked up a sale of about 3,000—an impressive total for a proletarian novel.

The events in the first half of *The Land of Plenty*, called "Power and Light," occur in something like an hour's time in a Washington veneer factory standing on a tideflat. It is the night before the Fourth of July holiday, and the machines are humming with a rush order. A power failure plunges the mill into darkness. Though they can see nothing, the conscientious operators move swiftly to shut off their already-stopping machines. This will prevent damage when the current is turned back on. Familiar with the place, the workers move about with ease. Not so with Carl Belcher, the pudgy and neurotic efficiency expert acting as night foreman. He dashes about, bumping into things, and hysterically blaming the electrician Hagen. Hagen calmly gets the power back on again, but

Carl, enraged by what he takes to be deliberate slowness of the men in returning to work, discharges both Hagen and Winters, a half-breed Indian who has been worried over his sick wife. Winters has been indiscreet enough to talk back when Carl abuses him. Pressure by the workers causes the superintendent to cancel the firings.

Part Two is called "The Education of a Worker." This refers mainly to the electrician's young son, Johnny Hagen. Johnny's ambition to go to college has been thwarted by the necessity of contributing to the family income. In the blackout he had encountered Walt Connor, a boy he remembered from high school days. Walt is a college dropout, also an economic casualty, but he still talks in superior fashion about the "good men" in the "Dekes" fraternity house. Johnny is impressed: "He sat back and listened to Walt, dreaming of the ivy-covered halls, the long slopes of green lawn, the beautiful coeds, each with her own sports roadster, giving herself so gaily and passionately with a true F. Scott Fitzgerald abandon. . . . Yes, and real hard work too, cramming for exams in the spring, when the air was raw and the leaves off the trees, staying up all night drinking hot coffee and cramming for exams tomorrow morning."

At home, Johnny is compelled, coming in late, to creep past his sister and her husband, an unsuccessful but desperately optimistic real-estate salesman. He is embarrassed in passing by their bed, especially when his sister giggles: "He's so funny. He must think we do it all the time." Hagen senior complains about the light bill, and Gerald, the sister's husband, discourses on the necessity of keeping up appearances if you want to stay in the game. The penny-wise pound-foolish salesman "starts economizing on little things, you know, he wears a shirt another day, he don't keep his shoes shined, he don't give away cigars and he begins to figure he can't spare the money for lunch so he gets out of touch with other men."

Walt Connor, would-be man of the world, gets Johnny in trouble when he takes him on a wild car ride with two of the factory girls. Ellen, the one with whom he has his first sex experience at a later date in the factory during a one-night sit-in, doesn't please him much when she dismisses him as "harmless."

Johnny's education as a worker is continued when the men return from the Fourth of July holiday to find that Hagen and Winters are going to be fired as Carl originally intended, and that in all, 20 men of the night shift have been let go. During the spur-of-the-minute strike that erupts, Johnny feels the weight of a policeman's club and learns that the strikers stand alone. The management, the respectable citizens, and the press are united against them. A driving rainstorm emboldens the strikers into forcing their way into the closed factory for shelter. They occupy it for one night during which Ellen permits Johnny to take her in the warm darkness behind the huge cylinders of a press. *"Promise me you won't talk about me,"* she begs. *"Oh, that's easy,"* he whispers, *"Why didn't you ask me something hard."*

The next day, bloody and violent, finds the workers massed in fights with the police on the tideflat. Johnny sees Ellen felled by a policeman's club. Led by Vin Garl, the seasoned Wobbly, he flees the battlefield. "They remembered the coarse blotched faces of the police, distorted with fury as they swung their clubs or ran after the few who were separated and lost, and the dull sickening smash of the clubs on human flesh. . . . So they rushed blindly through the brush, afraid of what might be ahead of them, and sick at heart with their fear for the ones who had been left behind." Johnny's fears are well-founded, for a beaten-up worker arrives at the hiding place to tell him his father has been shot. The book ends with Vin Garl and Johnny sitting in the drenching rain, waiting for the cover of darkness under which they may strike out in search of a safer hiding place.

Harold Strauss was dismayed by Cantwell's venturing into a wider area than he had covered in *Laugh and Lie Down*, which Strauss had admired. He grumbled in the New York *Times* Sunday book section: "There is not a line in *The Land of Plenty* that refers directly to a condition of heart, mind, soul or imagination in any of the characters." Strauss knew where to place the blame for Cantwell's artistic failure. "That none of the characters emerge as human beings is the direct result of Cantwell's service to the Marxists and their essentially non-literary purpose," he charged. "The moral we have promised should be obvious: it is high time that Cantwell strike out for himself."

Curiously enough, at least one of the maligned Marxists was in substantial agreement with Strauss. Jerome Mellquist wrote a letter for Mike Gold's "Change the World" column in *The Daily Worker* in which he said: "The American revolutionary writers do not state themselves simply enough. I found Cantwell's *Land of Plenty* practically unreadable. I sympathized with its subject matter, with what it had to say, and with what he was trying to do. But the result was one of the weakest, greyest things I have ever read. I've tried it out on other sympathetic people (one of them the boy who organized the National Students League at Harvard) and had a similar reaction."

It is significant that those who find Cantwell's labor novel dull are a professional literary critic, a Marxist intellectual, and a radical college student. Shortly after it was published, I tried the book out on a number of industrial workers. Among those of serious bent, appreciative interest was the common reaction, Cantwell's factory, though accurately set down, did not fit into the expected pattern of intellectuals who had never worked in one. As to the alleged obscureness, a condescending viewpoint then was that everything must be made ultra-simple for the worker. It was a forerunner of the Rudolph Flesch-ly school of "readability" that infested editorial offices a few years ago.

Cantwell was always dissatisfied with what he had written. I wrote him in October, 1932, praising a sketch of his in *The New Republic*—one with a factory setting. He replied that the mixed feelings he always had upon seeing something of his in cold print were worse than usual in this case. The real incident had been in actuality much more intense than he had been able to make it in writing. And he feared that he had recorded only the least impressive aspects of the experience from which the inspiration came. In April, 1934, his wife Betsy wrote Malcolm Cowley to say that Bob was glad to have Cowley's favorable opinion on a section of *The Land of Plenty*, but he feared that the novel dropped so at the end that it would be a letdown.

The conclusion of the novel was plainly defeatist, but few if any of the Marxists attacked it on that score. Writing in the *New Masses* (July 3, 1934), Cantwell made this explanation: "I tried to imagine what would actually happen, in the sort of community I pictured, when the workers entered the factory, what new factors entered a strike situation, what advantages were gained, what hazards encountered. . . . I couldn't imagine clearly what would happen, and the novel suffers as a result. But I wanted at least to state the problem, in the hope that it might be discussed, critically, that the imaginations of others might be directed to envisioning it more clearly than I could."

The sit-down strikes in Detroit were in the future, but the abortive seizure of the factory in *The Land of Plenty* plainly was a portent of things to come. Cantwell for some time was interested in writing a novel about the 1934 San Francisco longshoremen's strike to be called *The Enchanted City*, but irresolution and doubt (as well as his demand for artistic honesty) seem to have stayed his hand. In the years that have elapsed since publication of *The Land of Plenty* it has had no close rival for authenticity and accuracy. For one who has worked in a factory from necessity, as I have, it rings as true as a well-tempered bell and is as fresh and strong as it was more than 30 years ago. He has taken the various types one would expect to find in such a factory, deftly sketching their character traits and investing each one with recognizable humanity. Though prudence at that time decreed that he use a dash for some four-letter words now blossoming boldly on the printed page in current novels, the language is salty enough to be credible. Most important of all, his workers walk and talk with a dignity few of the other proletarian writers gave them. Too often they were like galley slaves chained to a machine they hated and yearned to be away from. Cantwell's workers are proud of their work and their ability to perform it.

Jack Conroy's *The Disinherited*
or, The Way It Was

ERLING LARSEN

I DIDN'T READ *The Disinherited* when it was first published; I waited for it to come out in paper. It was a long wait. The circumstances of the wait are not difficult to understand. In 1933 I was not buying books. Like many other people, I couldn't afford, or thought I couldn't afford, to buy them. And the libraries I had access to certainly weren't interested in *The Disinherited*. But I did, during those years, see *The American Mercury* once in a while, and I did know most of the Conroy stories that were appearing there, and I knew that *The Disinherited* incorporated some of them.

When the Hill and Wang paperback reprint appeared in 1963, I bought a copy of it immediately, being reminded of Jack Conroy and *The Anvil* and of a sporadic correspondence that we had carried on, mostly about Conroy's reasons for rejecting the short stories I once in a while sent him. And not long after reading the book, I set about trying to resume that correspondence. One reason for my trying was that I had for some months been affected by or afflicted with a concern about the Thirties. One reason for *that* was that I had recently become editor of *The Carleton Miscellany* and, because between the Thirties and the Sixties I had not been much involved with little magazines, a comparison of the decades now seemed important to me. I had, in fact, made a kind of comparison, after rereading James Agee's *Let Us Now Praise Famous Men*, and written a long nostalgic essay

about it. The reappearance of *The Disinherited,* together
with these other things, made it seem logical to me that
the *Miscellany* should run a symposium on the Thirties.
We thought, besides, that this might be something new
and daring, that interest in the Twenties had just about
run its course.

The people we invited to participate in our symposium
(*The Carleton Miscellany,* Winter 1965) were writers (or
jazz musicians) who had been active in the Thirties and
were still more or less productive in the Sixties. Among
them was Jack Conroy, who agreed to contribute, and
with whom I had begun to carry on that resumed and still
sporadic correspondence. A few good things came out of
it. We got our contribution to our symposium, and I got
from Conroy copies of some of the reviews given the
paperbacked *The Disinherited,* reviews of a novel that had
been in existence for thirty years and out of print for
perhaps twenty-nine.

Most of the reviewers in 1963 looked upon *The Disinherited* as a matter of historic curiosity. They gave brief
résumés of Conroy's career, explained that he was "now in
his sixties . . . identified with an educational publisher
and occasionally teaches writing courses at Columbia College, Chicago." So wrote William Hogan in the *San Francisco Chronicle.* Mr. Hogan, when it came to a discussion
of the work itself, said: "It seems old-fashioned today, and
improbable. But that's how it was in Conroy's Missouri
home country of the time he talks about. And today's
bright young novelist might study his book with profit, for
archaic as it may seem, it projects a vital, Jack London-
type approach to style, language and story. It remains a
curiosity piece, surely." Other reviewers were syntactically
and perhaps literarily more sound. Warren Beck, in the
Chicago Tribune Magazine of Books, pointed out that the
story line is concerned mostly with "the search for work"
and that this search "was also a quest for normal and
stable personal existence, not theoretical solidarity but
genuinely human relations." In *The Industrial Worker* a
reviewer who signed himself JS wrote that "the author

certainly has first hand knowledge of picket lines and soup lines." In the *St. Louis Globe-Democrat,* Howard Derrickson wrote that Conroy "does not complain, and he does not distort; he just uses an artist's resources to bring home the truth of the life of the poor in the 1930s."

Reviews like these raised questions about the meaning of "distortion" and "artistry" and "truth." I had myself been wondering about Conroy in such terms since I had read the novel. And my wondering became the greater when I asked some of my students to read the book, and learned that their lack of interest was so evident as to be impressive, or depressing. Twice, once at the close of each of two terms in which I had asked my students to read *The Disinherited,* I asked them to list at the end of the final examination the three novels of those we had read that they liked best—not those they thought most important or impressive, just those they liked best. The classes, alas, had been rather large and in these two polls I therefore got over a hundred responses. And only one student put *The Disinherited* at the top of his list, while many of his compatriots put it at the bottoms of their lists. This response I had not expected.

My reading list for the course, called "Twentieth Century Fiction," had been designed not to show what *the* novel of the twentieth century is but rather what *kinds* of novels have appeared during this first part of the twentieth century. We had therefore, I admit, put Conroy into some pretty fast, or strange, company. But I was not sure that the company had put Conroy to shame. Something more was at work. In a series of very short exercises in "practical criticisms," for instance, I did not get any Lawrence-Conroy comparisons, despite my own belief that such a comparison might be fruitful, that something might be learned from discovering how a common dislike for industrialism stemmed from quite different backgrounds, arose for different reasons, was put to different aesthetic and philosophic uses. Instead, the only nearly imaginative paper that I received compared *The Disinherited* with James Gould Cozzens' *The Last Adam,* published as was

The Disinherited in 1933. This paper pointed out the differences between the Cozzens' conservatism and what the writer called the Conroy optimism. Cozzens, the student wrote, looked back to the good old days while Conroy looked forward to the proletarian millennium. The New England of Cozzens, she wrote, was decaying while the Midwest of Conroy was on the verge of a revolution. Cozzens, she said, was a defeatist and Conroy was a meliorist. She did, however, write that she thought both these works were inordinately dull. I do not have the copy of this paper, nor do I suppose that one exists now, so you will have to take my word for its having ever existed and for its having said a number of sensible, more sensible, things about *The Disinherited* than I have cited here.

Perhaps the most sensible recent essay on *The Disinherited* is that by Professor Daniel Aaron, which appears as an introduction to the Hill and Wang edition of the novel. Professor Aaron gives a brief history of the work and of its inception, of Conroy's relation with H. L. Mencken, and documents Conroy's lack of interest in theoretical Marxism by quoting Conroy as saying, "Just to look at *Das Kapital* on the shelf gave me a headache."

As a critic, Professor Aaron paid closest attention to the realism of the novel. He points out that "the casual laborers who appear and disappear . . . are precisely the men one might have met in the early thirties working in the mines and railroad shops and rubber plants. . . . They are not splendidly impossible; they are as short-sighted, selfish, coarse, brave, irresponsible, and thick-headed as other Americans, and they speak authentic Americanese. . . ." As historian *and* critic, he points out that "Conroy's lack of formal education was by no means an unmixed blessing." According to Professor Aaron, Conroy had in 1933 told a reporter that he had "picked up a lot of education on freight trains, in the shops and in the mines too. It's been a pretty long course." In the course of this education, Professor Aaron writes, Conroy "had learned how excessive work brutalizes and breaks down the human spirit and how chronic unemployment can sap a man's self-respect. . . . Finally, he learned to set down his discoveries good humoredly and without self-pity in plain and energetic language."

Jack Conroy himself sees his novel in much the same light as does Professor Aaron. When he came to write his essay for that *Miscellany* symposium he said of his editorship of *The Anvil* that "*The Anvil* looked for material from the 'minds and mills and factories of America,' and it found it." *The Anvil* in an early editorial according to Conroy's essay, said, "We prefer crude vigor to polished banality."

Critics and reviewers, however, did not always understand. And in his 1965 *Miscellany* essay Conroy is still angry about that. He writes that "some of the stuff—rough-hewn, but bitter and alive from the furnace of experience—invited the jeers of the more esthetic urban and academic critics." He reports that James T. Farrell in 1935 told Whittaker Chambers that "neither man nor God is going to tell me what to write." Concerning this, Conroy says, "presumably, neither God nor man has to this day, which finds Farrell writing long and incoherent complaints to critics who feel that nobody, either mundane or divine, has ever yet succeeded in telling him *how* to write."

This present bitterness is apparently a long-enduring result of the Farrell review of *The Disinherited*, which appeared in *The Nation* for December 20 of 1933. Farrell wrote: "Mr. Conroy . . . has chosen the field of American life that is rich in literary possibilities. As reporting his work is satisfactory. As a novel, it is superficial. He has described a number of things. He has created almost nothing." Although she was apparently trying to be friendly, Margaret Wallace in the New York *Times* in the same year wrote, "In his very rejection of special pleading, on the one hand, and of literary artifice, on the other, lies the strength of his story." One might be inclined to agree more with Farrell than with Wallace here for the rather simple reason that a novel which has neither special pleading nor literary artifice might not have a very great deal to recommend it. Or one might try to discover what kind of strength a story that lacks both pleading and artifice might possibly have.

What is curious here is that the arguments we have thus far observed are concerned mainly with three ideas—artifice, special pleading, and realism. In 1933 Farrell and Wallace both agreed that the work was realistic enough, and in 1963 most of the reviewers, with Professor Aaron, also see the realism. But none of them has tried to define realism or explain what makes a work realistic. In fact, many of the little magazines of the Thirties, and many of the writers, made the simple assumption that realism meant proletarianism, or, if you will, "special pleading." A curious version of this assumption might be found in a comparison of *The Anvil* and *Kosmos*, for instance. *The Anvil* was openly proletarian, and *Kosmos* was equally openly precious and on the side of the sunflowers. Jay Harrison, editor of *Kosmos*, wrote in an editorial in the August-September issue of 1934 that although "economic conditions have tended to make the modern writer class-conscious . . . there is still room for . . . the writer of literature [who is] cognizant but unswayed by [the?] economics of today. In literature beauty is more important than utility—and *Kosmos* votes for beauty and preciousness."

Some evidence exists that at times Conroy fell between these two stools. For *The American Mercury* he was in the Thirties writing those hard-minded stories—"Rubber Heels" and "Hard Winter" and "Life and Death of a Coal Miner"—that later went almost word for word into *The Disinherited*. But he also wrote that most aesthetically self-conscious, perhaps "precious," of the Conroy stories that I know, "The Siren," which also appeared in the *Mercury* (May, 1933). "The Siren" did not go into *The Disinherited*, perhaps because the "I," no doubt Larry Donovan, is here only an observer and narrator and not a heavily involved participant. And the substance of the story would not have fit into the book Professor Aaron calls "a good example of the American picaresque novel."

The setting for "The Siren" is still Monkey Nest. The Donovan family and mining background serve only to introduce the main character, or one of the main characters, a pack peddler named Hassem. We learn in the first paragraph that Hassem is a Syrian and that he "became known as the Siren, not because he was thought to be a beguiler, but because that was the way the miners thought a Syrian should be called." As the story goes on, however, we know very well that this title "Siren" does mean "beguiler." Indeed, in the second and third paragraphs of the story we are given one of the strange symbols of beguilement that Conroy uses in this piece. Near the narrator's house is a "rank patch of jimpson weeds" in which at dusk "the air whirred with the wings of humming birds that came to sip from the long evil-smelling flowers." For a reason that is not given, the narrator has tried and tried to catch one of these birds and, also for reasons that we are not given, the narrator finds himself among these weeds one evening in company with the Siren who is intent also on catching a hummingbird. The Siren, apparently using the net of gunny sacks that the narrator has made, creeps "stealthily toward a ruby-throat poised for a blossom," swings the net and crushes the blossom, "shearing it from its stalk," only to discover when he puts his hands beneath the net that the bird is not there. The incident ends this way: "After a moment he arose slowly, looking as incredulous as a rustic who bets the wrong way on a shell game at a country fair. He could not believe that the bird had escaped."

Now the Siren does not have any fixed habitation, but spends the nights in barns on the various farms where he peddles his wares. One night he comes to the house of Lafe Towels and, after being searched for matches, is permitted to sleep in the hay. The hummingbird that meant so little at the beginning of the story begins now to take on significance when we learn that Lafe has a club-footed and shrivel-handed daughter named Birdie. In a perhaps excess of symbolism, the Siren contracts smallpox. Lafe, after the disease has run its course, says to the Siren, "You look like somebody has peppered you in the face

with an eight-gauge shot-gun. Looks like the good Lord
has made you jest as ugly as he could an' then slapped you
in the face." It is easy to see that Conroy wants to put the
Siren and Birdie into the same class of disfigured, mutilated, rejected people. But it is not quite so easy to see
why, while suffering from the smallpox, the Siren lives in
Lafe's barn and is frightened by a large snake that Lafe
forbids him to kill because it has lived in the barn for ten
years and has been "death on mice an' rats."

What happens, of course, is that Birdie and the Siren
fall in love. At what might have been an assignation, the
two are interrupted by Lafe, who becomes very angry and
drives the Siren from the place. The Siren goes back to
Syria and writes letters to Birdie that arrive in a rural
mailbox in which "at one time an English sparrow had
built its nest." Early in the story we learn that Birdie
writes poetry, sometimes published in the local paper, and
the story ends with Lafe's finding some unpublished
Birdie verse. One of the opening lines is, "Your love was a
fountain of strength to me." As Lafe reads, Birdie comes
into the room and the scene is described this way:

> "He paused, startled, as I was, by a queer choking cry
> from the kitchen. Birdie limped in, holding out both her
> good hand and her claw, her face screwed into an agonized
> protest. She stumbled and went down, clutching wildly at a
> chair.
> " 'Paw! Paw! Pleeease don't, Paw!'
> "She lay on her face, her thin shoulder blades almost
> punching through her dress, her hands scratching at the rag
> rug muffling her sobs."

Certainly we have learned that "Siren" may mean many
things. It is easy to play games with the hummingbirds,
the sparrow, and Birdie herself. But Conroy makes the
story even more complicated by showing that Siren is a
music-lover and a befriender of penniless strikers while
Lafe is a scorner of the arts and a member of The American Legion. Conroy has the peddler start a store, run
heavily into debt because of his giving credit to miners,

and eventually find himself forced into bankruptcy. Finally, something like "good times" returning and some of the miners having paid their debts, the Siren goes back to Syria where he is later reported to be "mixed up in a regular revolution" and in danger of being shot. It is in an attempt to learn whether Lafe thinks anything can possibly be done in Monkey Nest to help the Siren that the narrator arrives at Lafe's house in time to be given his final, dramatic look at Birdie.

If we see in this story the kind of split that early reviewers felt to exist in *The Disinherited*, if we reject the revolution story as extraneous and the bird-snake symbolism as overwrought, we have left to consider the realism and determine what sort it is. And we will then perhaps have a clue to what makes *The Disinherited* seem dull and remote to many modern students and readers. Modern students find in *The Disinherited* the too-pat propaganda of the ending, and readers of Joyce and Kafka dislike the mixed-up preciousness in sentences like this one in the opening paragraph: "Cold and white like the belly of some deep-sea monster incongruously cast out of the depths, the dump dominated Monkey Nest camp like an Old World cathedral towering over peasants' huts." But I think we can also see more—perhaps that which Conroy himself talks about in his *Miscellany* essay.

In that essay he defends himself against James Wechsler who in *The Age of Suspicion* (1953) writes that "we read the proletarian novels of . . . Jack Conroy and of countless others who had sprung to their typewriters to herald the final conflict." Conroy calls this a "flippant vulgarization of my purpose in writing *The Disinherited*" and says that it is "symptomatic of an attitude that prevailed for a great many years. I, for one, considered myself a witness to the times rather than a novelist. Mine was an effort to obey Whitman's injunction to 'vivify the contemporary fact' "—which is *one* way of defining realism, one way of stating a desire "to make you see." And Conroy does indeed in *The Disinherited* make us see a great deal. And we, seeing, can forgive him his opening pages, his "belly of some deep-sea monster" and his "Old World cathedral" while we thank him for vivifying at least some of the facts of the Thirties.

The Disinherited is essentially an artless book. It is, quite simply, the story of a young man's life. It begins with his becoming aware of the difficulties under which his family is existing and it ends with his becoming aware of the propriety, historic propriety, of his becoming a labor organizer in order to make those problems, as they affect not only his own family but all lower-income families, less difficult of solution. The narrator, who is also the hero, escapes going down into the mines to die as his father did, but he moves off into a world filled with jobs almost as difficult and as dangerous as those of his father. He works in the railroad car shops, in rubber-heel factories, and automobile factories, and one of the last jobs he holds is that of a high-iron worker, a job that very nearly costs him his life. His account of his fall from one of the bridge girders reminds one, necessarily, of his having been held out over the mine shaft as a boy and being frightened by the depths below him. Almost any of these adventures, these jobs, could have been eliminated from the story without affecting at all the contrast that Conroy sets up between the boy's innocent childhood and his politically and economically sophisticated young adulthood. For sophistication comes not in any way as a result of personality, of psychological necessity, but, the reader surmises, because of Conroy's intellectual conviction that all good people should at the end of all good novels come to the aid of perhaps not the party but certainly the class.

What I have called an "intellectual conviction" was perhaps not a conviction at all. It was instead, in Conroy, a mistaken notion that a proper novel needed a proper proletarian ending, and had no more basis in intellectuality or in psychological insight than did the "inevitability" of Helen's becoming a prostitute because *she* was in economic difficulties. Similarly, we may argue that the fancy writing came into existence because the author was essentially artless and had an artless conviction that "art" was necessary to a proper novel. The "special pleading" and the unnecessary and intrusive "literary artifice" have been imposed on the novel from without. They do not arise from within the work itself.

What does arise is the "vivifying of the contemporary fact." Where the strength of the novel lies is in its simple, poignant descriptions of a life that Conroy obviously knew very well. If it is to be remembered for another thirty years it will be not because of its propaganda or its preciousness but because of its success in achieving what many of the young uneducated and unsophisticated writers of the Thirties were trying to do—simply to tell other people about the way things actually are. It will be remembered for its account of Larry's devotion to his mother and his mother's devotion to him, of the boy's worry when he inadvertently ruins a washtub full of clothes that the mother was doing in a vain attempt to keep ahead of the butcher bill, and, perhaps more than for these things, for the vividness with which the narrator recollects the small things that made up the world through which he moved—the ticking of the rails at night after the passing of the large passenger train, and the slow quiet dripping of the water from the tank across the tracks.

Perhaps one of the dominating fears in the minds of those living during the Thirties was the fear of isolation. And a host of writers were trying to explain to the world what it meant to be a lonely harvest-hand, a friendless miner, a defeated small-time prize-fighter. Those of us who remember the isolation and the sense of loss will recognize quite easily that Conroy, economics and the precious aside, knew very well, "the way it was," and was quite able to tell us about it. And it may even be that when and if we recognize this achievement we will also understand as well the reasons for those qualities of the work that our education has led us to label "pleading" and "artifice."

Daniel Fuchs' Williamsburg Trilogy
A Cigarette and a Window

IRVING   HOWE

EVER SINCE THE END of the nineteenth century there has
been an outpouring of fiction about the life of American
Jews. Most of it has been predictably mediocre: journalism draped as art, "problems" blotting out experience,
sentimentalism corrupting memory. Yet the subject has
kept a certain hold on the imagination of both readers and
writers, and during the last few decades there has arisen a
talented "school" of novelists—or what to an outside eye
may seem like a "school"—that has taken as its main
concern the experience of immigrant and first-generation
Jews in the American city.

At a time when a good many American novelists
seemed anxiously uncertain as to their true interests or
themes, writers such as Saul Bellow, Isaac Rosenfeld, Del-
more Schwartz, and Bernard Malamud enjoyed notable
advantages. They have composed their work under the
pressure of inescapable subjects that came welling up in
memory, subjects they had neither to improvise nor discover but merely submit to. They have rested their fictions
in local worlds intimately known and sharply contoured,
so that the very settings of their stories seem a force
making for dramatic control and personality. They have
written at some intellectual distance from the main assumptions of our society, thereby gaining the perspectives
of nostalgia, irony, and contempt. And by drawing from
the idiom and rhythms of Yiddish which some of them
know and others still hear as a half-echo of their youth,

they have been able to develop new prose styles, some of great rhetorical virtuosity and others of a plainness so severe as to constitute a kind of anti-rhetoric.

These writers have recently been much praised, perhaps overpraised. We are all eager for the appearance of new talent—watching for it is a mild American disease; and even those of us who know how facile and dangerous is our national desire for "greatness" cannot help being somewhat subject to it. What tends to be forgotten in discussions of "American-Jewish writing" is that it did not begin a few years ago: there have been writers, in the earlier decades of our century, who have used the same materials with occasional success. Only recently has one begun to meet people who know Abraham Cahan's *The Rise of David Levinsky* (1917), a neglected ornament of our literature, or who have heard of Henry Roth and Daniel Fuchs, both of whom made their literary debuts in the Thirties and deserve as much recognition as Bellow and Malamud. Roth published only one book, a master-piece entitled *Call It Sleep*, while Fuchs turned out a trilogy that constitutes a miniature *comédie humaine* of Jewish life in Brooklyn. Well-received by critics, the works of these two men were commercial failures, and soon, wearied by the assaults of political ideology and literary fashion, disappeared from sight. Roth retired to farming in Maine and Fuchs to script-writing in Hollywood, their names all but forgotten, victims of the frantic amnesia that besets our culture.

Now, a good many years later, they are slowly being rediscovered. *Call It Sleep* has been reissued by Avon and Fuchs' three novels by Berkley. As with all belated acts of justice, there is something bitter in the thought of all the years that have had to go by; but still, reprinting them *is* an act of justice, and a welcome one.

At the foot of the Williamsburg Bridge in Brooklyn lies a grey and dreary slum. During the years of Daniel Fuchs' adolescence and young manhood, Williamsburg was the home of the poorest New York Jews, those who were even more deprived than the Jews of the Lower East Side or the East Bronx. It was the cramped and harried life of this slum that was to be decisive, even traumatic, in shaping Fuchs' career as a writer. I doubt that one can find another American novelist, except perhaps James T. Farrell, whose image of life was so tightly bound by his adolescent experience, whose entire creative effort was so painful a struggle to come to terms with his memories—yet whose achievement, in the bruised serenity that marks the best of his work, seems finally so much more than the growl or whimper through which the young writer has traditionally affronted his fate.

For the adult imagination, memories of formative years are both a rich source and a destructive temptation. The writer who has not thoroughly worked out for himself, in both thought and feeling, his relationship to the world in which he lives will make such memories the center of his work rather than an absorbed part of his total perception. As one picks up *Summer in Williamsburg,* the novel Fuchs published in 1934 and which he had written during several summers while freed from his job as substitute teacher in a Brighton Beach public school, it seems almost as if the book is still marked with the prints of his adolescence, as if the heat and smells of a Williamsburg summer continue to cling to its pages.

All of Fuchs' novels are dominated by a sense of place—the sense of place as it grasps a man's life and breaks him to its limits. *Summer in Williamsburg* may look, at first glance, like still another naturalistic genre study dealing with the troubles of disadvantaged youth, but as one reads into the book, it becomes clear that Fuchs is not merely subject to a dilemma, he is actively developing a novelistic idea. And that idea is the way the power of environment, the tyranny of conditions, can take over a segment of human life to become an overwhelming presence. In the grimy Williamsburg summers young people scurry about, seeking ways of escape and avenues of pleasure but soon learning that escape is unlikely and pleasure brief. And that, insists Fuchs with a quiet but self-tormenting passion, is the law of Williamsburg life, the trap of its youth. From the first to the last word of this novel, Fuchs is obsessed with a single theme: escape and trap. Yet at no point does he slide into self-pity, for he is at once too clever and too grim a writer to pose as the sensitive youth or the tormented intellectual. He is not, in the trivial way, a "sensitive" youth at all, and he has no claims to intellectuality. His object is more impersonal: to release a sense of fatality which, oddly but suggestively, reminds one of the work of Edith Wharton.

As a novel, *Summer in Williamsburg* is conventionally made: a series of set-pieces, forming not a consecutive plot but a scheme of contrasts and reinforcements. It is a structure with obvious dangers, and Fuchs, only 24 when he wrote the book, does not avoid them all. There is a tendency toward sketching for its own sake; an excessive lingering over the pleasures of dialogue; and a resort, at the end, to melodrama, perhaps to summon a climax that seems slow in coming. Yet these are minor, even amiable faults, and anyone now opening the book will be struck by the sureness with which Fuchs validates his world and quickens his characters. Totally unsentimental, Fuchs was nevertheless able to bring to his picture of Williamsburg a wry and disenchanted tenderness, perhaps because he possessed that capacity for accepting "the given"—the life one sees, the only life one has, no matter how wretched it may be—which even the most rebellious novelist, if he is to be a novelist at all, must have. It is not exactly love for his world or his people that is at stake here, but something that for a writer like Fuchs is more important: a total absorption in his material, so that his rendered world creates an illusion of coming not from the writer's craft or contrivance but from some deeper necessity. A reader's protective skepticism is always softened when the recollections of a writer seem to result from some unavoidable pressure.

At the center of *Summer in Williamsburg* stands Philip Hayman, a decent young man raised in Williamsburg, who can neither take his experience for granted nor provide it with some intellectual order. Contrary to the *Erzie-*

hungsroman formula, Philip is not a precocious intellectual; he is only an earnest chap who is aware of his conflicts of will, but thinks of his will as something almost apart from himself, subject to the alien and dispossessing powers of Williamsburg. Encircling him, and representing a series of possible paths into life—probably, traps within life—are a number of finely-drawn figures: his father, whose honesty has melted into helplessness; his brother, who decides it is better to earn a living than to live decently; his uncle Papravel, a racketeer handy with knives; and his friend Cohen, a youth racing through postures as if he were bolting bad food. At the end Philip reflects:

> That was the choice . . . Papravel or his father. Papravel, smoking cigars, piled up money and glowed with sweat and happiness, while his father sat with his feet on the window-sill in the dimness of a Williamsburg flat. . . . He was heading in his father's direction. . . . Look at him, Philip said, he's old, he's skinny, and all he has after all the years is a cigarette and a window.

Without pressing a point that is inherently speculative, one is inclined to look upon Philip's dilemma as in part a reflection of Fuchs' problems as a writer. In his first novel Fuchs looked back upon his experience with a mixture of fondness and loathing, and in the end had to admit that he was helpless before it, helpless to change and helpless to understand. Like Philip, he was not an intellectual: he could not claim the solace, such as it may be, of theory and speculation. All he knew was that his experience was *there*, with its "marks of weakness, marks of woe"; that people in tenements "lived in a circle without significance, one day the duplicate of the next until the end, which occurred without meaning"; and that, so far as he could tell, there was no exit.

In Fuchs' second novel, *Homage to Blenholt* (1936), all these vexing problems remained, but now mainly to be teased and laughed at. Naturalism, with its massing of detail, somberness of voice and gloom of vision, was not really Fuchs' most congenial mode; he had turned to it in his first book because in the Thirties it seemed the most likely way of recording the pains of youth. Now, in his best novel, he would release his true gift, which was for an exuberant if slightly embittered comedy, a mocking play with daydreams, a marvelous twisting of Yiddish rhythms as these came to inhabit and haunt American speech. The book rocks with zest and energy, those impulsive spirits that, in the world of Williamsburg, must soon flag. But if *Homage to Blenholt* is happily the work of a young man enraptured by the discovery of his mimetic powers, there is also within that young man another and much older one, Jewish to the core, who is never able to forget the essential sadness of things. And one mark of the novel's distinction is the poise with which Fuchs balances these two sides of himself, young and old, gay and weary.

Reading *Homage to Blenholt* I have been struck not merely by Fuchs' ability to register Jewish life in the depression era, but also by the extent to which he is a "pure" novelist devoted to the pleasure of observing the human spectacle in its own right. *Homage to Blenholt* is totally caught up with the milieu of the Williamsburg Jews, yet is notably free from tendentiousness or special pleading. Not only is Fuchs innocent of theories concerning the destiny of the Jews, he seems also quite indifferent to those modern notions which transform Jewish characters into agents of the human condition, symbols of estrangement, heroes of consciousness. He writes about Jews, quite unremarkable people, because he has lived his life among them; and in this freedom from preconception, this relaxed indifference to folk ideology, he is closer to such Yiddish masters as Sholom Aleichem than are most of the later and more intellectualized American Jewish writers.

Max Balkan, the *schlemiel*-hero of *Homage to Blenholt*, is a Brooklyn Harold Lloyd, a charming, befuddled daydreamer who yearns not for mundane wealth but for spiritual glory. As the novel opens he is on his way to the funeral of Brooklyn's Commissioner of Sewers, Blenholt, a man who had risen above this "flat age" by building a political machine of flunkies and gangsters. Musing upon the fate of this great figure, Max thinks back to the words of Tamburlaine, "*We will reign as consuls of the earth / And mighty kings will be our senators.*"

What little action there is follows the rhythm of the pratfall: Max, having naïvely interfered with the ceremony of Blenholt's toughs, is beaten up and left gasping with disenchantment, so that in the end, allied with his winsome entourage of *Luftmenschen,* he must return to the dust of reality. And meanwhile it is the women in his life who most urgently represent the principle of this-worldliness: Max's sister Rita, who snares her fiancé by "close dancing," and his girl Ruth, the sort of female who will perpetuate the race no matter what foolishness men may dream. Max will now slice salami in a delicatessen store and his father, "Mr. Fumfotch," who earns a few pennies carrying a sandwich sign for Madame Clara's beauty parlor, can only whisper to himself, "Max was dead already for now he would live by bread alone."

For Fuchs women are this-worldly sex, the child-bearers chaining men to earth. Far from being romantic, they are the personification of the earth force, the champions of the reality principle. They bind men to the sort of life that ends with a cigarette and a window.

Max's final defeat is unmistakable. When he receives a letter from a company expressing interest in his scheme for bottling onion juice, his hopes soar: Max Balkan, onion king! But the company has already been bottling onion juice for years, and all it offers him is a three-pound bag of onions in gratitude for his interest. . . . Reality, or what Williamsburg takes for reality, is vindicated.

Fuchs allows only one concession to the meek: little Heshey, Max's juvenile double, gains a victory. In an exuberant scene, he traps his tormenter, the bully Chink, in a dumbwaiter and bombards him with rotten grapefruit. But once having impressed Chink with his shrewdness, Heshey proposes a predatory alliance between his brain and Chink's brawn. Even if the meek do triumph momentarily, they must forego the purity of motive that had sustained their meekness.

Begun as a lark, and for long sections (most notably, in its high-spirited and rapid "overture") sustained as a work of brightness and play, the book ends on a note of subdued resignation. You may fancy yourself a modern Tamburlaine daydreaming your way out of Williamsburg, but life will bring you back, back to the inevitable store, back to the cigarette and window.

Low Company (1937), the last of Fuchs' novels, is skillfully composed: its plotting tight, its prose sharp and efficient, its characters conceived with greater complexity and firmness than in the two previous books. Clearly, Fuchs was steadily gaining in mastery of his art, those tacit skills difficult to label but easy enough to perceive. *Low Company* is not, to my taste, quite so enjoyable a book as *Homage to Benholt,* if only because Fuchs' comic gift is now bent to the needs of a well-made novel; but by way of compensation, it is a more reflective work, bringing its author deeper and deeper into the crisis of his career.

Low Company starts with a passage from the Yom Kippur prayer: "We have trespassed, we have been faithless, we have robbed . . . we have committed iniquity, we have wrought unrighteousness." The characters are drawn in twilight greys, colors more somber than we have come to associate with Fuchs: for the world is closing in and the moments in which it can be forgotten are vanishing. It is as if in his five or six years of composition Fuchs had run through the cycle of hope, exhaustion, and resignation; as if the pleasure of imaginative resolution cannot keep him at a sufficient distance from the dispiriting shabbiness of reality in Brooklyn.

But if the tone of defeat sounds through *Low Company,* it is surely wrong to say (as did Irving Howe years ago in *Commentary*) that the novel is slick in method and cynical in outlook. It does, to be sure, keep repeating Fuchs' cry: *See what a world I come from, see what a world I would escape!* But there is also a modest, self-chastising emphasis upon the possibility of decent relationships among men, which comes through in Fuchs' delicate handling of the gambler Karty, the moral complexity with which he presents the brothel-keeper Shubunka, and the concluding glimmer of humaneness which leads one of the characters to believe that "it had been insensible and inhuman for him, too, simply to hate Neptune Beach and seek escape from it. This also was hard and ignorant, lacking human compassion. He had known the people . . . in their lowness and had been repelled by them, but now it seemed to him that he understood how their evil appeared in their impoverished dingy lives. . . . It was not enough to call them low and pass on."

Yet the moral resolution of *Low Company* is more problematic than this quotation might suggest, for there is also another side of Fuchs, corrosive and mocking, that speaks throughout the book. The petty deceits and meanness of a lower-middle-class neighborhood, men lost in their small desperations and defeats, form the substance of Fuchs' plot. And when the brothel-keeper Shubunka cries out, "We must not be like animals to one another! We are human beings living together in this world," it comes as a bitter shock to remember that the immediate point of these words is to defend small-scale prostitution against a syndicate. Earlier in the novel there is another incident which seems to sum up Fuchs' view of things, his kindness and despair together: an aging Jewish intellectual, disturbed by a street fight, spills a pail of water from his window in order to restore quiet. When the crowd stares up, he delivers "a lecture, impassionate and burning, on the decencies of human life. Everyone quite forgot the fight to hoot and yell at the intellectual." Without sentimentalism or tough-guy posturing, Fuchs knew the acrid reality of our urban life, the measure of low company.

Beyond this, it seems, Fuchs could not go. If *Summer in Williamsburg* presents a dilemma, and *Homage to Blenholt* is a high-spirited attempt to delay or evade the problem of choice, *Low Company* marks an acceptance of the burdens of commonplace reality. For what constitutes both a major strength in Fuchs' work and a reason, perhaps, for the abrupt termination of his career as a young novelist, is his grim and ironic appreciation of the power of the commonplace, everything in daily existence that erodes ambition and spirit. As Albert Halper, a novelist who is Fuchs' contemporary, remarked of him: "he is a man with a burden. I do not envy him . . . he is a child of sorrow."

Perhaps so. But this child of sorrow, this poet of the Williamsburg streets, wrote some of the most winning fictions we have about American Jewish life. His scope narrow but his tone pure, Fuchs was that rarity, a "natural" writer with a gift for spontaneous evocation and recall. He stopped writing; he went to Hollywood, where he has now spent several decades; and during the last few years he has published a few stories, ironic and painful sketches of Hollywood life, in which, as it seems, the young drifters and dreamers of his novels now appear in their sagging middle age, hearts eaten away by success and memory. One hopes that he may still turn his gifts to the world of Hollywood, which by now he must know only too well. But no matter what he does in the future, or does not do, the work of his youth deserves honor. This is the time to thank him for the pleasure he has given to that small band of readers who have always been faithful to him, always remembered the turmoil of his Williamsburg and the immortal funeral of Blenholt.

Dalton Trumbo's *Johnny Got His Gun*

LEONARD KRIEGEL

WHATEVER ELSE can be said about the literature of the Thirties, it should be apparent by now that it was both far more complex and far more varied than has generally been assumed. The decade's complexity cannot be excessively stressed, which is one of the things that make such books as Alfred Kazin's *Starting Out in the Thirties* so peculiarly discouraging; such memoirs succeed only in making of the decade a kind of never-never land to be approached with whispers of celebration. And if the Thirties seems to be on the verge of becoming literarily fashionable once again, this, too, seems to be for the wrong reasons. The fact is that we continue to be embarrassed by the literature of the Thirties, treating it as an unwanted legacy discovered in some unlamented aunt's attic, some poor relative for whom we apologize with all sorts of gestures about her good intentions. Even those books which have survived the general critical condemnation of the generation — much of it a *mea culpa* breastbeating — have frequently been praised for the wrong reasons. The recent revival of James Agee's *Let Us Now Praise Famous Men*, for instance, focussed far too much on Agee himself as a kind of American *Wunderkind*, tragically dead before his time, tragically unfulfilled as an artist, a kind of natural cousin to Fitzgerald and Hemingway. The focus should have been on the book itself, on the fact that *Let Us Now Praise Famous Men* is probably the single most painful documentary in our literature, and that even to read it today from cover to cover demands an act of will that goes beyond what art may legitimately demand of us. In the same way, Henry Roth's *Call It Sleep*, now evidently selling in the hundreds of thousands as a paperback, seems to be slated to serve as the official precursor of the Jewish canonical revelations that have played so significant a role in recent American fiction, a glimpse into the childhood of Moses Herzog rather than what it is, a nakedly sensitive portrayal of the immigrant child's terror in the face of all that this America, this *goldena medina*, actually represents.

Dalton Trumbo's *Johnny Got His Gun* has suffered a similar fate. It was reissued in 1959, but after reading Trumbo's flippant introduction to the new edition one is not quite sure why. There is a myth about the novel which such flippancy does little to dispel. According to the myth, the novel was put together as a kind of contemporary *exemplum* to be used by the American Communist Party in the days of the Hitler-Stalin Pact—one envisions old men who smell of garlic and wear horn-rimmed glasses secretly plotting the overthrow of god, mother, apple pie, and J. Edgar, and all by insidiously trying to get the public to read a book which portrayed the mutilation produced by war. This is, of course, to ignore the history of the Thirties, when revulsion over the First World War swept not only the campuses but the country at large. Still, if one subscribes to the myth instead of to the reality, all that prevented our blood from turning to water was Hitler's invasion of the Soviet Union, an act which made American Communists even more ferocious than John Wayne.

It is, one sees, a rather ironic fate for a novel whose very ugliness possesses power as excruciating as Zola's. Simply as a *tour de force*, *Johnny Got His Gun* is remarkable. In its successful use of the mind of a basket case as its point of view, it can stand comparison to Faulkner's use of the mind of the idiot Benjy as the point of view for the opening section of *The Sound and the Fury*. No novel, however, can exist as a mere *tour de force*, and if this were all that could be said of *Johnny Got His Gun* it would probably be better forgotten. After all, a television newscast on which we see an American marine applying a cigarette lighter to a jungle hut in Vietnam offers a far more graphic portrayal of the horror of war than Mr. Trumbo ever could have. We watch such newsreels every evening, while the professionally reportorial tones of Huntley and Brinkley assure us that even if this is not the best of all possible worlds it certainly is the most natural.

Mr. Trumbo is an American novelist and American novelists have rarely been particularly squeamish about death, at least not in our century. But other than Hemingway, for whom death and the prospect of death remained from the first some sort of mystical apotheosis, our novelists tend to avoid the more mundane realities death demands that we admit to our daily lives. Our novelists are fascinated by death, but only our newspapermen, those men of brick-and-straw talents, have understood that its possibilities are more than biological. And for all the vaunted gothicism of our literature, physically and mentally deformed characters are usually meant merely to shock the reader rather than to increase his awareness of life's possibilities and dimensions. Let the reader compare the world of a Carson McCullers to that of a Genet. And so Trumbo's ability to make a Joe Bonham human seems even more remarkable. To create him so that the revulsion we feel is, at least in part, the same kind of mixture of fascination and disgust that we feel when Proust's Charlus parades before us like some homosexual peacock, to force the reader merely to admit to himself Joe Bonham's awareness of his existence—to do this is a substantial achievement for any novelist.

This is not to deny that by any critical standards, even those incorporated in such Marxist semantics as "socialist realism," *Johnny Got His Gun* is a novel which contains a multitude of sins. Even worse, so many of the sins are boring: much of the novel is sentimental; the stream-of-consciousness is often faked; the simplistic good

guys-bad guys view of the world is apparent from the very
first page; and the Rousseauistic nobility of the much-
heralded "common man" has become an increasing liability as that creature spits in Martin Luther King's face
when he doesn't burn down huts in Vietnam. But the
power is there. And the novel still lives, both as a pacifist
plea, perhaps as relevant today as when it was written
(although for entirely different reasons), and, even more
important, as a work created around a thing, a consciousness endowed with a humanness which we see as being so
revolting that it tests our humanity. As contemporary
readers, we recognize life's complexity; we are even victims
of that recognition. Our sophistication, our refusal to be
taken in by the myths of a previous generation—each
forces us to respond cautiously to Dalton Trumbo's novel.
Johnny is certainly not a difficult book to read; its trouble
is that it remains so personally embarrassing.

What remains most significant about modern fiction is
its intensely personal vision. Tolstoy spoke for the world;
Joyce spoke for Joyce. And Joyce's *Portrait* remains the
artistic *modus vivendi* for our century's fiction; we see the
world through Stephen's eyes and what is most significant
about Stephen is that he is himself. Not that Stephen is
not also a number of other things; his is, after all, a
portrait of *the artist*. But his world is created in one man's
brain, his own. And so is Joe Bonham's. But the brain of
Joe Bonham is unlike any other brain in all of literature,
for it is a brain without a body. *Cogito ergo sum*, wrote
Descartes, thus changing the nature of western reality.
How vicious a parody *Johnny Got His Gun* offers on that
famous syllogism. For Joe Bonham's is the reality of caricature, the kind of reality which so distorts the world that
we see it as a hall of mirrors until truth is thrust upon us
by the very insanity of the angles. It is caricature, but so is
the reality with which it deals. The brilliant English critic,
Raymond Williams, in distinguishing between types of
realism speaks of how in contemporary literature realism
can be seen as "a principled organized selection" of "observed reality." A basket case is the *sine qua non* of war as

an action engaged in by men. In Williams' words, Joe Bonham is, as he lies on a hospital bed trying to make contact with the world around him, our "principled organized selection" (minus eyes, legs, arms, face, etc.); the "observed reality" is the war, the First World War—and all wars—which produce the Joe Bonhams. The dead who are living are an embarrassment to all of us. Who wants to be reminded of Hiroshima or Buchenwald, especially of their survivors? How nauseated we are when, after years in darkness and isolation, Joe finally does manage to communicate, and the finger that taps against his chest asks him, "WHAT DO YOU WANT?" What an absurd question!

To attempt a critical analysis of *Johnny Got His Gun* seems just as absurd. One can speak only of his reaction to the continued existence of Joe Bonham. Now this is a reaction we can better imagine if we think of ourselves as sitting in a darkened theater watching the first newsreels which depicted the heaped bodies and parts of bodies which greeted the Allied armies when they entered the German death camps near the end of the Second World War. Suddenly, a voice from a part of a body, say some stray leg or arm, begins to address us in matter-of-fact tones to tell us what it was all like. In the face of this kind of thing, literary criticism, like history or political science or sociology or even physics, is simply inadequate. It is even useless, for it cannot even conceive of a reaction to such a horror. Read, say, any essay by T. S. Eliot and then read this novel. It is certainly not Eliot's fault that Joe Bonham exists or that what caused Joe Bonham to be what he is exists. But Joe Bonham is that voice; he is that voice despite the overblown rhetoric, despite the sentimental nonsense of his remembering how his mother "read the story of the little Christ-child of the baby Jesus," despite the overly propagandistic ending (not that the ending is a total failure, for one of the questions we must learn to ask of novels accused of being propagandistic is how accurate their propaganda is). Joe Bonham simply *is*, and, in creating him, Trumbo succeeded in creating our nightmare.

The power of the nightmare is especially evident in Book I, "The Dead," where Trumbo carefully works the mind of a basket case becoming aware of exactly what his situation is into the life he has come out of, a life that seems typical enough. In fact, it is this very typicality, Joe's apple-pie and mother origins, which is one of the aspects of the novel which justify the charge of sentimentality. But Joe has to be typical because the very atypicality of the horror he is to become must emerge from the everyday world itself. Trumbo's sense of detail is unusually skillful here. It is one of the better lessons that the novelists of the Thirties learned from Hemingway. As he awakes to the ringing of a telephone, Joe's first memory is of a night he was working in a factory in Los Angeles when another ringing telephone brought him the news of the death of his father. He leaves the factory and heads for "the place." (Even before the First World War, Americans did not have homes.) "The place was on the alley above a garage behind a two story house. To get to it he walked down a narrow driveway which was between two houses close together. It was black between the two houses. Rain from the two roofs met there and spattered down into wide puddles with a queer wet echo like water being poured into a cistern. His feet squished in the water as he went." This is the way death is meant to be. Joe feels the pain of remembrance, the pain of a young man's sense of loss, of fragmentation, of the passing of a father who was loved and needed and who failed, as all fathers inevitably must, to provide for his son a buffer against the knowledge of death.

Trumbo learned his other lessons from Joyce and Dos Passos. The modified stream-of-consciousness of Book I seems natural enough; in Book II, "The Living," it frequently seems forced, perhaps because Trumbo is beating us over the head with his message. Dos Passos' weaving of American history and contemporary events into the narrative is also quietly made part of Joe's memory before the shell that made him into what he has become exploded. "Lincoln Beechy came to town. It was the first airplane

Shale City ever saw. They had it in a tent in the middle of the race track over in the fair grounds. Day in and day out people filed through the tent looking at it. It seemed to be all wire and cloth. People couldn't understand how a man would risk his life just on the strength of a wire. One little wire gone wrong and it meant the end of Lincoln Beechy. Away up in front of the plane ahead of the propellers was a little seat with a stick in front of it. That was where the great aviator sat." In the jingoistic patriotism of "the people who are willing to sacrifice somebody else's life," Lincoln Beechy is the American ideal. But it is an ideal of heroism without the true recognition of death, with neither questions asked nor emotions permitted. The growing consciousness of Joe Bonham is to become revolted by that same kind of super-patriotism which Dos Passos scathingly envisions for us in the concluding line to the section of *Nineteen-Nineteen* entitled "The Body of an American": "Woodrow Wilson brought a bouquet of flowers." Of course, both Trumbo and Dos Passos are guilty of oversimplification. Novelists generally are. There undoubtedly was a purpose to the war. Not all generals, as Hemingway writes, die in bed. And not all politicians are soulless automatons eager to send thousands of men to their deaths for the sake of mere abstractions. So what? All Joe Bonham knows is, "You're dead, mister. Dead."

Political rhetoric is a denial of death's reality, just as it is a denial of war's reality. Ultimately, it is an extension of the child's view of the world. Joe Bonham, a living consciousness, is physically dead. In a country which pretends to as much religious faith as ours does, such a reversal of traditional Christian immortality seems deeply ironic.

Book II is definitely something of a falling off as far as the novel's power is concerned. It is here, I suppose, that Trumbo lays himself open to the charge of writing propaganda. Book II is devoted to Joe's attempts to communicate the consciousness within him to the world around him; at times, it is done with a kind of grueling humor. Joe Bonham's tapping with his neck comes to seem, even to him, a kind of insanity. And yet, like so much "black humor," it is the insanity of life. "There were times when he knew he was stark raving crazy only from the outside he realized he must seem as he always had seemed. Anyone looking down at him would have no way of suspecting that beneath the mask and the mucus there lay insanity as naked and cruel and desperate as insanity could ever be."

And then, as Joe finally manages to make himself understood, that terrible question comes: "WHAT DO YOU WANT?" The furious rhetoric of the last two chapters of *Johnny Got His Gun* are an attempt at an answer. Joe wants himself seen, recognized, perhaps exhibited as the end result of Woodrow Wilson's Fourteen Points. Let us admit that this is propaganda of a rather elementary sort. Meant to be an impassioned plea against war, the rhetoric falls short of the mark. Trumbo is too conscious of what his objectives are, too much in control, to create the kind of surrealistic explosion that is needed. It would have been better if Joe had wanted simply to die, really to die, to end his suffering and his isolation. It is rhetoric; it is propaganda; it is, one reminds oneself, not very different from that other simplification, the patriotism of such groups as the American Legion. All of this is true. But as I write this, entire villages in Vietnam are being sacrificed to the expediency of accidents. Like the shell destined to make Joe Bonham a basket case, napalm is its own logic. It needs no defense. One begins to suspect that it is the logic of existence itself. All we can do is to react to the rhetoric, just as all we can do is to react to Joe Bonham's existence. But if one must think in choosing between such rhetoric, admittedly futile, and the rhetoric of a Lyndon Johnson as he, too, saves the world for democracy, then the failure is far more than a failure of art.

B. Traven, Pure Proletarian Writer

CHARLES H. MILLER

WE HARDLY USE the good Latin word "proletarian" in our green-backed land, but let's say that a proletarian is a working person possessing no negotiable capital. It isn't easy not to possess some capital in today's capitalist society; so, perhaps, the best way to become a proletarian is to be born one, and millions are. But the only writer I can name who worked with, fought for, and continues to stand for, the proletariat is B. Traven. He says that he is a proletarian, "indistinguishable from the others," and his work proves his point.

Much of the American confusion over Traven's image as writer and man is due to our slowness to recognize him as a pure proletarian; for we hardly recognize the proletariat, the drone class left at the outer edges of the glittering but anguished American Dream. Or the proletarian is directed toward an escalation of the American Dream where he will become a little capitalist, if a mortgaged one. But Traven the outsider, the exile, the philosophical revolutionist, and benevolent anarchist, rejected the American Dream. His world and his works are of the true proletariat of the Americas.

In his early autobiographical books, the young Traven tells how he became an international revolutionist and a philosophical anarchist. Traven Torsvan wrote stories, novels, poems, revolutionary pamphlets, essays, and speeches in English and in other languages before he first appeared in print as "B. Traven," in the liberal Berlin daily *Vorwartz* in 1925, with a series of informal stories about his work adventures in the booming Mexico of the Twenties. Seeing this work (which appeared in German), the editors of the pioneer Buchergild Gutenberg, or Gutenberg Book Guild, wrote to Traven and asked to see more. From Mexico he sent the manuscript of *The Death Ship*, which they promptly accepted, and it appeared in German as *Das Tottenschiff* in the spring of 1926 as a Book Guild selection.

Rejecting publicity, the young Traven refused to meet press or public in person or to furnish photographs of himself; pursuing his career, he published eight books in five calendar years, some of which were written or drafted previous to his first publication. The Mexican sketches and stories which introduced him to the German reading public were speedily expanded into a picaresque proletarian novel, *Der Wobbly* (Berlin, 1926); it was published in a bad English translation as *The Cotton-Pickers* (London, 1956), but is yet unpublished in the United States.

A work-quest begins with the first sentence of this "first" novel: "I stood on the station and looked about me." From the station platform he sees only Mexican bush and ragged men, all of whom seek work. A Mexican, a Spaniard, a Chinaman, and a huge Negro speak to him. No local Mexican knows exactly where the promised work is to be found, but the men walk in the direction advised, and after several days of marching, sleeping on the ground at night, and eating almost nothing, they find Mr. Shine's cotton plantation. So the first quest ends within twelve pages.

Each of the ragged men is described in detail. "Then there was me, Gerard Gales. . . . I was indistinguishable from the others, and I was going cotton-picking . . . because there was no other work and I badly needed a shirt, a pair of shoes and pants. These'd have to come second-hand, for fourteen weeks' earnings at cotton-picking wouldn't buy new ones." So young Gales-Traven stoops under the blazing tropical sun to pick cotton, each kilo made up of "two to five hundred pods," at four centavos per kilo. After many days of drudgery, they realize that their wages barely pay for their food and that they will have hardly enough cash to get out of the bush and onto the next harvest job. So they strike.

That is, they sit in the shade and look at the cotton while Mr. Shine fumes and protests. But the strike is soon settled, the men are granted eight centavos per kilo of cotton picked, and they return to work. This is perhaps the first sit-down strike to be described in the literature of the Americas; it is a basic, pertinent episode, for it is the "direct action" of the Wobblies, a tactic the C.I.O. used so effectively in its formative years.

Yet the Wobblies remain characteristically invisible, being present in spirit but absent in person. Several other strikes follow in nearby Tampico, all conducted on Wobbly principles. "The Cotton-Pickers' Song" written by Traven was used by Wobblies and revolutionaries in several nations, and the novel gives evidence that the I.W.W. was an effective invisible force, just as B. Traven was to become.

In the course of the novel, many international and native proletarians are described, always in relation to the work they do, or the work they seek, and in relation to their beliefs. A Louisiana Negro goes into the egg business as a sideline to cotton-picking and proves—by a catch—that hens lay more eggs for proletarians than for capitalists. A Mexican and Spanish worker indulge in an Aztec duel; the Spaniard wins the money-stake; the Mexican dies of the duel wounds. Some writers might have stretched the story into a symbol, but Traven didn't. Gales-Traven goes to work in an oil field, then in a Tampico bakery, and at last drives a herd of range cattle across the Mexican hinterland. The narration is picaresque, the theme is work, and the life is vital, various. The fresh Mexican countryside is both kind and cruel, but it never persuades the canny narrator to be sentimental or to relax his necessary judgment of individuals with whom he works. In a formative, revolutionary Republic, his judgments are invariably whole; while he works for and with the proletariat, he shows the "gringo" capitalist-ranchers, Shine and Pratt, to be likable human beings. From the first, Traven's vision of individuals and society is round, whole, and always vividly realistic.

Young Traven leaves no doubts about his philosophical status: "I was forced to become a rebel and revolutionary . . . out of love of justice, out of a desire to help the wretched and the ragged. The sight of injustice and cruelty makes as many revolutionaries as do privation and hunger." Yet his only "revolutionary" act in this early novel is to accost a policeman who is beating a defenseless Indian in a public park; the higher action is embodied in his pledge "to help the wretched and the ragged," a pledge he amply fulfilled in his six related novels of the Mexican Revolution.

The Wobbly is a rural, provincial proletarian novel, such as Hardy and Dickens would have enjoyed. Although Traven is a man of ideas, and a cataloguer of endless details, he sees men as individuals looming over the dawn light of any idea. His ideas are moist with mankind. His apolitical views are uttered with passion, never in duty to party line or ideological framework. It is clear that Traven was a gifted storyteller who became a revolutionist, and *The Wobbly* is a whole proletarian novel of the Americas because Traven loves mankind even while he admires radical and revolutionary remedies for the obvious ills of society.

While *The Wobbly* is very much the "first novel" of an adventurous young man in a new green world, his real first novel, *The Death Ship*, is vastly different. It was written over a long period of time in various ships and ports in the form of notes, journals, and episodes; then it was written in the form of a novel in Tampico, one of Traven's first permanent homes in Mexico. Subtitled "The Story of an American Sailor," it is a quest in search of a passport (that is, identity), a quest which ends in self-identification with fellow sufferers.

The plot is as simple as the silhouette of a ship on the horizon, but the nature of the voyage is as complex as life going toward death. Young Gerard Gales ships out of New Orleans on the freighter *Tuscaloosa,* but is left in Antwerp without passport or belongings; the time is post-World War I. Unable to prove his identity as an American citizen, the young sailor becomes a man without a country. He is shunted across borders and jailed; released, he goes wandering and scrounging in the Low Countries, France, and Spain, but never retrieves his passport or sailor's papers. From a Barcelona dock he boards the tramp freighter *Yorikke,* which proves to be a "death ship," itself without legal papers. Crewed by passportless sailors from many nations, it is smuggling arms to African rebels and is subject to no laws on the high seas. Like other ships of its kind (some of which still exist), it is liable to be sunk at sea without many telltale survivors, so that its owners may collect its rich insurance. In Dakar, Gales and his buddy Stanislav are shanghaied onto a newer death ship, the *Empress,* which is run onto shoals in the Atlantic, with "Pippip" Gales the lone survivor left to tell the tale.

This epic tale of modern mariners is as easy to define as *Moby Dick,* to which "Pippip" Traven refers between the lines; he likewise refers to Shakespeare, Dante, Goethe, Kafka, Conrad, O'Neill, and others. But the sailors, stokers, jailbirds, farmers, workers, petty officials, and cops whom Traven describes and to whom all his books are directed are not concerned with lofty literary names, and the author is primarily concerned with his proletarians and with ideas which apply to their condition and destiny.

The first documented idea is that most societies, including our American one, tend to be criminally careless about lowly members on the outer fringes. And the strongest thematic idea is the young hero's apocalyptic vision of death, that real horizon toward which all of us are sailing, with oppressed proletarians outsailing the rest of us. These two ideas are related in Traven's consciousness as a result of his personal experience; for *The Death Ship,* according to Traven's own statement at the time of its publication, is autobiographical.

The *Ship* carries a grand cargo of ideas, individuals, and issues, but, as Traven said in a letter to one of his editors, "The sailor peeps out from every page in the book." Yes, and the sailor speaks as a whole man whose vital ideas are voiced in slang, with the accent of a self-educated worker or immigrant. Even while the passportless sailor is getting the bum's rush through bureaucrats' offices, customs, jails, frontiers, trains, towns, and situations, he turns loose strong opinions:

> Each age and each country tortures its Christians. That which was tortured yesterday is the powerful church today and a religion in decay tomorrow. The deplorable thing, the most deplorable thing, is that the people who were tortured yesterday, torture today. The communists in Russia are no less despotic than the Fascists in Italy or the textile magnates in America. The Irish who came five years ago to the States and who took out citizenship papers yesterday are today the most ardent supporters of all the narrow-minded God's-country-praisers who want to bar from these United States everyone who did not ask his parents to be hundred-per-centers. Whose fault is it that a Jew was born a Jew? Had he a chance to ask to be born a Chinese? Did the Negro ask the English or the Puritans to bring him to the only country worth living in?

Gales soliloquizes on many things, including the nature of American proletarians: "Workers are not all as chummy towards each other as some people think when they see them marching with red flags to Union Square and getting noisy about a paradise in Russia. Workers might have a big word in all affairs were it not for the middle class ideas they can't shake off." This is logical for young Traven, whose sharp insight and firm opinions have already marked him as an apprentice anarchist. The many ideas in the book do not obtrude, for they derive from "The Story of an American Sailor," with a worker's stream of awareness which is one of the most remarkable in proletarian literature.

From the moment that Gales sights the *Yorikke* by the Barcelona docks, there is a change in the novel's tone. The physical description of that particular death ship is a

gothic masterpiece, one of the most literary and provocative set pieces in all of Traven's books, but the real change
comes when Gales descends into the stokehold. The ship
stinks of death, but Gales is fascinated; the stokehold
looks fatal, but Gales goes to work: "Wherever any other
human being can live and work, I can." He is no longer
just a wily bum; he has found a ship. The quest for
personal identity is postponed, for the gypsy proletarian
has become a proletarian slave. Henceforth, Gales speaks
more of "we" and less of "I." He is concerned for his
fellow workers.

A passportless stoker, Stanislav Koslovski of Poznan, becomes Gales' buddy and tells his life story in detail. Stanislav's homeland was simply wiped off the map by the
Treaty of Versailles, and Stan was doomed to a life of
wandering without proper papers or even the opportunity
of returning to his homeland which became a "foreign"
nation. Traven gives Stan hero status and imagines him
confronting the Great Skipper: " 'Can you read what is
written above the quarters, Stanislav?' "

"And Stanislav said: 'Aye, aye, sir. He who enters here
will be forever free of pain.' "

The Death Ship transports pain, but there is purgation
in Gales' ironic acceptance of the order of things in this
world, from which order the only release is into death.
This is the attitude of a young benevolent anarchist. Yet
while it sails, the death ship is full of life, not only the life
of the forgotten workers, but the life of the mind. Trav-
en's mind is never anchored in any cozy harbor of theory,
but is free as the trade winds of philosophy, as liberated as
empiric anarchism can be. The reality of the book is so
stark, so relentless, as to seem unreal to persons unaccus-
tomed to the workers' world or the workers' mind as
Traven epitomizes it without transcending or traducing it.
The "strange air" of the book is achieved through a double reality: the reality of the workers' world and the more
insidious reality of the mind, that is, the supremely alert
mind of young Traven who, experiencing what he did,
became opposed to many of the world's ways and so
became an anarchist in his own way.

Because *The Death Ship* is a big book written from the core of a young man who defies governments, gods, ideologies, and even his fellow men, it can mean different things to different readers. Some editors, whose timing is poor, recently wrote that Traven had slipped into the quagmires of communism; it happened that they were speaking of his third book, published in 1927 (*The Treasure of the Sierra Madre*), and they quoted no proofs, but they proved that they knew little about Traven's works. The very essence of Traven is that he is apolitical, being too philosophical to be cooped up in any party or ideology. In *The Death Ship* he attacks communists, fascists, Catholics, Protestants, bureaucrats, and bureaucracy. He soliloquizes, "I should feel unhappy in a communistic state where the community takes all the risks I want to take myself." And in his work he takes all the risks of the creative thinker who is anarchistically above and beyond any system or set formula of thinking and writing.

Only a few of the important critics who have discussed some of Traven's books complain about his use of language. These did not include H. R. Hays, Granville Hicks, V. S. Pritchett, and Cyril Connolly, who were more concerned with Traven's ideas and effectiveness, but A. Calder-Marshall and John Wain have protested that Traven was murdering the king's English. My contention is that Traven's books in general, and *The Death Ship* in particular, are written in true pitch for his proletarian world; of course *The Death Ship* written in ivy-hall English would never have made its remarkable 40-year voyage in 31 languages.

Traven says that he was born in Chicago in 1890 of Scandinavian worker parents, and he claims English is his mother tongue. Since he also writes well in German, Spanish, and other languages, it is easy to believe that the young Traven did indeed travel, work, and live in various nations. And from the evidence of the original Traven manuscripts in English that I've studied, I believe that Traven wanted to cross over into English as Conrad and Nabokov crossed over, but that he succeeded only in a primitive way, as befits his nature. His English has the flavor of the immigrant or second-generation worker, but it has the same power of eloquence found in the words of Sacco and Vanzetti when they spoke on matters of life and death. Traven's language is usually work language, but it has powers of suggestion, allusion, and eloquence.

His death ship is a "tub . . . a bucket . . . a coffin . . . a deathmobile . . . . a bob-tail." His fellow workers speak a bit of all the languages of the globe they sail. The ship is a floating babel, and Gales is concerned with language, soliloquizing on the captain's too-correct grammar and the differences between real and literary English. Gales speaks common American English. The captain is "the old man," the workers "knock off" and "bring in the grub." The language is dated but effective. It is the dialect of the underdog; it is part of our vital, melded, American idiom.

This "Story of an American Sailor" is told from the outside by an outsider who looked toward the American Dream but belonged only temporarily to "the only country worth living in." He lost his passport and eventually his citizenship, but never lost his affection and his hopes for America. While *The Death Ship* remains a great underground paean to proletarian victims, it also sounds the triumph of the human spirit over dreary, deadly conditions. "Wherever any other human being can live and work, I can," said young Traven. He lived and worked there, and he came out of that world to take us back into it.

Each Traven book is different, the first two differing as land from sea, and the third, *The Treasure of the Sierra Madre*, has a mountainous reputation as an adventure story. It happens to be a proletarian adventure story, beloved by millions of non-proletarian readers.

This time the hero (or antihero) is a third person, an ambiguous anarchist throned on a broken park bench: "Dobbs had nothing. In fact, he had less than nothing," for his rags branded him a white outcast in a nation of dark skins. Even the Tampico bootblacks are capitalists, with their kits and stools worth three pesos. Dobbs can't even fish: "Having grown up in a bustling industrial

American city, he hadn't a bit of the patience so essential for crab-fishing" in the river.

Dobbs and his new acquaintance, Curtin, are befriended by old Howard, a veteran gold prospector. Howard is one of Traven's most lovable heroes; he knows that "you never can buy love with gold," and he repeatedly warns the younger men of the corruptive powers of gold. Howard knows how to dig gold, and he also knows how to lose it; he rocks in "Homeric laughter" when the wind blows their gold dust back into the Sierras from which it came. Howard, an amiable anarchist, becomes a great healer who gallops off with the Indians to begin a new life quite different from the retirement he planned in a "small house in a quiet town" in his native Midwest.

From the proletarian scenes of Tampico the adventure mounts swiftly into the Sierras; all is flooded with mountain sunlight and busy with the drudgery of gold digging. In three massive digressions, Traven increases the suspense of the treasure hunt; the stories of the Green Water mine in northern Mexico, the murderous but abortive train robbery, and the Huacal mine of Don Martin and Doña Maria (whose blood-stained gold disappears into the viceroy's palace) are told in superb style.

This treasure novel has many facets and many nuggets of natural, unpolished wisdom. Certainly it is a more important book than its world-wide popularity suggests. It is what adventure stories ought to be, and then some: it is a kind of mature *Treasure Island* for adult proletarians and anarchists. I suspect that many of the millions of Americans who read this book do not know that they are ingesting anarchist ideas, for sardonic Traven has tossed gold dust into their eyes; but the real treasure from Traven's pen may sift into their gold-hungry hearts and work its magic by means of the ancient alchemy of storytelling.

Mr. Traven tells me that he lived in Mexico off and on for years before he received his first recognition and consequent earnings from European publishers, which came on the heels of regular rejections from the United States. Rather than speeding for the literary capitals with his new fame, he invested in horses and equipment for exploring his beloved southeast Mexico. From this expedition came a unique book of travel-exploration with anthropological bias, *Land of Springtime*, written in but unpublished in English; it appeared as *Land des Frahlings* in German in Berlin, 1928. It describes various Indian nations, including the Lacandones, Tseltals, and Tsoltsils; it discusses native life and customs, archeological sites and treasures yet new to the world at that time. Like all his books, this travel book bristles with Traven's awareness of and affection for his new world.

In the same year he published his first collection of stories, which appeared in German as *Der Busch* with the provocative "Bush" song in English and in German in the front flyleafs: "Down we hiked from Illinois / Full of hope three jaunty boys / In the bush in Mexico." The closing story of this collection is "The Night Visitor," which appeared as the title story of a newer collection in English in New York, 1966. In this casual but revealing story, a certain Doc Cranwell writes eighteen books, enjoys his creation, thinks about it, then revises, perfects, and destroys it. Doc counsels young Gales: "Be like God, who destroys with His left hand what He created with His right." Another neat notch on the anarchist handle.

During this eventful expedition, which was made mostly solo, Traven lived and later wrote about an incident in the near jungle. Published in German (Berlin, 1929) as *Die Brucke im Dschungel*, it appeared in Traven's basic English in New York, 1938, as *The Bridge in the Jungle*, and was reissued in New York in 1967. The novel tells how a native boy falls from a bridge and is drowned, how his body is recovered, and how he is buried. That's all. But the bridge was built by a United States oil company, the boy falls because he is wearing his first pair of shoes (brought from Texas by his half-brother), and so the implications follow. Young Gales plays the perfect role of observer. With his love for and sympathetic understanding of native Mexicans, he enters their settlement, their huts, their lives, their dreams, and subconscious minds; he bridges their primitive and our complex cultures.

Traven has said many times to many friends that this is his favorite book. And perhaps it is his most perfect. With Traven, art is truly a branch of philosophy; ideas are the skeleton of his strong fiction, and here the fiction is fleshed with love and pulsing with passion, but always a controlled passion, always casual, always as real as the bereaved mother and her friends swigging harsh tequila from a common bottle in a hut before the funeral march. And the march has its moment of mirth—a terrible, choking mirth, product of a most ironic author—when the teacher, drunk (through no fault of his own), gives his divinely idiotic speech and topples into the grave.

In this novel Traven shows us the universal pathos of a boy's death. The Garcia family consider neither their own lives nor their loss of Carlito as tragic, but rather as fate, as "destiny's orders." This book is a tragicomedy on death and love; Traven reaches the height of his power to reveal the nature and spirit of proletarians from the lowest social level. Such a novel never has and never will be written under the influence of anything less than brotherly love.

Here again Traven had a perfect symbol: the bridge. But to him, a bridge is a bridge; let the critics label it, swing it, and suspend it as they will. The reader sees a bridge over which trucks roll and from which a child falls to his death. It is the boy Carlos we remember, and the love he enjoyed from his mother, and from every mother and every civilized human being who knows his story. Adios, Carlito: "No king was ever buried the way you were. Adiosito!"

Among the Traven books yet unpublished in the United States, *Rosa Blanca* is particularly important. Oil is mentioned in his first six books, and oil is the sacrificial earth blood of his seventh. Translated from Traven's original English, it first appeared in German as *Die Weisse Rose* (Berlin, 1929). It concerns a tract of land in Vera Cruz State which natives own but American oil exploiters covet; its Indian owners have subsisted very well on its lush acres for centuries, until oil derricks appear on the horizon. The Indians, who have no use for oil or money, regard their land as a sacred trust, but oil capitalist C. C. Collins swears to get the land at any price and pump the oil out of it. The results are tragic for the traditional families on hacienda Rosa Blanca.

Young Traven knew the hacienda and its people. He calls this novel a document, for it is a true account of land seizure in the Mexico of this century. The novel's theme is land versus money. In the opening chapters, we discover a warm, bucolic little community which Traven describes as humanly short of perfect; self-sufficient, but not quite utopian, it is demonstrative of family life, tribal security, and parental if paternalistic love.

From the flowering hacienda, the story swings to the United States, where the life of C. C. Collins is traced in grey and savage lines. Traven usually portrays his characters through their words and actions, tracing their physical appearance in one or two Chekovian phrases; but Collins gets the treatment, and charges through this big book, a man as evil as a human being can be. Yet Collins is believable. As a financier who came from rags to riches, Collins deceives investors, buyers, and the public. Publicity is his trump card. He knows how to turn the public against striking workers, how to create confusion in labor's ranks, how to influence and bribe labor leaders, and how to increase his capital on all this.

Through Collins' tactics, Traven considers and compares the great anthracite coal strike and the historic Chicago construction strike. He examines various wolf and bear tactics in the Stock Market and gives us a prophetic rehearsal of our Stock Market crash of 1929. Among the remarkable scenes are Collins' confrontation with John D. Rockefeller, Sr., an orgy planned and staged (or bedded) by Collins' favorite mistress, and the murder of a Mexican landowner on United States soil.

Rosa Blanca rambles yet manages to become a rough epic of land versus oil. It is Traven's most ambitious social novel; it ranges far and wide in issues, ideas, and historical fact. Broad in scope, it is even broader in its implications. But its greatest achievement is its note of personal passion, which places it above other social protest novels, and a world above Sinclair's skillful, informative, but impassioned *Oil! Rosa Blanca* can best be compared to Zola's masterful *La Terre,* but Traven's land-ownership novel picks up terrible force when it swings back and forth over the border, castigating our culture, indicting the civilization that tramples individuals for the sake of progress. Finally, as in all of Traven's books, this story triumphs because it is founded on knowledge of human individuals and related with love. Some readers may want to forget C. C. Collins if they can, but who can ever forget hacienda Rosa Blanca or her people?

Rosa Blanca is one of Traven's most controversial books. It appears in eighteen languages about the globe, it is a classic in Latin America, and it has been rejected by some New York publishers. Each of Traven's books has a vital publishing history, but the world-wide record of *Rosa Blanca* is lengthy, disputatious, and far from ended. English readers who hope to read the novel will have to wait, for *The White Rose* version of it, published in London in 1965, is a badly butchered and tampered text, from which two hundred pages were "edited," including big scenes important to American readers. Look for it in one of the other seventeen languages and in American English in the near future, for it will come home to roost.

Rosa Blanca is the only novel I know which significantly portrays and compares segments of our two hemispheric cultures, the brown and the white, and this is done with a large passion compounded of patriotism and exile, hatred and love.

Within the four calendar years 1926 to 1930 young Traven published the seven books we have discussed. His Old World fame was sudden and solid; he seemed assured of financial independence, and, considering his years of hardship and homeless wandering, he was eligible for a rest. But he had different plans. During his expedition in the southeast interior, he learned much about the region and met many veterans of the Revolution; he was determined to write a big work based on his new knowledge of the region and its people. The result was six related novels, each self-sufficient but together forming a whole work which documents in powerful fiction the social and economic causes of the Revolution in that region.

Had Traven written nothing else but this loose epic of the life and liberation of the rural proletarians of southeast Mexico, his reputation in the Americas would be secure. Unfortunately, only one of these novels appeared in hard cover here, *The Rebellion of the Hanged* (New York, 1952); it is the fourth of the group.

The first, *The Carreta*, appeared in German as *Der Karren* (Berlin, 1930); it is a fresh, pure story of the native carters who guided caravans of ox-drawn carts through countryside and over so-called roads which caused "unrelieved martyrdom" to man and beast. Though hardship is the general condition, the young natives forge ahead in life and love, even while they are passed from owner to owner like slaves, never dreaming that they are heading for a rebellion which will topple the entrenched dictatorship of Porfirio Diaz. This novel is distinguished by a tender love sequence in which Andrew meets the homeless Estrella and accepts her as his *compañera* or common-law wife; she relates the Indian legend, which appeared later as *Sun Creation*.

The second of this group, *Government*, is a strong sociological novel of local dictatorship. Appearing in German in 1931 in Berlin, it was the basis for the later Nazi ban on Traven's books and confiscation of his German earnings. *Government* is particularly provocative in showing how outside owners fail to govern and control the illiterate but wily and spirited natives of an isolated locality.

Not a trace of Gerard Gales-Traven is to be found in this series, though he could have doubled as "the Professor" in the later books; he dedicated himself to his third-person characters, just as "Pippip" dedicated his conscience to fellow workers on a death ship. Celso Flores, the Indian hero of *The March to Caobaland*, is one of the many who were tricked, framed, or actually lassoed and marched off to work under armed guard in the coffee *fincas* and mahogany lumber camps, from where one laborer in four returned alive. *The Troza* (a *troza* is a log or tree trunk fit for lumber) depicts the actual mahogany camps near the Guatemala border, the laborers, the owners, and the product, along with global glances at the nature of society which prizes mahogany wood without questioning the fate of the workers who got it out of the jungle.

The Rebellion of the Hanged unites some of the heroes of previous books into one "monteria" camp where they are tortured for failure to fell huge quotas of mahogany. Because there are rumors of the Revolution's inception in the North, the owners are sadistic with the workers, hanging them alive by four (and sometimes five) members in the trees. The workers at last rebel, execute the owners, and make ready to march out against towns, cities, and the Dictator's armies. *The General from the Jungle* shows them in action, but still isolated from the revolutionists far to the North. It describes the natural tactics and strategy of the native guerrillas on their own terrain and the wiliness of a young uneducated "general" who defeats the Dictator's well-equipped and trained troops. It is a brilliant if bloody novel of guerrilla warfare, even while it damns war of any kind; it leaves the regional natives on the road, traveling toward a nebulous future with only their battle cry of "land and liberty" to guide and govern them in an Hispanic world where democracy is a foreign dream with no local or regional examples to prove its existence. And so, to the tune of prophetic or admissive anarchism, the curtain falls on this bloodstained saga.

With the series of Revolution novels completed in 1939, Traven rested most of his Mexican campaign in our hemispheric literature, but he continued to publish stories, essays, and articles and completed more than one nonfiction work which, for his own private reasons, remains unpublished. *Macario* appeared in 1949, and we will discuss it presently. During the Fifties, Traven spent a great deal of time on play and film scripts; Seki Sano staged *Sun Creation* in Mexico City, and a total of seven films based on Traven books and Traven scripts have appeared to date, including such international successes as *The Treasure of the Sierra Madre* and *Macario*. Ufa of Germany filmed *The Death Ship* with Horst Buchholz and Elke Sommer at their best, but the film ran into litigation and is now restricted to German territory. *Rosa Blanca* was filmed in Mexico with top national talent under an all-time record budget of millions of pesos and promptly banned from Mexican screens by the government that subsidized it. Such things can happen in any nation with a strong, chauvinistic government, but the *Rosa Blanca* controversy still rages in film and diplomatic circles, with a possibility of the controversial film being shown outside of Mexico any day now, or even mañana.

In 1959, *Aslan Norval* appeared in German in Hamburg; it is a novel about the United States. Mrs. Aslan Norval is an American heiress plagued with proliferating wealth. Having an urge to do something epic, she undertakes the project of a canal across continental United States to be financed by an open corporation which welcomes wage-earning investors and shareholders, a kind of civic capitalism, so it meets with opposition from leading capitalists. The project is investigated by Congress, but public-spirited Americans swarm to its defense and ensure its possibility. Mrs. Norval hopes that the canal will solve such problems as unemployment, demobilization of the Armed Forces, world shipping troubles, the Cold War, and the Berlin schism! She is a rich dreamer, and her Texas-bred man Friday is a practical dreamer. The novel is a modern comedy of hemispheric problems, but it is out of the mainstream of Traven's passionate concern with oppressed minorities of the Americas.

In 1966 *The Night Visitor and Other Stories* appeared in New York and was very well received, having complete critical success, but (as usual in the U.S.A.) small sales. I saw none of the old critical complaints or slurs concerning

Traven's radicalism, and this would appear to be critical progress, but to my amazement, hardly a reviewer or critic remarked on the obvious anarchistic aspects of various stories in this collection. And, of course, the term "proletarian" was not called into use when our reviewers attempted to place Traven in our hemispheric literature. Some of the reviewers found the stories "fresh," even "superb."

Of these stories, "The Cattle Drive" is as fresh and green as it was when Traven wrote it in 1922; "Assembly Line" promises to live on the power of the basket weaver who is a delightful indigenous anarchist; in "Midnight Call" everybody (except the confused policemen) is outside society and the law; in "Conversion of Some Indians," Christianity proves to be too far in for the far-out Indians. Most of the characters are proletarians, even "The Night Visitor" charcoal burner who is descended from royalty that ruled his land before white conquerors came to take it over. These and most all Traven stories will endure because they have solid philosophical bones of contention, because they are based on radical and anarchistic ideas that dwell in the depths of human nature, and because they are examples of the oldest art of all, that of pure storytelling.

One of Traven's latest heroes is one of his grandest, Macario the woodchopper. With his sandaled feet treading wood chips and his back bent from carrying wood to village buyers, with his belly empty and his mind unhampered with dreams of material gain, Macario deals with the Devil, the Son of God, and Death in a very satisfying manner. He can do this because human nature is expansive and because Traven (who was well-trained in hunger, work, and the powers of death) tells his good friend Macario exactly what to do. Everything Macario does is completely Mexican and yet wholly universal. When we've tired of a jumping frog with its ass full of lead, when all the biggest fish and spotted horses have been rounded up, we will admit that "Macario" is the great folk tale of the New World, for it is compounded of folk wisdom and timeless folk in their living struggle against superstition, hunger, and death.

B. Traven, a political proletarian author of the Americas, is too big to shoehorn into an essay. He doesn't need to be criticized or analyzed, but to be read. What a shame it is to talk about important books rather than read them! But here we have talked about them because we couldn't read them, and Traven himself (ever the anarchist) is partly to blame for his spotty publication in the United States. That is another story, and a fascinating one for bibliographers, but the four-decade story of Traven's achievement is now taking a turn for the better. In the United States, editors, librarians, scholars, and readers are seeking his titles. A Traven boom, American type, is in progress.

What is his place in our literature? Happily, it is too early to place Traven, for not only are we a decade behind in reading his books, but he is writing others. Besides the unpublished Traven manuscripts I've been privileged to see, there are hundreds of remarkable letters, a few of which have been published about the world. There are uncollected essays, stories, poems, and scripts, some of which were published under still other pen names. Any serious student of Traven's full body of work will discover as I did that he is confronting a most unique major writer.

Traven is more than just a proletarian writer of the Thirties, for he straddles that decade and others. Half of his work to date was published before the Thirties, but his six related Revolution novels appeared during the Thirties, and paradoxically, our readers have yet to "discover" them. Tremendous as the Thirties were, no major writer can be assigned only to the period. The ideas, issues, and philosophies that raged and warred through the Thirties were imported or improvised from other decades and other nations, just as internationalist Traven improvised his individual philosophy from tested (if embattled) Old World philosophies.

It might be argued that Traven is a regionalist, for more than half of his work deals with southeast Mexico, but one might as well try to prove that Dickens was a regionalist of surrounding London Counties. Like Hardy, Traven stood for a while in the forum of a region while he addressed and judged the universe. From the global awareness of *The Death Ship* soliloquies to the peasant wisdom of Macario conning the world, Traven proves himself to be that man of today and tomorrow, an internationalist.

Of course Traven is a proletarian writer, as surely as the proletariat is still with us: millions of marginal and seasonal workers, impoverished minority groups, a whole region and several generations of colored proletarians, a whole segment of our society sprinkled through fifty states with no negotiable capital other than manual or operative ability. Millions around us are still fighting for food, shelter, jobs, education, and the vote. Clearly, the proletariat is a proper and challenging literary subject. Young writers with sympathy, insight, and brotherly love for fellow human beings have great material waiting for them, and a world of readers waiting for news about the neglected proletariat.

From the proletarian level, or depression, the view of our rich nation is startlingly sharp: all is not well. We need more and better writers to represent the proletarian minorities and to tell us what our changing America looks like from down there. We need whole writers to present the whole picture. It will be interesting to see if we get any writer as passionate, as full of brotherly love, as dedicated to the proletariat as is our great neglected author of the Americas, B. Traven.

If "brotherly love" is too exotic a label to describe the core of Traven to a materialistic world, let me say it in another way. Traven has achieved a status which shines above all classes and categories: he is a liberated proletarian who wants all proletarians and all oppressed minorities to share his status of enlightened liberty.

The Roots of Radicals
Experience in the Thirties

MARCUS KLEIN

THE CAUSE WAS AFTER all literary as well as proletarian, and proletarian literature was among other things a new episode in the literary modernism which had come into being at least as long before as 1912. On the one hand, much of the history of modernism—comprising the great formal innovations, the general hardening of sensibility, and the great joy of various iconoclasms—had by the end of the Twenties already been written. On the other hand, there was a new generation nearby, which apparently was quite willing to share in the modern lessons, but which must have found them also to be somewhat alien. What—to take an example from the terminus of the Twenties— could Hemingway's tough disaffection with the words "sacred," "glorious," and the expression "in vain," mean to a young man who had not actually, come to think of it, been reared in those particular pieties? Again, almost all of the most impressive writers of the Teens and Twenties— Hemingway, Fitzgerald, Faulkner, Willa Cather, Pound, Eliot—had turned at some point to the verities of Christianity, and what were they likely to mean to a young man who had never by any reach of imagination known the lure of the Church? The revolution of modernism had at the beginning consisted of two major parties, one formed around Van Wyck Brooks, the other around Pound and Eliot. The latter group, with its conservative politics, its fillip of aristocracy and exclusiveness, was by the end of the Twenties certainly the more in charge of modern literature, and it was the less likely to speak directly to the new men. What, to put it bluntly, did a man named Thomas Stearns Eliot, on his way from St. Louis to Harvard to Anglo-Catholicism, have to say to a young man named, let us say, Irwin Granich?

Let us attend to the prophet.

> I have seen many cults come and go in bourgeois literature—escapists, abstractionists, Freudians, and mystics of art, foggy symbolists, clowns and trained seals and sex-mad pygmies of the pen.
>
> But even at their best, in the supreme expression of the bourgeois individualist, in a James Joyce or a T. S. Eliot, defeat follows them like a mangy cur. They are up a historic blind alley and have no future. But year after year I have seen the great proletarian dawn unfold over the world, revealing new human miracles. . . . Literature will aspire and live again, as it did during the depression.—Mike Gold, "The Writer in America"

So spake Mike Gold in 1953, when he was lonelier in both his wrath and his radiance than he had been, and the cause was threatened on every side by nostalgia. There is pathos in this posture, of course. The human miracles in this moment adduced by Gold are Herb Tank, a playwright, Lloyd Brown and Philip Bonosky, writers of fiction—who if they were not up a historic blind alley with a mangy cur, were evidently not about to bring the dawn, either. Even Mike Gold must have known that. But if there is testimony here to the fate of the particular leader become aged in his low-brow captiousness, his blatancy, and his loyalty, and if Gold was still mechanically greeting the good news which had long since been withdrawn, there is suggestion here also of large historical truth. Inevitably, in 1953 Gold was writing a memoir. Perhaps the very failure of proletarian literature to become a movement, not to speak of the political misfortunes of the Communist Party in the United States, meant for him a measure of freedom from distractions. In any event, he paid tribute to a radical sensibility much greater in scope than anything possibly contained in the dogma of "proletarian literature," and much more extensive in time. In this lowest, and therefore basic, proletarian celebration, the enemy is modernism. That, clearly, is what Gold means by "bourgeois individualism." Its threat, clearly, is the obfuscation which it imposes, with its escapism and foggy symbolism, on what Gold knew were the important actualities.

But not only does Gold locate his enemy among the moderns, in the same place he also finds the basic tactics of his own thought. It is the history of literary modernism which totally engages him. Gold's essay, with its title taken from Van Wyck Brooks, is an exercise in that kind of energizing melancholy which Brooks had invented long ago. It is so quite explicitly. "Our literature is one long list of spiritual casualties," said Brooks and so says Gold in this essay, and "The blighted career, the arrested career, the diverted career, are with us the rule." The specific careers which Gold uses for illustration are, naturally, different ones. He names Hemingway, Caldwell, Sandburg, Upton Sinclair, and Steinbeck. Brooks' elegance, transmuted by Gold, is bitter gall, and the air of noble striving naturally has become Marxist one-upmanship. Hemingway, Caldwell, and the rest, have failed simply because they got rich—"Brooks made a certain *mystique* out of the process, not seeing too clearly its material base." But it is the pattern and the echoes of the argument which are significant.

Those whom we call our poets, Gold was in effect saying just like Brooks before him, have failed because they are remote. They do not fulfill their promise of spiritual leadership. While they impose their sovereignty, they do not speak either to us or for us. A true literature will express the people. The new literature is to be built on the usable past, which has somehow been obscured by the actual past. The test of a literature for Brooks, and for Gold after him, is its adequacy to the nation as a whole. Brooks had subscribed himself to youth and Socialism, but in literature he was a conservative and a nationalist—and so, remarkably, was Gold. Neither of them would abide literature as a progress of technical experiments, and both regarded literature as existing within national boundaries. For both it was the current task of the American writer to pick a quarrel with the culture, in order to lead the culture to right values.

And if in this essay Gold derives himself particularly from Brooks, his argument is taken even more generally from the very modernists whom he attacks. The sense of fact, a sense of the moral role of literature, the sense of an adversary position within the general culture—all these constitute a great amount of what modernism meant. The implication to be discovered in Mike Gold, finally, is that modernism has failed because it failed to live up to its own valid premises. And no matter what Mike Gold's limitations and narrownesses, by this much he discovered conspicuous truth which still embarrasses us. The values of the best of the moderns had at one extreme reached expression in blatant insult—as in Eliot's "Bleistein," some of the early poems of E. E. Cummings, the anti-Semitism of Pound. At another extreme those values had led beyond all actualities—as in the case of the twelve Southern Agrarians who proved to be the most likely heirs of modernism, who in *I'll Take My Stand* composed a politics based on a myth of feudalism, which they then treated as a literary metaphor. At best those values were not likely to have any immediate social context for this new generation.

Proletarian literature was a literary rebellion within a literary revolution, to which it was loyal. It had as its aim refreshment of that revolution by way of bringing it to a knowledge of current realities. That is the implicit case of "proletarian literature" even in the most confined definition of the phrase, as it indicates not even a body of literature but only a polemical activity, a slogan distributed by the American Communist Party for a period of about five years. What the slogan actually signified was a subject, of course, of constant and cunning dispute among proletarian critics—could a bourgeois write proletarian literature, was the material to be revolutionary or could it be

merely descriptive, what in American terms was the proletariat, did the subject of the writing necessarily have to be
proletarian, and so forth. But whatever the failure of the
phrase to become a defined ideology, there can be little
doubt that the ideologues had something definite in mind,
to which the dogma was virtually addendum.

The most nearly official statement of a position was the
anthology *Proletarian Literature in the United States*
published in 1935—ironically, after the period of the
United Front had begun and the phrase "proletarian literature" had been withdrawn from the Communist vocabu-
lary.[1] The characteristic tone of the collection, as is to be
expected, is aggressive self-congratulation. ("What we are
seeing today is the emergence of a galaxy of young novelists who happen to be artists, even by the admission of the
enemy." ". . . we have here the beginnings of an American literature.") The contents have a range for the most
part of only three or four years, as is to be expected. Like
any other avant-garde, the proletarians were as soon as
possible certifying the fact that they existed, although the
crudity and the derivativeness of much of what is here
given a second existence puts the matter actually in some
doubt. Much of what is presented of course has only
dogma to justify it—the anthology reaches what is in one
way its essential moment in a play about the Scottsboro
case, by John Wexley, when a character sings out: "Pray
fo' yo' life an' fo' the blessed N.L.D."

Nevertheless, *Proletarian Literature* had a conspicuous
literary ambition. Beyond, and within, all the much fierce-
ness about parochial matters by the six editors and by the
contributors, it is a matter of constant insistence that
literature must live, and the life of literature is its involvement with ordinary, insistent, real experience. Experience,
indeed, rationalizes everything. A knowledge of the class
struggle and participation in the Marxist vision are good
for a writer, for the reason that they contain experience.
So, after some thrusts at bourgeois liberal critics, when he
settles down to the matter of the book, Joseph Freeman in
his general introduction says: "The best art deals with

specific experience which arouses specific emotion in specific people at a specific moment in a specific locale, in
such a way that other people who have had similar experiences in other places and times recognize it as their own."
That is his major premise. Today's specificity is not yesterday's. The minor premise is that "the teachings of communism correspond to the realities of the contemporary
world," and it is Freeman's merely inevitable conclusion
that the best art is written now by communists and their
followers. But experience is foremost.

Therefore one of the sections of the book is given to
"Reportage," which the particular editor says is the characteristic literature of the age. Reportage is valuable because it "helps the reader *experience* the event recorded."
"If you come from the middle class, words are likely to
mean more than an event," says one of the reporters,
Meridel Le Sueur. "Now in a crisis the word falls away
and the skeleton of [the] action shows in a terrific movement." Poetry, according to the poetry editor, must in the
same way have exact reference to the experience; poetry
must deal with the "actual battlegrounds" or with the
actual effects of the real battles. And in a piece of con-
trived doggerel, "Life of the Mind, 1935," Genevieve Tag-
gard writes: *The words in the books are not true / If
they do not act in you.*" Proletarian fiction in its turn, according to the fiction editor, is built on the premise "that
art is more than a parlor game to amuse soulful parasites."

Given such statement, literary communism comes to be
a vast metaphor for new expression of an aesthetic long
since become honorable. Meridel Le Sueur indeed might
have been writing a program for Imagism, rather than
about the literary effects of a strike. The word, she in
effect says, is to be of the event, and not a gloss upon it.
Except for the politics, Joseph Freeman might have been
prescribing the early Hemingway. The aesthetic was still
honored. Quite specifically, Joseph Freeman as general
spokesman for this anthology claimed the inheritance. In
his telling of history, proletarian literature was what happened when modernism met the depression.

From the poetic renaissance of 1912 until the economic crisis of 1929, literary discussions outside of revolutionary circles centered on the problem of Time and Eternity. The movement associated with Harriet Monroe, Carl Sandburg, Ezra Pound, Sinclair Lewis, Sherwood Anderson, Gertrude Stein, Ernest Hemingway was one which repudiated the "eternal values" of traditional poetry and emphasized the immediate American experience. . . .

The economic crisis shattered the common illusion that American society was classless. Literary frustration, unemployment, poverty, hunger threw many writers into the camp of the proletariat. . . . Poetry, however, tends to lag behind reality. Suffering opens the poet's eyes but tradition ties his tongue. . . .

In the past five years many writers have fought their way to a clearer conception of their rôle in the contemporary world.

Their role was to wield art as a weapon in the class struggle, of course. And if the role was created by new knowledge, it also provided the new men with a way to use the old knowledge which they had inherited. The class struggle carried conditions of immediacy, and of direct and exact references—and for that reason, there can be little doubt, the proletarian movement was exciting, even to that majority of writers who shared in no ideology. The class struggle could make modernism contemporary. In fact the point of the literary protest in *Proletarian Literature* is, precisely, the failure of the old revolutionaries to remain contemporary. Revolutionaries become reactionary with age and success. The "T. S. Eliot of *The Hippopotamus*," Freeman says, "becomes the T. S. Eliot of *Ash Wednesday*," and that is a descent. The fiction editor of the volume glancingly refers to "the futile drunkards and Paris expatriates of Ernest Hemingway"—a subject which of course in 1935 he finds trivial, as in some obvious way *The Sun Also Rises* was trivial in 1935.

In truth the great revolution in modern letters was in some danger of retiring into ancient accomplishments or into classic serenity, and by that much there is validity in, for instance, Mike Gold's attack, reprinted in *Proletarian*

Literature, on Thornton Wilder. In this most famous of
Gold's fits of overflowing energy, "Wilder: Prophet of the
Genteel Christ," [2] after all the mayhem and the snarling
and the stricture, what is at stake is the sense of literature
as something which imperatively exists now. The trouble
with Wilder is that he did not write about modern America; his use of the past was an escape from specifici-
ties—"Is Mr. Wilder a Swede or a Greek, or is he an
American? No stranger would know from these books he
has written." More particularly, Wilder's expressed ambition was a revival of religion, an ambition which was
necessarily offensive to Gold writing in 1930 because—
ideology quite aside—it was not unique with Wilder.
Clearly the object of Gold's attack was T. S. Eliot when
he accused Wilder of dealing in "that newly fashionable
literary religion that centers around Jesus Christ, the First
British Gentleman." "It is," said Gold, "a pastel, pastiche,
dilettante religion, without the true neurotic blood and
fire, a daydream of homosexual figures in graceful gowns
moving archaically among the lilies. It is Anglo-
Catholicism, that last refuge of the American literary
snob." More particularly still, Gold's own stylistic blatan-
cies clearly were meant, here and elsewhere, to constitute
an assault for the sake of assault, and freshness, and blood-
iness. Literature was growing pale. It needed an excite-
ment.

Beneath all of the garbled dogma of proletarian criticism, there is this implication, that literature is made with
the materials of current verifiable experience, and only
when it is so created is it active. The idea was not new,
certainly, nor was it comprehensive—small wonder that
proletarian criticism often had trouble accounting for the
value of the literature of the past. But within its own
literary historical context, the idea was just and energizing.
In the absence of any binding definitions, one may say
that the proletarian movement as a whole is primarily
characterized by this sense, that literature is of the present, that it is to be rescued into contemporaneity. The
idea is inherent in those novels of the Thirties which deal,

explicitly, with such proletarian subjects as the adventures of industrial workers and embattled farmers and Communist converts. But it is not only in them. In fact, not a great many novels did deal with those subjects. The idea, and the sensibility for an emphatic attachment to the hard facts of the present, are much more extensive.

That sensibility is common to novels of the Thirties so disparate in subject as, for example, Mike Gold's *Jews Without Money*, Jack Conroy's *The Disinherited*, Ira Wolfert's *Tucker's People*, and Nathanael West's first struggle toward literature, *The Dream Life of Balso Snell*. *Balso Snell* is particularly illustrative, just because it is so clearly an initial effort within a new moment of history. West may have written the novel during his college years, prior to 1928, but he rewrote it before its publication in 1931. It was written by a markedly unproletarian young man who had devoted himself to much of the matter of modernism. In college West had read Baudelaire, Verlaine, Rimbaud, Huysmans, and he had discovered Joyce, Nietzsche, medieval Catholicism, and magic, and then he had had his time, two years, in Paris. The first literary results, predictably one would say, was an effort at freedom from his education, which turned out to be so strenuous as to be crippling. *Balso Snell* is all irony, which becomes so complicated and which builds upon itself so constantly and so self-consciously, that the narrative is lost. Balso, by profession a "lyric poet," wanders through the entrails of the Trojan Horse, and has encounters. He meets a Jewish tourist guide, a man who calls himself Maloney the Areopagite; a twelve-year-old schoolboy; and the boy's teacher. These characters tell him tales of other characters. The teacher actually becomes two other characters. Balso himself has a long dream, within the dream, in which there are echoes and reflections of characters named previously while there are inventions of new ones. The book is not only labyrinthine, but evasive; at no point within the interior of the novel will West join an issue by making a declarative statement. Or in any event, all statements are so hedged in ironies as to be suspect.

But the ambition for a narrative and a thematic line is clear. Balso, the dreamer, enters the wooden horse through its anus. At the end he deposits himself in the embraces of the schoolteacher, and West says: "His body broke free of the bard. It took on a life of its own; a life that knew nothing of the poet Balso." The book enacts a wet dream ending in orgasm. It begins in sodomy and culminates in something at least closer to wholesome nature. At the beginning, the Jewish guide had told him that "A hand in the Bush is worth two in the pocket." Balso has his schoolteacher behind a clump of bushes, thereby reduplicating the lesson. And indeed the whole of the narrative, involved and skittish as it is, does serve to bring Balso through a series of hot mental perversions to a dream of full genital thrill. Balso's adventures, sometimes his own and sometimes those of the persons he invents, are scatological, homosexual, Oedipal, sadistic, masochistic, and they are marked by other peculiarities. The series is not in any cogent way progressive, but it accumulates disgusts and thereby comes to a desired natural end.

More to the point, these adventures are continually invested with literary referents and with allusions to the fashions of thought among modern literary people. At a moment in his wanderings, Balso realizes that the wooden horse "was inhabited solely by writers in search of an audience." In fact the *mise en scène* of the action is hardly the wooden horse at all. After an early joke about a gigantic hernia, West mostly forgets about it, and what is projected instead looks like Paris of the day of the expatriates of the Twenties. The Jewish tourist guide, who might be Gertrude Stein, invites Balso to have discussions about Picasso and Cézanne. The Areopagite, fashionably Catholic, tries to interest him in the mysteries of early Christian love—he tells the story of St. Puce, the flea who lived in the armpit of Jesus Christ. The schoolboy parodies Dostoevsky and then Gide. Along the way there are references to symbolists and surrealists, and to Huysmans, Rimbaud, Nietzsche, and for good measure, George Bernard Shaw. Balso's adventures therefore make an equivalence between modish literary chatter and sexual perversions. And given that discovery, of course the aim of Balso the poet is to get free into a firm natural reality. "The world," he mourns, "was getting to be a difficult place for a lyric poet." He advises Maloney, after hearing him out, " 'Don't be morbid. Take your eyes off your navel. Take your head from under your armpit. Stop sniffing mortality. Play games. Don't read so many books. Take cold showers. Eat more meat.' " He says to the twelve-year-old Raskolnikov, " 'What you ought to do, child, is to run about more. Read less and play baseball.' "

The characters invented by Balso are all perverse because they are all derivatives, without flesh and blood of their own. They are frustrated, self-conscious poseurs—in a couple of instances characters do break forth to inveigh against the infection of literature, but of course that too is a pose. And the necessity faced by West, behind Balso, is to get free of this posturing, into something new. Which is to say that *Balso Snell* declares an aesthetic requirement: literature must rid itself of a literary inheritance. The particular inheritance has become a prison, for the author, of hothouse imaginings. It is overbearing, forcing derivativeness. In this book the author has his revenge, as it were, on the body of learning. When Balso falls on his schoolteacher, who protests in a diminuendo of "no's," he seems to be demonstrating the proper love of education, which in turn leads him from his vapors into reality.

Given this kind of self-consciousness on the part of West, it is likely that the next book, *Miss Lonelyhearts*, would have been just the kind of novel it was, stripped, precise, and outrageous, though even in that novel the hero is continuously accused, by the newspaper editor Shrike, of falling into attitudes which are clichés. And given West's self-consciousness, it is likely too, just as a literary matter and all imperatives of conscience aside, that he would have involved himself in Communist activities. As he did. He picketed, and he was one of the many involved in the first American Writers' Congress, in 1935, and he worked for Loyalist Spain, among other things. He also wrote a political novel, A *Cool Million*—he did not have a talent for political expression. The author discernible in the first book was straining toward unimpeachable experience, which necessitated his rejecting his own literary past, which was the revolution of modernism.

West's sensibility by that much is not different from what is to be discovered in such a novel, for instance, as Albert Halper's *Union Square*, which deals explicitly with the question of the nature of proletarian art. Halper's answer to the question was, seemingly, that proletarian artists first of all had to be good artists, but then anyway they would probably not be useful to the class struggle because proletarians don't need art. That is the hopeless content of a long set speech delivered by one of the protagonists, to a group of artistic aspirers:

> "Comrades, if you will allow me to say so, all of us here are nothing more or less than parasites, we're barnacles on the bottom of a boat. The Revolution doesn't need us at all, what it needs is militant workers, militant intelligent workers. . . . What I say, and I say it for the last time, is, that, if you want to help the movement, you must first be capable in your craft. The Party doesn't want bad posters, in fact, the movement really doesn't need you at all. Two or three intelligent, articulate workers could do more good than a whole hall full of 'class-conscious' painters or writers."

But if there is a dismal contradiction in this position, still the conditions of art which Halper has in mind and for which he strives are clear. He has two heroes in this novel, both of them artists. The one, a painter, is a faithful and helpful member of the Party, but he is a pipsqueak. He is referred to constantly as "the little fellow." He is a-tremble with excitements, but he does not know the score about some basic things, and obviously he is not going to make the Revolution. The other is an ex-Communist and ex-poet, and also tubercular, who has fallen into the purlieus of cynicism. He has taken to writing sexy potboilers. Behind these protagonists the novel develops a number of stories, which abut on each other without quite intersecting. They provide more or less a cross section of life on Union Square in the year 1931, and it is one of the ironies of the novel that neither of the artists knows anything about this life at their doorstep. What the minor characters have in common, moreover, is an inability to meet the demands of reality. There are a businessman and a dapper little barber and a laborer. The businessman, a widower, has taken into his home a vulgar tart. He knows that he is being demeaned, used, and cuckolded, and he can do nothing. The barber is called upon to rescue a childhood sweetheart from a terrifying husband. Conscience and love demand, but he has syphilis. He commits suicide. The laborer, wholesomely named Hank Austin, is fired from his job and refuses to believe that he is one like others, one of the masses of the unemployed. More generally, because he is the exemplary proletarian in the book, he is the most proper object of concern by the Communists in the book; but they do not know him, and he goes along believing in Herbert Hoover.

Everybody fails to meet the unimpeachable reality. Beyond the circumstances of plot and motivation, they are frustrated, too, by the unremitting ironies of Halper's telling. (As: "And Hank, good old ivory-headed Hank Austin, there he sat with his six-foot Yankee build." Or: "Someone was speaking there, haranguing away, none other than Comrade Irving Rosenblum, who was giving the citizenry the lowdown on the whole rotten situation.") Given the density of the irony, there is little opportunity for the actual. All of the characters are reduced to posturers. Despite their sorrows, they border on the condition, for instance, of a Mr. and Mrs. Otto Drollinger, who have gone Russian—they have surrounded themselves with Russian knickknacks, they call each other Vanya and Natasha, and they speak to one another in the manner of a translation of Chekhov.

As much as it was for West, the obsessive enemy is the cliché, and the necessity is to burst through lies. In Halper's novel the milieu is different and therefore the clichés are different. Halper is particularly hard on the modish

Russianism of the moment and place. He is hard on the rhetorical monotonies of the Communist Party. The clichés of the left command much more of his attention, it happens, than do those of the right—significantly, because they are closer to home—but it is the cliché which is the problem, and much less the politics residing therein. The problem is basically and specifically an aesthetic one. The husband of the Russianized couple draws advertisements for his living, and the wife is an advertising copywriter. They rebound between clichés. The ex-poet, having sickened of Party polemic, now writes not merely potboilers, but aggressive parodies of potboilers. The leftish boys and girls who aspire to make the masses classconscious through their art are just "bohemians." "Fifteen or twenty years ago," the ex-poet tells them, "you would, if you had been born earlier, been living in Greenwich Village, fighting for the 'new freedom,' free love, and all that sort of stuff." That sort of stuff has now become the common property of the bourgeoisie, and so the new radicals have "shoved off with the Party." They are not radicals at all, because they are trite.

In this constancy of derivativeness, the real proletariat would be an aesthetic relief. Early in the novel Halper has a janitress of Union Square say, "Artists. . . . There was a time . . . when this neighborhood had only working people, now it's lousy with phony folk. Artists, phony people, I calls them." The novel reaches one of its climaxes in a scene of a Party mass meeting for aid to the Kentucky coal miners. While some writers who have been down to Harlan County are speaking, the audience suffers torturing longeurs. When a real miner speaks, flatly and simply, the audience, so it is indicated, is electrified. Of course by indicating that, Halper would seem to have closed the possibilities of a deliberate art. It is immediately after the scene of the mass meeting that the large set speech on the nature of proletarian art occurs, with its impossible paradox. Still, the problem of sensibility is credible and emphatic. The novel in fact seeks relief from derivativeness in some ways other than by appeal to the real proletariat.

One of the lesser characters in the book is a mad printer, a Jeremiah who appears every once in a while to make enigmatic prophetic statements. Another character, called The Man Who Walks Backwards, walks backwards and watches the world in mirrors attached to his eyeglasses. These characters are not very well attached to the book, but the supernatural intensity of the one and the deliberate perversity of the other serve a function just like that of the proletariat, of breaking through the clichés. And then Halper's general scheme, of multiple stories strategically selected according to the class background and place of national origin of the characters, surely is meant to provide the novel with the clear reality of sociology.

In this latter design, Halper was of course far from alone among the new novelists of the Thirties. The appeal to a broad sociological reality was simply the most apparent way of securing the sensations of fact and immediacy, as the most apparent device was a multiplicity of stories, contained usually by geography. *Union Square* in this measure is like such ghetto novels as Mike Gold's *Jews Without Money* and Meyer Levin's *The Old Bunch*, and it is like such conscientious Left novels as Clara Weatherwax's *Marching! Marching!* and Josephine Johnson's *Jordanstown*, which confine themselves to a single town, and it is like such city novels as John T. McIntyre's *Steps Going Down* and *Ferment*, and like the fiction which ranged over America, such as the trilogy written by Josephine Herbst. Small wonder that *U.S.A.* was the acknowledged masterpiece—it managed so much larger a perimeter than any other novel. The technique might have been the result of doctrinal necessity. How else call attention to the class struggle except by putting together in a locale representatives of the classes? But in fact the doctrinal class struggle was in a good many of these instances just an implication, if so much as that, of a purpose which was first of all literary.

Indeed, the hero of the new novel of the Thirties was again and again an artist, and the issue was the shaping not of his politics but of his sensibility. Dos Passos' "Camera Eye"—who if he is not explicitly an artist, is anyway a very sensitive young man—moves outward from Proustian introspection. Larry Donovan, the hero of Jack Conroy's *The Disinherited*, is revealed at the end to be a poet, but now he will be a poet with a difference. The character in the novel who is an organizer says to him: "I just wanted to make sure you had no romantic ideas. You used to live in a world of poetry, you know. The kind of poetry we live and see is terrible as well as majestic, sometimes it's bloody and grim and it takes a stout heart to keep knocking away." But that is poetry still. In Edward Dahlberg's *Bottom Dogs*, Lorry Lewis "wished he knew enough to be a writer." In *Jordanstown*, a compulsively lyrical novel, the sensitive young aristocrat and writer chooses social activism. His reasons are as vague as the rest of the novel, but it is clear that social activism means for him real activity. In this particular novel, that is virtually all that it means. It is a chance to have a responding sensibility. Jonathan Chance, the protagonist of Josephine Herbst's *Rope of Gold*, is a writer seeking to improve his writing by organizing the farmers of his neighborhood. He wants to "touch actual people." He calls upon the examples of Jack Reed and Jack London, but not for the correctness of their social opinions, rather indeed as failures, as examples of what happens to writers who remain away from the source of their beliefs.

Given the prevalence of an ambition which was primarily literary, it is after all to be expected that much proletarian fiction found opportunity and value not among the workers of the world, but among rural and small-town folk. The "actual people," according to a tradition much older than literary Communism, were likely to be farmers. So the Communist Jonathan Chance feels falsity weighing upon him when he is not among the farmers, and Josephine Herbst behind him takes every opportunity to make the point that in New York City all things are hypocritical. Conroy's *The Disinherited* goes up and down among a number of milieus, but at the beginning and end the poet hero is a pastoral poet, and in the climactic scene of the novel when the masses organize, it is a group of farmers which organizes. Even Mike Gold's *Jews Without Money*, confined as it is otherwise to the Lower East Side, finds its emotional center in a scene in which the family takes an outing at Bronx Park. The young protagonist's mother reveals suddenly a profound knowledge of mushrooms; she is a peasant, still, here in America!

And the peasantry had the further advantage that it could be conceived to represent the real America. The discovery of America, in turn, was absolutely the characteristic subject of the new writing of the Thirties. It is to be found everywhere, in criticism, "Reportage," drama, poetry, and fiction. In the presence of an ideology that was international or nothing, there is some irony in the fact that the one significant book of Marxist literary criticism to be written during the decade, Granville Hicks' *The Great Tradition*, should have been about the national tradition. The "Reportage" ran to titles which contained "America"—*Puzzled America, Tragic America, Behold America!*, and so forth.[3] The new drama was in some good measure another version of the same reportage. In poetry, from Hart Crane's *The Bridge* to *John Brown's Body* to any number of poems of more and less accomplishment, the subject was most likely. And it is to be found in the fiction of all varieties.

No doubt this discovery of America owed something to Russian nationalism, in letters and movies, with its emphasis on the peasantry and the land. No doubt it was in part a political activity—the country was falling apart, and an effort was to be made to discover what in the country had gone wrong. Certainly the subject was fostered by the WPA projects in the arts. But it was also a new opportunity, a new way of touching the real. It was the other alternative which had been provided by literary modernism in America, Brooks' invention of the "usable past," which had not been utilized by either Anglo-Catholics or the expatriates of Paris. Americanism was the other traditionalism, and because it was traditional it was attractive in many ways. It equipped reality with history, and it also promised the writer the possibilities of rootedness, acceptance, and large participation. It made the writer and the experience of the moment vastly important.

The sense of history which this Americanism in particular provided was itself traditional—and it had little to do with American politics and nothing to do with the historical dialectic. What was to be discovered in the purposes of this moment was that idea at least as old as James Fenimore Cooper, of an America fallen from its purity, from the sturdiness, openness, and large freedom of its pioneering. That idea of history informs all the characteristic novels of dispossession and homelessness. *The Grapes of Wrath* in its large movement and emphatic concern for geography is as much a tale of westering, certainly, as it is a thesis on agrarian displacement during the Depression. The Joads are of that pioneering stock which has endured, although it has been obscured, and the hard times which have put the family on the road is a contemporary version of an old corruption, as familiar as the family's simple desires. Again, more modestly, the aimless, feckless boy who is the protagonist of Nelson Algren's *Somebody in Boots* is, as Algren has said, a "Final Descendant," the end of the line of those Kentucky hunters who had moved into the Southwest after Shiloh and built their shelters in the valley of the Rio Grande, and the first title of the novel was *Native Son*. There is great irony in this ascription. Cass McKay, the offspring "of that wild and hardy tribe that had given Jackson and Lincoln birth," [4] drearily rides the rails and takes to dismal petty crime. He is whining, belligerent, callow, and not much better than dim-witted. But even that irony holds a traditional nostalgia. Unbeknownst to Cass, the frontier has closed. His little efforts at individual initiative are anachronistic. He is exposed to an amount of polemical social and economic analysis, and Algren's message might have been that the *Lumpenproletariat* is to be educated from its dim lethargy into mass action—but in fact Algren constantly, at times it seems perversely, prevents that education from happening. Cass is perfectly enclosed in the story of the corruption of the American dream.

Again, that American myth of the Fall is the affective

content of even so seemingly class-minded a novel as Conroy's *The Disinherited*. At the end Larry Donovan reaches the standard epiphany: "I knew that the only way for me to rise to something approximating the grandiose ambitions of my youth would be to rise with my class, with the disinherited: the bricksetters, the flivver tramps, boomers, and outcasts pounding their ears in flophouses." His ambition specifically, as it had been set forth to him by his father some pages back, was to be a lawyer or a doctor. But in this closely autobiographical book, the lyrical moments suggest that he has a different dream. The novel begins and ends with scenes of Larry at home. Home is a mining town, presumably in Conroy's native Missouri. Peculiarly enough, despite the recounted terrors of the mines, the recklessness and the tyranny of the Company, the union-busting, the facts of poverty—despite all that, there is a pervading loveliness in this town. The particular house in which the young boy lives is simple, but it is neat and rather superior to the other houses in the neighborhood. With the other boys, young Larry plays games of rather a literary cast: "Diamond Dick rode valorously to rescue his sweetheart Nell from scalping at the hands of the redskins just in the nick of time; while Handsome Harry, the old sarpint of Siiskiyou, proclaimed to the world that he was an extremely pisen rattler possessing sixteen rattles and a button; moreover, he was not a bit averse to biting viciously if he were provoked sufficiently." The woods are nearby, and Larry hunts for birds' nests. The young bucks repair to the woods to play their accordions and flutes. A girl comes into Larry's young life, a girl who is a farmer's daughter, and she has all of the flouncing and charming righteousness of a Becky Thatcher. Indeed, this town is not far removed from St. Petersburg, Missouri. (Before he wrote *The Disinherited*, Conroy had begun to work on a biography of Mark Twain.) Almost a third of the novel is devoted to this scene of Larry's childhood. When at the end of the novel he returns to it, the mine has moved away, the camp is almost deserted, the girl has gone to college and become a social activist, and sheriffs' sales are about to take the nearby farms. But inevitably, the emotion appropriate to this return is nostalgia, and given such a general movement in the book, *The Disinherited*—which is dedicated to "the disinherited and dispossessed of the world"—takes on a significance different from its obvious one. Young Larry Donovan has been disinherited from that spacious time and place, the American boyhood of the myth.

Such appeal to sustaining myth has a value in all times. In the Thirties it was likely to mean more just because the new writers needed it more. Conroy was unimpeachably American, but not many of the others were. In a large number of instances they were Jews and the children of immigrants, or immigrants themselves, as in the case of Henry Roth. In the same instances, they were likely to have learned their literary and social aspirations while coming of age in the ghettoes of Chicago or New York. These circumstances apparently sharpened the whole question of culture, and also, incidentally, the question of language. Home was not really an isolated enclave within the majority culture. Home was in America, but still it was different enough to be a foreign country. In this situation there was necessity to bridge the difference, either by full-tilt going in for Americanization, or by exploring the ghetto, by way of saying that this, too, was a part of America, or by exploring the ghetto for the purpose of rejecting its restrictions, or by effecting some combination of ways. And the same was true in various measure for all of the many new writers who had no assured inherited place within the majority culture.

Alfred Kazin, in *Starting Out in the Thirties*, testifies to his feelings "almost of duplicity" as a young literary fellow, traveling between his family in Brownsville and the literary personages with whom he was engaged in mid-Manhattan. His apparent solution was *On Native Grounds*, a formulation by a Jewish radical of the modern American tradition. Some years earlier in the Thirties, more desperately, the aspiring novelist Nathan Weinstein—heeding, so he said, Horace Greeley's advice to "Go

West, young man"—had become Nathanael West. Michael Gold, born Irwin Granich, made perhaps the most complicated effort of all. By the name he chose for himself he retained his own Lower East Side identity and also secured a sense of its apparent opposite: according to his testimony, he took the name from a certain Corporal Michael Gold who was an old veteran of the Civil War living in the Lower East Side. His symbolic value for the new Mike Gold, who grew up reading Mark Twain and Walt Whitman, must have been that he was an authentic native of two places at once. He involved the Yiddish Lower East Side in American history.

And it was by the impetus of such intricate displacement that the most intensely realized writing in the Thirties, in all genres, was accomplished. The novelist in particular, in these circumstances, was under pressure to clutch for the sense of culture, because the novel anyway is more dependent than other genres on the facts of culture. So the triumph of Henry Roth's *Call It Sleep* is Roth's possession of the distraught culture in which young David Schearl lives, which is not hyphenated Yiddish-American but rather an impossible contradiction. The virtual schizophrenia of the life of Brownsville and the Lower East Side confirms the boy's ordinary troubles about the nature of sex and love and religion, and transforms them into terrors. And Michael Gold's *Jews Without Money*, while it is in no way so fierce as *Call It Sleep*, is a surprisingly vivid book because the same kind of pressure is to be discovered in it. The Lower East Side, in that novel, is infiltrated at every point by Americanism, and all of the characters are forged by their attempts to fashion a cultural coherence. *Jews Without Money* certainly is not the political statement which it pretends to be. The young hero eventually is converted by a man on a soapbox, but that is a matter of a last few exhortatory sentences tacked on to the end of the book. Indeed, the book scarcely has a plot. Its content is a series of vignettes in which the *stetl* tries to meet America. In one way of this meeting, boys are likely to become gangsters and girls to become prostitutes. ("It is America that has taught the sons of tubercular Jewish tailors how to kill.") In another way of meeting, men take comfort in outrage. ("A curse on Columbus!" the boy's father shouts. "A curse on America, the thief! It is a land where the lice made fortunes, and the good men starve!") In another way, the *stetl* retreats far into gentle wonder. ("Ach, America! Who can understand America?" says the old holy man Reb Samuel.) The boys in the neighborhood inevitably take as their model of success the sleek Jewish pimp who speaks perfect English.

And it is the solidly circumstantial effort to possess such cultural fact in its meeting with history in modern America, that makes such a novel as Meyer Levin's *The Old Bunch*, for instance, so much more imperative than, for instance, *U.S.A.* With all of its devices of topicality and with all of its great efficiency in narrative, and with all its anger, *U.S.A.* does not have the sense of *The Old Bunch* that history is something that happens to *me* and to *my* friends and *my* family. With all its externals of authenticity, there is something abstract about *U.S.A.*, something which is exemplified perhaps most pointedly in the fact that Dos Passos' narrator, the "Camera Eye," is just what he is supposed to be, the observing eye of a camera. And even so, sensitive aristocrat that he is, the angle of his vision is oblique, and his disillusion is self-conscious. No doubt Levin learned from Dos Passos. *The Old Bunch* is made of multiple stories. It is very long; like *U.S.A.*, it intends to be gigantic. It interweaves public events with its narratives. But unlike *U.S.A.*, it is written from a personal center—the "old bunch," precisely, of Jewish boys and girls in Chicago, the children of immigrants, coming of age in the Twenties and Thirties. The members of the bunch go outward in various directions to meet American history—one becomes a sculptor and another couple become doctors and one is a bondsman and another is a professional bicycle rider and another is a radical lawyer, and so forth. But the center pulls them back, and that is the movement of the novel. Significantly, it is the

radical lawyer, who should be least affected by the cen-
tripetal force of this sensibility, who at the end of the
novel utters the theme,

> "Think of the people you know," and you found yourself
> thinking not of the people you knew today but of the
> people you grew up with. Because you really knew their
> class background, Sam decided. Or was it because they were
> the people you really lived with all your life? Whether near
> or away from them, you measured yourself by their stand-
> ards, for these were the ideas you had grown into, when you
> first became aware of the social world. They were the
> unchangeable flesh of your mind.

But the theme has still greater imperatives, because the
old bunch itself has no stability of values or standards.
The members of the old bunch participate in history,
more than most of them know, but whether they know it
or not, they are shaped by double histories, and they are
uneasy in both because each, in all matters, is a denial of
the other. There are few large events. The small events
sometimes have a perfectly cozy smallness, but they have
also the weight of the complication of cultural fact. So in
the beginning, when Estelle Green gets a bob, that is
funny, but her girlish and excited bid for freedom inevitably is more than a delightful scandal. It is a betrayal, of
the *stetl* in which her mother imaginatively lives. The
children, among the bunch, who have the richest father,
bear a perfectly ambiguous stigma and honor. Their father
does business with Chicago's dirty politicians. Thereby he
has made a place for himself, a Jew, in America; on the
other hand, he is at the mercy of gentiles, and his family is
more Americanized than any other. The bunch begins to
bear children of its own, and then there is the terrible
problem of names—will it be Jacob or James? High and
low, the question of doubleness is constant. At a Passover
ceremony, to which *goyim* have been invited, the hostess
is careful to mispronounce "matzoth." In another instance, a proposal of Communism must be met by the
arguments not of anything related to it, but of Zionism.
Members of the bunch are shaken when they are shown a

similarity between Hasidic Judaism and mystical Catholicism. With the weight, then, of all that irony, the members of the bunch are made to meet newspaper headlines, like Leopold and Loeb, the Lindbergh flight, the Lindbergh kidnapping, boom and depression, and the coming of war. That trick clearly is borrowed from Dos Passos. The sense of the absolute experience derives from Levin's struggle to possess the provisional, demanding, unique cultural fact.

Clearly this is not to say that there was no social impulse behind the new writing of the Thirties, but only that social discovery was generally not so abstract nor so dogmatic a matter as has been often supposed. Willy-nilly, writing in the Thirties had a class bias, because for whatever historical or sociological reasons, the new writers in the Thirties tended to come from a social experience different from that which the writers of the Teens and Twenties typically knew. Not one of them came from the absolute bottom, like Theodore Dreiser. They tended to come from the emerging disestablished. For that sufficient reason—confirmed by the public events and the politics of the Thirties—reality apparently had a class basis. Ironically enough from one point of view, these new writers were likely to be fully aware of and excited by literary modernism; but the known reality had not been liberated into being by the revolution of literary modernism which had liberated everything else. Modernism therefore was to be redefined, recaptured, and in part rejected, just for the sake of seriousness, so that literature might express the known.

Character and Self in Fiction on the Left

CHESTER E. EISINGER

THIS ESSAY DEALS with various literary strategies used in the treatment of the individual or the self by authors writing during the Thirties and early Forties in the general ambience of Marxism.

I am deliberately avoiding the use of terms like proletarian fiction or radical fiction because criticism has not yet worked out a generally accepted meaning for them and may never do so. As early as 1939 Philip Rahv had remarked the confusion generated by these phrases, and in 1957, Irving Howe and Lewis Coser, in their history of the American Communist Party, were still unable to untangle their meaning.[1] Not only are they ambiguous, but they are too rigid and delimiting for present purposes. The concern of this essay goes beyond the orthodox Marxist authors to include people who were writing fiction when Marxism and the Communist Party were, at least for them, vital parts of the general culture. The protest character of the fiction here considered predisposes its authors to reflect or draw upon Marxist ideas, although neither the writers nor their characters may be committed to Marxist ideology. The fiction reflects the presence of the Party even though no one concerned may be a member of it. These are the conditions that describe what I mean by the ambience of Marxism. The writers I discuss wrote fiction generally representative of the treatment of the individual or the self in the body of work produced on the left. And the writers are representative of those who wrote in the ambience of Marxism in the measure of their understanding of Marxist ideology and in the degree of their attachment either to the ideology or the Communist Party or both.

The idea of the individual or the self is, of course, immensely complicated. Space permits only a kind of shorthand description of what the relevant terms mean in the context of the discussion to follow. The individual is distinguished as over against the group or society. The superiority of the individual to the group and the drive toward full self-realization by an individual are forms of individualism. Each individual has a self, which he seeks to define and realize; this effort is the quest for identity and is carried forward in the individual's subjective being. The notion of the self in the beginning rests upon process and choice: it is a process of becoming or self-realization in which the will is the instrument by which identity is discovered. The impulse generating this act of will is related to death. To assert the self is to be alive and not dead. But more than this, as Frederick J. Hoffman says in *The Mortal No*, the choice of dying is linked to willing the persistence of self-identity. In Jung's terminology, the process that makes a human being a unique individual is called individuation. Jung describes this process as the play, the conflict, and the collaboration of the conscious and the unconscious, of the reason of the one and the chaotic life of the other out of which comes the individual, who must learn to know himself in order to know who he is.[2]

The relationship of the self, of the defined, self-conscious individual, to the Marxian ambience is paradoxical and challenging. Let me outline briefly some of the theoretical problems implicit in this relationship. Several years ago, in an essay on changing patterns in American thought, David Bowers argued that traditional individualism in this country was undermined by the Hegelian emphasis on *Volk* and state and the Marxian emphasis on class.[3] Attention to the individual, to development of the self, withers before the overwhelming importance of the group or corporate entity. What that can mean for literature and the self is suggested by this remark in a Frederick Engels letter: "Realism, to my mind, implies, besides truth of detail, the truthful reproduction of typical characters under typical circumstances." [4] This emphasis upon the generalized and the typical is destructive of any writer's intention or desire to portray an individual character in all his idiosyncratic complexity. A reasonable expectation, on the basis of such doctrine, would be a concentration upon mass-man rather than upon the individual. And as we shall see, some novels written in the ambience of Marxism clearly fulfill this expectation.

Another problem with regard to the self in Marxian thought lies in the materialistic philosophy of consciousness advocated by Marxism. Marx held that life is not determined by consciousness but consciousness by life, that real life processes and the conditions of life determined the inner world of individuals, their beliefs, and their value schemes. The implications of this view are very damaging to notions of subjectivism and self-consciousness, obviously, since such materialism can only look with contempt upon solipsistic preoccupations with spiritual concerns. What this philosophical view leads to in literary criticism is illustrated by this passage from George V. Plekhanov's well-known essay, "Art and Society": "The idea that our ego is the sole reality has always been the basis of subjective idealism; but it required the unbounded individualism of the period of the decline of the bourgeoisie to convert this idea, not only into an egoistic rule of conduct, governing the relations between men, each of whom 'loves himself like God' (the bourgeoisie has never been distinguished for excessive altruism), but also into a theoretical basis for the new esthetics." [5] Idealism, subjectivism, egoism, and individualism are all anathematized together. The result is that the resources of man's inner world are excluded in the enterprise of self-definition, and the loss of these resources is crucial.

The discussion thus far would make it appear that Marxism was not concerned with the self or with the fate of the single individual, but only with classes and types and some mass concept in a materialistic world. We know, of course, that such is not the case. The revolutionary idealism of Marxism and Marxists was born of faith in a new order that would bring justice, dignity, and economic and psychological security into the lives of men. The utopian thrust of Marxism can be seen as an effort to free the individual from coercive forces that maim him both economically and psychically. The informing spirit of much literature written in the Marxian ambience was indeed both idealistic and utopian and revealed a concern, as one might expect, for the freedom and development of the self. More specifically, the Marxist doctrine of alienation is clearly centered on the self.

Marx inveighed against the alienation of man because he refused to accept the dehumanization and automatization of man. He advocated instead the full realization of man, who makes his own history, who is what he does, and whose labor is an act of self-creation and an expression of life. I draw these ideas from Erich Fromm's "Introduction" to a volume entitled *Marx's Concept of Man*, which is part of an ongoing movement to uncover the existential and humanistic content of Marxist thought. It is in this context that Fromm defines alienation. "Alienation (or 'estrangement') means, for Marx, that man does *not* experience himself as the acting agent in his grasp of the world, but that the world (nature, others, and he himself) remain alien to him. They stand above and against him as objects, even though they may be objects of his own creation. Alienation is essentially experiencing the world and oneself passively, receptively, as the subject separated from the object." [6] In the *Economic and Philosophical Manuscripts*, an early work that Fromm reprints in this volume, Marx defines alienation in three stages: from the products of the worker's labor, from the productive activity itself, and from nature, from other men, and from himself. Later, in *The Poverty of Philosophy*, Marx tells us that with the coming of capitalism everything that men had considered as inalienable became an object of exchange and could be alienated. He deplored the loss of the self in an economic system in which money and the machine impose indignities and inflict humiliations upon individuals. These psychic disabilities rob men of a sense of their being and so destroy them. In fact, he goes so far as to recognize that this destruction of the self takes place in the inner man and is not confined to the materialistic world.

It is apparent, then, that the Marxist conception of man encompasses polarities and strains under tensions. Now let us assume fiction writers of varied degrees of commitment to Marxism and knowledge of it, but all of them working in the ambience of Marxism. The question to be considered is, how did these writers cope with the tensions generated by the demands of Marxist ideology on the one hand and the demands of fiction on the other, especially in the light of this complicated and ambiguous conception of man as individual? And the answer, to anticipate for a moment, is that some writers virtually abandoned the individual for some mass concept or group entity; some made passing efforts to individualize their characters, but with indifferent success; and one at least achieved a fine imaginative synthesis of humanistic or individualistic aspects of Marxism.

Albert Halper is one writer who deals very little with the individual but at length with a group entity and at the same time seems to have hardly any ideological commitment. Yet he is fully aware in his fiction of how an urban-industrial environment dwarfs and often crushes the individual, of how capitalism exploits and oppresses the workingman, of how the competitive spirit of capitalism destroys human beings, and of how the machine feeds on man. Such perceptions give the radical or protest quality to his work; they float in the fiction, free of rigid, doctrinaire considerations and of the demands of rhetoric. The possibilities for attention to character, to the effect on the individual of these various social forces, are therefore very real for Halper, but he has little creative talent with which to exploit them.

Halper's first novel, *Union Square,* was flat and formless and offers scant opportunity for comment. *On the Shore,* a volume of short stories issued in the same year, 1934, is useful for one piece, "Young Writer Remembering Chicago," which is essentially a memoir. Here Halper, who is a kind of Chicago Saroyan, combines memories of immigrant relatives and of diving for pennies in the park with more somber scenes from the raw, slangy city in which he was born. He tells us about the neighborhood where he grew up, smelling the stockyards and hearing the trains. What he remembers of Chicago is mixed in quality, then, but dreariness and failure predominate in this apparently autobiographical selection. The writer remembers the broken men in Chicago; the quietly desperate people with whom he worked at stultifying jobs in the post office and the foundry—dead jobs for dead men; the strippers and the whores; the poor seeking relief from the heat on a crowded excursion boat sailing along the shore. His is an evocation of the city as product of a culture that is inadequate in satisfying the human needs of its people. The memoir is full of implicit protest stemming from a proletarian bias, but it does not speak to the problem of the self or the individual. What it does do is anticipate Halper's novels about workers where the problem is given some attention.

But it is not the overriding concern of these books, *The Foundry* (1934) and *The Chute* (1937). In Halper's imagination, the electrotype foundry in the first of these and the mail-order house in the second loom larger than the people who work in them. Both novels are written in the collectivistic manner, and the result of this technique is to subordinate the characters to the industry or the business. The people in the books derive their importance, then, from their relationship to that larger entity which directs their fate. When business and industry become deterministic agencies, human beings lose their individuality and their centrality in the scheme of things.

It must be understood that Halper does not regard the subordination or exploitation of the individual as a good thing but just as a fact of life, a fact that he protests. For example, in *The Foundry*, an errand boy is fired. "He was now jobless; he had, at one stroke, become a piece of straw whirled by a mighty wind and whisked into the gigantic sea of unemployment." Never mind the melodrama and the bathos. What is of interest is that the errand boy is faceless, and the injustice of his firing and the terror of his plight are essentially abstractions. The same failure to make experience meaningful in terms of individual character may be seen in the episode in which the caster goes slightly mad from the pressure of work, the heat, and the unjust accusation that he cannot keep up with the rest of the plant. The work, the heat, and the bloated employer (he really is bloated) have greater reality than the worker's berserk seizure. In the hands of another writer, each of these scenes might have been played internally, and the psychic shock of the experience registered upon the individual. One thinks of Jack London, in an autobiographical fragment and not in fiction, to be sure, describing his terror at falling into the bottom of the pit, represented by unemployment, and the vicious, determined scrambling he undertook to escape this fate. The reader has a genuine sense of individual struggle as London tells of his experience, but as Halper treats his scenes, the reader must feel mostly the reality of impersonal forces as they affect various worker-stereotypes.

The Foundry treats still another kind of subordination imposed upon the worker—that of the machine. The history of conflict between man and the machine is full of threats to human identity. The machine is regarded as a force that will not only displace man but will also eliminate him. The worker has felt these threats at least from the beginning of the Industrial Revolution. Halper treats this problem in his novel more like a historical phenomenon than like an episode in the life of man. For him, a scene depicting workmen sabotaging the machine is conceived as part of the class war; the total strategy of his novel prevents him from assessing the meaning of this conflict through the felt experience of one of the characters whose idea of his self might be at stake.

The chute, in the novel of that name, is like a machine in its polarization to the worker. Halper is reasonably successful in making of it a symbol of magnitude and power. In the mail-order house, the workers must pour a certain quantity and kind of goods down the chute at stated intervals throughout the day, a task that is always just beyond their capacities. The chute becomes an insatiable maw, consuming the lives of those who must strain themselves in an incredible way to keep it full, who feed it, as it were, their very own lives. The chute is the rapacity of big business. It offers any character in the novel a magnificent challenge: he might pit himself against the omnivorous chute as Ahab pitted himself against the white whale. But Halper is not interested in this contest of the individual against the chute that might lead, in its intensity and destructiveness, to a definition of the self. The protagonist in his novel feels the demands of the chute, but no more intensely than other characters; and, in fact, it is others who actually fall down the chute and are destroyed by it.

Halper's reality is primarily external and social, and his attention focusses upon business and industry, which he depicts as living forces in his fiction. Although he understands the threat to the individual, he tends to neglect him, especially disregarding the workings and substance of his character's consciousness. Halper's literary method does not seem to be the result of doctrinaire Marxism, but of a glancing impact of Marxism that supports a personal bias toward protest against what these social forces do to the individual. But it would be misleading to suggest that Halper ignores his characters altogether. In *The Chute*, at least, one is made to feel the deprivations of poverty and the frustrations of ambition as they work upon the protagonist, a consequence of the system in which he lives. To a certain extent Halper shows how fulfillment of the self is thwarted by the working of capitalistic society.

The orthodox Marxist novel, in all its tendentious simplicity, not only ignores the complexity of the relations between self and society in both the real world and fiction, but also, as a consequence, manages to resolve all tensions in a straightforward way. John Hyde Preston's *The Liberals* (1938) is a neat example of such a novel, written with competence within its limitations. It concerns among others a patriarchal factory owner, Marston. He wishes to do well by his workers, according to his own lights, but cannot understand why they should want a voice in their own destiny. Preston equates Marston's feudal ways with liberalism. "The liberal lived in a world where he thought all things were solved by the individual—by his enlightened understanding, his love of justice, his powerful and balanced sense of the good. It was true that the rare liberal could advance the cause of humanity, could approach perhaps almost to perfectibility of human unselfishness and justice. But he could not carry the world with him, could not advance, save in his own sphere of influence, the general good." The trouble with liberalism, the author says, is that it does not understand the basic nature and means of progress; progress has to be viewed realistically as a mass force and as a mass demand of men whose need and dignity mean they must win for themselves what they must not be merely given. Marston's liberalism is the sickness of individualism.

This novel is quite explicit in its attitude toward individualism, especially in literature. The protagonist is a dramatist. In writing about him, Preston is able to work into the novel a discussion of the nature and function of literature. Predictably, Preston claims that literature must deal with the "real" problems of our society, and that such real problems are bound up with the protest that workers must make against capitalism; that as an instrument of protest, literature is on the side of progress; and that a literature devoted to the individual problems of human beings is myopic and sick, leading the writer to corruption. In every way, Preston stands opposed to the examination of the individual and the quest for the self.

Two other orthodox Marxist novels which minimize the self might be mentioned briefly here. One is by Josephine Johnson, whose characters, in *Jordanstown*, are murkily conceived, one suspects, partly as a result of her inadequa-

cies as a novelist. But more important, and clearly within
the range of her intention, is the fact that the theme of
the book is the indomitable strength of the people, and at
the end of the book the people rise phoenix-like from
defeat. The concept of the people as mass is central to the
book and destructive of the individual as realized character. Of greater interest is Leane Zugsmith's *A Time to
Remember* (1936) which uses a department store setting
the way Halper uses the foundry or mail-order house and
which employs a collectivistic technique a little reminiscent of Dos Passos. In an effort to make technique contribute to the theme, this author deals with several characters and tries to prevent any single one from becoming
important. For the point of the novel is that the strike
against the department store, which is at the center of the
action, is carried on through mass action. It is made
possible when individual members of the white collar
group identify themselves with workers and thus lose their
individual identities through absorption into the working
class. This shift in class loyalty and identity constitutes in
the novel a rejection of middle class individualism. The
novel is at some pains to demonstrate that such individualism, whereby a man tries to succeed by virtue of his own
talents and industry, is illusory and ineffectual. The corollary of such rejection of individualism in this book becomes a determination to reject individual characters.
While the novelist does not wish to show us a single
protagonist, her novelistic impulses nevertheless draw her
to treat one person in the novel, the daughter of the
middle-class Jewish family, with more sympathy and care
than is expended on any other; and this individualization
of experience is perhaps the most persuasive portion of the
novel.

   The Old Bunch (1937) and *Citizens* (1940), by Meyer
Levin, are also versions of the collectivistic novel. The
individual is not much attended to in either one, but
where the problem of identity is considered, it is related to
the social context in America.

   In *The Old Bunch* Levin had an opportunity to deal

with the problem of identity by bringing his several characters to a sense of themselves through their Jewish culture, especially through religion and their Old World heritage, but he does not exploit these possibilities in his book. His characters are a group of first-generation Jews who are trying to enter the mainstream of American life. Levin depicts the process of acculturation for these people as it moves on an unsteady course, divorcing most of them from their parents, from Judaism, and from the old country where their roots might have been. The existential crisis for Levin's old bunch lies in the way they have slipped the ties of the past but have failed as yet to identify themselves firmly as Americans. But Levin seems only peripherally interested in this crisis and treats it in a crudely satiric way.

If the Old World fails Levin's characters, so does the New. Levin seems to find that the idealism invested by the immigrants in this country of hope is dissipated and destroyed by a corrupt society in which the omnivorous law of competition governs everything, including human relations. The consequence is that the book centers, in its realistic and kaleidoscopic way, on the ills of American capitalistic society, and this precludes close examination of individual characters and development of their identities. Yet beneath the social criticism one may perceive Levin's conviction that men are alienated from their work, that is, denied satisfactions of a self-sustaining order in their careers, because their society twists and distorts them. The book tells us that men in business, in the law, and in medicine are forced to live by cheating, bribery, chicanery, intimidation, violence. Human relations are determined by the demands of business and politics in a capitalistic society, as Levin's use of Samuel Insull indicates. Insull appears in this novel as the friend of one character who wields his considerable political influence to forward Insull's designs. This fragile relationship collapses with Insull's downfall, and the financier simply uses and then runs out on his friend. As for those who work with their hands or those who would do a public good, the capitalistic system thwarts and frustrates them as well. The only fulfillment in work comes to the two characters who defy the system and move toward the social-political left. These men paradoxically achieve some degree of self-fulfillment by immersing themselves in group ventures. They are the promise that the good society—the cooperative society—creates the good self by encouraging selflessness. If I read Levin aright, the fuzziness of his hope probably justifies his neglect of the self-conscious and subjective individual. His real interest is in the disfigurement that man suffers in the competitive, Darwinian struggle in what Levin regards as the real world. The development of the individual is in a future that Levin does not choose to penetrate.

It is ironic that a writer like Levin should be so absorbed in social protest as to neglect the individual. But his collectivistic technique, the sense of outrage that demands protest, and the concept of reality in his novels, all combine to diminish his interest in the individual and his capacity to depict the self in the act of finding itself. In *Citizens*, which concerns the clash between police and pickets on Memorial Day, 1937, outside the Republic Steel plant on the outskirts of Chicago, Levin speaks of the fiction writer's approach to actuality. He believes that "the inner human truths of motive and compulsion can be found by examining experiences of reality. By using only actual, attested events as materials, the writer reduces the possibility of arriving at false conclusions." [7] This is essentially an external and materialistic view of reality that makes for a kind of social realism in literature. And it is inimical to the concept of the individual or the self.

Citizens demonstrates as much. It is permeated with a sense of outrage at social injustice, routine politics, and monopoly capitalism. Levin believes that the people of a democracy must come to see their own problems and take the responsibility for solving them. A responsible individual making free choice among several alternatives might well be a character whose interior life and whose idea of himself could be developed. But Levin's view of society denies the operation of responsibility and choice because men are the victims of society and not its masters. Much of the novel is devoted to bringing its protagonist to the realization that the whole system is larger than any individual man and depicting the individual, despite his good intentions, as helpless within the system. In this view, the importance of the individual is minimized. Even for Levin's own purposes of protest and reform, the relationship between the self and society is impossible, freezing the individual into immobility as it does. In a larger sense he has simply failed to find a suitable structure that will present self and society together, which is the problem of the novel generally, as Mark Schorer suggests. "The novel seems to exist at a point where we can recognize the intersection of the stream of social history and the stream of the soul," Schorer has written. "This intersection gives the form its dialectical field, provides the sources of those generic tensions that make it possible at all." [8]

Levin's disabilities as a novelist do not seem to stem from his ideological commitment to Marxism. On the contrary, he seems hostile to communists in *Citizens* and caught on undefined ground between communism and industrial capitalism, both of which he has rejected. Nevertheless, he wrote in the ambience of Marxism. Albert Maltz, who actually joined the Communist Party and tried to work out the implications of Marxist theory for literature, illustrates more dramatically the ambiguous relationship between society and self forced upon the leftist writer by his ideological preconceptions. Maltz is a competent writer, one of the best to join the Party in this country. He constantly holds before the reader the bad society, because the literary strategy dictated by his consciously held assumptions demands both a rhetoric and a climax that condemn unjust capitalism. But no matter how disciplined the effort of the good writer is to conform to such assumptions, he cannot ignore his own characters. Society is bad because it cripples and brings death to the self. The moving scene for the reader is often to be found in what happens to a particular man. In Maltz, especially in his volume of short stories, *The Way Things Are*

(1938), the conflict between craft and ideology both obscures and dramatizes the relationship between self and society.

The first story in this volume, "Season of Celebration," illustrates Maltz's problem. On New Year's Eve a young man dies in a Bowery flophouse. When the investigating policeman asks what he died of, one of the other characters replies savagely: "He died from not having a job. . . . He died 'cause he couldn't eat right an' he couldn't live right and 'cause he didn't have sense enough to fight. An' that's the truth!" This is the message of the story, the part where Maltz is dutifully performing according to the script Mike Gold had laid down in the "Introduction" to this book: what marks Maltz is his fraternalism and identification with the poor and suffering; he is a fellow-victim of "the great daily crucifixion." [9]

Maltz's rhetoric has the power arising from justifiable indignation. The reader is aroused by its revolutionary implications, although not in political or class terms; even in this scene, one is thinking of the dying boy as an individual. But the really moving part of the story is the death of the young man, because Maltz is an imaginative writer perceptive enough to know that death is a transfiguring experience for those who witness it; death both takes men out of themselves and plunges them more deeply inside themselves than they have ever been. Death is a uniquely singular and personal experience which brings with absolute finality the end of the self. And Maltz conveys an understanding of this phenomenon and shows the empathy of the others in the flophouse who imagine themselves dying somewhere, ill and alone and broke. Here in Maltz's penetration to the psychic reality of death is the power of his story, when each individual faces alone the end that all men must finally face.

Quite similar strategic problems plague Maltz in his well-known "Man on the Road." This too is an effective story, carefully planned to build toward the climax, which should be hatred for the careless system that is killing so good a man. Our emotional response is channelized by the narrator toward this end. But our emotions refuse to take instruction. Instead of a predominant feeling of wrath at the company which allowed its workers to contract silicosis from its own failure to provide masks and install a fan system in the tunnel the men were boring, one is likely to feel most poignantly the selfless love of a man for his wife. The disruption of a human relationship is more important than the social injustice. Yet the two are tied together. The semi-literate letter the miner writes to his wife expresses a self-abnegation that is embedded in the social scene. As with Vanzetti's letters, the miner's letter gains its impact from the contrast between the semi-literate form and the profound and delicate feeling. And as with Vanzetti, the agony and the triumph affect the individual character in a deeply personal way, but they also constitute a martyrdom that derives its meaning from its public impact.

It is possible to avoid the conflict between self and society, as Maltz shows us in "Incident on a Street Corner." It is not quite fair to say that the writer does this by eliminating the self or the individual from the story. What Maltz does accomplish, to put the matter another way, is to create stylized figures who perform an accepted ritual which arouses a completely predictable response. The characters in this sketch are not individualized; instead they quite literally wear uniforms or play roles. Two are Policemen who represent Law and Order, or Society. The crowd is made up of Irish Catholic Workers. The victim is a Drunk. The interest in this sketch lies in the possible ambivalence of the policemen, who are also Irish Catholics: will they identify with the police and the state or with the workers; that is, what role will they take? What we get is a sort of morality play in which the brutality of the police validates the conviction that justice is not embodied in the minions of law and order. The story presents the reader with a straightforward rhetorical proposition without involving him in the problems of character at all.

But the stories in *The Way Things Are* tend generally

to suggest that Maltz needs individuals as fully realized as his skill and imagination can make them to convey the ideas about society that animate and undergird his fiction. The theme of a story may be the deprivations and degradations of poverty, but what gives the story its interest is the degree of success Maltz has in making his reader feel the loneliness and yearning of a young man from Tennessee who is performing a killing job at the drop-forge in the auto plants of Detroit. The inner reality of the character and his personal needs, whatever it is that marks him as an individual trying to satisfy and express the self, are certainly more telling than concern with the objective social reality. Indeed, that objective reality has importance chiefly as it draws upon or refers to the other.

The failure of Maltz's novel, *The Underground Stream* (1940), may be traced to his neglect of the inner reality. The consequence is a novel about a conflict between opposing ideologies embodied in faceless creatures. The personnel director of one of the motor companies in Detroit is a sort of Jack London-Darwinian puppet who has "learned thoroughly the basic social creed of dog-eat-dog" that characterizes the capitalistic world. The failed businessman is the proto-fascist who works in the Black Legion, a terroristic organization opposed to labor, minorities, and so on; this figure, drawn to specifications established by Communist orthodoxy, is designed to reveal how fascism will rise from the frustrations of the middle class in a bourgeois society. The Communist is a worker with social vision who "lives in an age of social change when history plucks the business of vision out of the hands of the philosophers, away from thinkers and priests, and gives it over to the humble and anonymous." The novel never rises above or deviates from the rhetoric of proletarianism. Even the reluctance of the Communist to accept Party responsibilities cannot, in Maltz's treatment, make of him a man concerned as an individual with a genuine human dilemma; and his martyrdom in the end does not reclaim him as a figure who appeals to our sense of human terror and human loss. Without ambivalence between society and self, between objective and subjective reality, the novel written in the Marxian ambience (or the straightforward Marxist novel, as in this case) fails to give the imaginative satisfactions that we can legitimately expect from fiction.

As an anti-intellectual novelist, Nelson Algren is not a victim of the tensions that Maltz suffers from in writing. There is no question, however, that his first two novels, *Somebody in Boots* (1935) and *Never Come Morning* (1942), were written in the ambience of Marxism. In the first, the epigraphs to the chapters are all taken from Marx. The "Introduction" to the second, written by Richard Wright, claims that Algren's imagination has long brooded on the possibility of changing the social world; his strategy in this book is to depict the intensity of feeling, the dreams, and the longing for human dignity in the lives of his characters. But in neither book does Algren give overt expression to his desire to change the world. We must simply assume that, since Algren's world is so completely degraded and without hope, he would naturally wish to change it. Both books deal with what Marx would have called the *Lumpenproletariat*, in which he put very little trust. These protagonists are not, even in Algren's scheme of things, agents of revolution. They inhabit a world in which men are so stunted economically and spiritually that failure in self-fulfillment is a matter of course. Algren is content to allow the social implications of his version of life in America to speak for themselves. This means that the characters do not speak very much for themselves. Environmental determinism robs them of their individuality.

Yet occasionally Algren penetrates to the inside of each protagonist. Cass McKay of *Somebody in Boots* is brought most forcefully home to us as a human being when he yearns for love, but he becomes pretty largely a type-figure when he undergoes the brutalization that is the lot of the innumerable thousands of homeless boys to whom the novel is dedicated. The failed hero of *Never Come Morning* is Bruno Bicek, unemployed except for a brief period as a pimp. He is a part-time hoodlum who commits a murder, mostly out of self-hatred, and at the end is arrested for it, saying cryptically, "Knew I'd never get t' be twenty-one anyhow." The conviction of fatality hangs over Bicek, who knows that he cannot escape the fate prepared for him by the violence and degradation of the North Side in Chicago. Living in fear and insecurity under the foreknowledge of doom, Bicek is driven into the fantasy world in his search for self-realization and a role with status. Here he envisions himself as a powerful fighter in the ring or a great pitcher on the mound; he dreams of the day when the social worker will call him Mister. In the real world his life is a series of lusts—for tobacco, meat, sleep, whisky, women, ball games—and he is never satisfied. He becomes a refugee from that world and seeks for satisfaction and fulfillment in the dream world. Both novels may certainly be read as a condemnation of American society. Both suggest the basis on which Algren condemns the society—that it twists and corrupts the self, denying opportunity for reasonably full and free development of the personality.

The Unpossessed (1934), by Tess Slesinger, treats a dream world very different from Bruno Bicek's, inhabited by quite different characters. The people in this novel are described as intellectuals; their fantasy is to dwell in the avant-garde world of radical ideology and amoral behavior. Their existence is no more self-fulfilling for them than Bicek's is for him. The particular target of this novel seems to be intellectuals, especially of the left, who suffer from a condition that might be described as ideological dehumanization; it induces a flight from life and a paralysis of inaction. In their sterility, hypocrisy, and alienation, self-definition becomes an impossibility. Miss Slesinger, then, is concerned with the problem of identity in a more direct way than any of the writers I have examined up to this point.

One of the relevant problems in the book is the alienation suffered by Miles Flinders, a New Englander who has left his home and his God. As a child, Miles had known and feared the wrath of God and had needed the punishment that was meted out in His name. But God is dead for Miles, as Miss Slesinger says. He has lost his faith and his roots in place. "For those early days—and all his later life he failed to make it clear—held something (which he now supposed was God) that made living, if terribly painful, meaningful. Something was there, in black and white. One was damned or one was saved; and in between there were no finer shadings. There was always the rough soil to be struggled with; and in the Fall there was either food or less than enough. One faced the problems daily; there was no drugging oneself from final issues, either of the earth or of heaven—one lived, as one's neighbors did, by some guiding rote combined of practical and spiritual."

That stable if difficult world Miles can no longer dwell in; his existence is bounded by the depression, the trial of the Scottsboro boys, the terrible events in Germany. His new god under these new circumstances of life is economics. His new hope is to be a Communist. He seeks commitment, just as earlier in his life he had sought God. But communism and economics are inadequate and uncertain substitutes. He cannot commit himself fully to them and, since he exists in limbo, estranged from his traditional sources of self-realization, he cannot give himself to love. All these conditions combined make for an alienation that leads to the failure of self in Miles—a failure to release his creative energies as a father, to fulfill himself as an intellectual and as a citizen.

Maggie Flinders, Miles' wife, best reveals the sterility that attacks these intellectuals. She is concerned that the feminist impulse arising from a new freedom for women will in the end destroy her as a woman. She thinks she and her friend are too girlish for their age and too mannish for their sex: "O Economic-Independence Votes-for-Women Sex-Equality! you've relieved us of our screens and our embroidery hoops, our babies and our vertigo; and given us—a cigarette; a pencil in our hair." Fulfillment as a woman lies in having children, she thinks, and so becomes pregnant. But at the end of the novel, she aborts herself, because she and Miles decide they cannot bring a child into their desperate world. Together, they flee from life—from new life, that is, birth, and from new experience. This denial of the maternal impulse arises from a failure in commitment to life. In rejecting the deepest needs of the self, it is a denial of the self.

The theme of sterility is less powerfully revealed in Jeffrey North, a sometime writer, who typifies the synthetic and false lives, both emotionally and ideologically, of the unpossessed. He is without passion, but he tries to persuade women that they must rid themselves of bourgeois standards and sleep with him; he is without conviction, dabbling in revolution and Marxism as a parlor game but shunning the realities of genuine hunger and deprivation. As a character, North is largely caricature. He is deliberately made two-dimensional and so not in search of the self. Much the same is true of Professor Bruno Leonard, whose sexual and ideological passions are choked and stopped, and who says savagely, "you're not supposed to be human, you're an intellectual."

Although Miss Slesinger sometimes seems unclear about the nature of intellectuals, she is without any doubt at all about her distaste for them. Nor does she make clear that her intellectuals should take action along Marxist lines; she is much more sure of the imperative need to participate in life. Marxist ideology plays little part in the novel, but in the background looms the committed Party member who derives moral assurance, strength of purpose, and self-identity from a life of directed action. The fellow traveler and the phony Communist are contemptible in good part because they are only playing a role; they do not know who they are.

No one, among the several novelists considered here, handles the problem of society and the self more effectively than Ira Wolfert does in *Tucker's People* (1943). The achievement of this novel is to reconcile polar ideas of reality by showing the integral relationships between the world of the individual and the social world. More specifically, it can be claimed that Wolfert treats the

impact of society on the human consciousness, especially
as he deals with the wedding of psychological and economic phenomena. The problem of alienation of the self
from the modern American world is thus effectively and
dramatically presented. For these several reasons, *Tucker's
People* belongs among a handful of memorable novels
written, during the Thirties and Forties, in the ambience
of Marxism. It is remarkable for the richness of its themes,
its sophisticated and knowledgeable attitude toward urban
power relationships, politics, and crime, its deftly handled
plot, and its sharp and accurate ear for urban speech.

On the opening page Wolfert says this is a story of the
modern world, of what the world does to its people, and of
which people shall be the users and which the used.
Tucker is a user. Scrabbling for a place in the world, he
had been, in the past, a strikebreaker and had killed a
man. The company "fixed" the murder. When he understood what was happening, "There weren't any people left
for Tucker on earth any more—only himself and human
beings he could use or could ignore or must fight. Business
and its law of self-defense had taught him that." The
theme which Wolfert here pursues is the elimination of
the individual by the world of business. People—both
pursuer and pursued—are rendered lifeless by the quest for
money. Tucker is a pursuer, and "everything about him
was a businessman." He had a lust for money, and "best
of all—he had what insecurity and its fears can give, an
almost complete failure to feel that people were people or
anything at all except things." He destroys others, but he
will destroy himself as well.

The novel concerns Tucker's effort to take over the
policy or numbers racket. He moves into this field of
endeavor with the cold efficiency of a large corporation,
and he swallows all the small-time, independent entrepreneurs. Wolfert quite deliberately makes his action a para-
digm for corporate enterprise, and Tucker is as soulless,
bloodless, and modern as a corporation. To emphasize
how Tucker loses his self in his bitter economic world,
Wolfert contrasts him to Leo Minch, who had operated

independently in the policy game. Leo had run his business in a paternalistic way, had recognized the existence of people as individuals, and had tried to persuade them to do the right thing and to like him. Tucker's corporate efficiency is a means of alienating man from his world, while Leo represents business as old-fashioned paternalism that at least mitigates the harshness of the notion that the cash nexus is the only tie between men.

Tucker's first lieutenant is Joe Minch, Leo's brother. At the end of the novel, Tucker feels forced to sacrifice Leo to opposing gangsters. Joe is told he may either go along with this course or try to save Leo but thereby lose his place in Tucker's business. To protests at the inhumanity of this dilemma, Tucker replies, "I don't see what I'm doing is so wrong, so terrible. What about any corporation when a man becomes a liability to them?" Tucker not only points up the similarity of organized criminal activity to legitimate business, but in his insensitivity to fraternal love and to loyalty, he also repudiates human values that lead to definition of the self. Finally he flees the city, leaving the field to his opposition. It is a symbolic death of the self: Tucker degenerates from manhood to corporate entity, and then to nothingness.

The same theme—that business crushes the individual—is pursued with Bauer, a bookkeeper who works for Leo. As Tucker uses Leo in business, so Leo uses Bauer, forces Bauer to do his will and torments the man by robbing him of himself: Bauer "became aware, as Egan had been aware and Leo and as most contestants in the business game at some time must become aware, that he had been made into an animal in a trap." The world of business, which is a microcosm for the world at large in Wolfert's imagination, induces in all men a searing insecurity, which is in Bauer more intense than in any other character. Molded by insecurity, he is intellectually and spiritually crippled almost from the beginning. He is unable to define his place and role in society and becomes an office worker although his real talent is for mechanics. "The result, altogether, was that Bauer not only sacrificed his personality (as it might have been expressed through his talent for mechanics) in order to control his sense of insecurity, but he sacrificed with it any chance he had had to find security in business." And this uncertainty was the condition of all the people he knew. "His natural self loved them or was willing to be at peace with them. Fear forced him to love no one and nothing and did not allow him to live at peace with anyone. The best the business world permits the fearful man is an armed truce."

The Marxist view that fascism is the last gasp of a desperate capitalism leads Wolfert to impose a burden on Bauer that this little man cannot convincingly bear. Reduced by the world of business to something less than a man in his insecurity, Bauer comes to feel that death is the only way out. The will to self-destruction grows strong in him. It is nourished by fear of enemies he invents for the purpose. A corrupt leader appears to him (actually a young punk working for the rival gangster organization) and promises a solution to Bauer's problems which the latter knows is really a promise of death. And in fact he brings death to Leo and to himself. Wolfert designed this too-elaborate miniaturization of the rise of Nazism to show the parallel between fascism and business—both destroy the possibility of the self and hold the promise of wholesale death. These conditions are the climax toward which the modern world is heading.

Bauer suffers from insecurity, as does Tucker. So do Leo and Joe Minch and Wheelock, Tucker's attorney. This condition is induced by business and also by money. A second theme of the novel, closely related to the first, is that money destroys the self. Money can do its work because every man is reduced to fear and insecurity in a society in which money means survival. Leo is a good man as long as he is left alone. " 'I am friends with everybody up to money,' he told himself, and meant that when being 'good' aggravated his insecurity he stopped being 'good.' " He is a man who wants to live within the law but whose need for money is lawless, who needs money to breathe. The result is that he makes money in shady, nonproductive but legal ways that fill him with self-disgust.

Leo and Joe were born into a poverty that made them insecure; it determined their pursuit of money. The same was true of Henry Wheelock, whose family sacrificed deeply to train him as a lawyer and then waited for him to repay them. Under this intense pressure, Wheelock sat in his office and watched New York sweat money; the feel of money was all over the city, and everybody had his face in it like a hog. Except Wheelock. He is ripe for Tucker's criminal offers when they are made, although he does not admit to himself that he is a criminal. The corruption of the self goes on unacknowledged, but inevitably it goes on. In this passage about Wheelock and Doris, an inept chorus girl he is inexplicably attracted to, Wolfert reports Wheelock's unthought thoughts:

> For a sensitive man who had loved his father and regarded his father's way of life as heroic, to hunt down money was exactly wrong. Yet he became frantic for money and frantic to hunt it, as Doris seemed frantic to dance well. The harder Henry tried for money, the more he degraded his natural self, just as the harder Doris danced the more she degraded her self. The more degraded Henry felt, the more money he must try to get. The more money he got, the more degraded he must feel. The harder Doris danced, the more degraded she felt. The more degraded she felt, the harder she danced. This was what Doris meant to Henry, although as yet it could not be clear to him.

In Wolfert's unrelieved vision of the destructive power inherent in a business and money society, two other matters are worthy of comment. One concerns the inefficacy of morality, a point hinted at earlier in discussing human values. Egan, a detective, finds himself trapped and so turns, Wolfert says ironically, desperately to truth. But he is adhering to a "morality that had been invented before the game of marauding for profits had grasped up the whole earth. Now this morality was no more use than a sword to an admiral. . . . What use could morality be on an earth given over to profit except to ornament a life or fill a grave?" The breakdown of morality is laid to capitalism, which eliminates a guide to life and a way to self-definition. Another factor destructive of life and therefore of the self is the urban landscape Wolfert provides for those who have money—Tucker and Wheelock. This setting is symbolically arid, as with the hedge near Wheelock's apartment house, which grows in boxes chained to the sidewalk and encloses a concrete plot where a fire hydrant "bloomed like a bush." Tucker lives on a street that looks like a path through a petrified forest and seems drowned in stone. In its darkness and stone-shrouded quietness, his apartment house conveys a feeling of death.

Tucker's People sees man in a deterministic framework, driven and goaded by a society that leads him to exploit and destroy others and finally to destroy himself. That destruction is both psychic and physical so that the idea of the self is dead before the body actually loses its vital warmth. Business, which is warfare carried on as cheating and gambling, and the pursuit of money are the mainstays of this society. They reduce people to things and rob men of the self.

It is reasonable to say that in the Thirties and early Forties in this country, Marxism was in the air. And for those fiction writers concerned with social protest, it was a particularly heady kind of air to breathe. Marxism was exciting and intoxicating because it seemed to offer alternatives to a culture that had suffered shellshock. But not all the fiction writers understood Marx. The evidence suggests that writers did not read him carefully; even if they had wished to make of his ideas a theoretical basis for their fiction, not all of his work was available to them in English. Further, no American literary critic had explained in an adequate way the subtle relationships between literature and economics that a sophisticated reading of Marx might uncover. In the light of these conditions, it is not surprising that while writers turned to Marx, they read him in partial and simplistic ways.

The fiction examined here suggests that writers by and large failed to exploit the deeper possibilities of Marxism. In part, the difficulty lies with Marx himself. He made it easy to believe that the essence of his thought lay in ideas of class and in the fate of mass-man in the revolutionary struggle. The frequent appearance of mass-man in the fiction of the Thirties and the frequent occurrence of the collectivistic technique in the novel are reflections of this rather direct and unsophisticated reading of Marx. At the same time, the humanistic implications of Marxism were barely recognized by the writers of the period. In the crucial matter of character, personality, and the self, writers on the left generally failed to seize the opportunities latent in the Marxian doctrines of alienation. Such writers sometimes managed to smuggle into their fiction a consideration of subjective states of consciousness and ideas of identity; or despite themselves, despite their ideological convictions, they dealt with character simply in obedience to the imperatives of their craft. The tensions within Marxism generated by the polarities of humanism and collectivism are certainly reflected in this fiction. But, on balance, it must be said that individual character is not sufficiently explored and defined in the fiction written in the ambience of Marxism.

Aesthetics of the Proletarian Novel

FREDERICK J. HOFFMAN

IT IS NOT EASY to set the limits of a subject of this kind. For one thing, we discover through hindsight that the Thirties were a much more varied decade than they appeared to be at close range. That there was a proletarian novel, and that it conformed (or responded) to certain conditions, are facts we must accept. Just what was the "proletarian novel"? In the best book on the subject, *The Radical Novel in the United States, 1900–1954*, Walter Rideout limits the subject rather severely: "A radical novel, then, is one which demonstrates, either explicitly or implicitly, that its author objects to the human suffering imposed by some, socioeconomic system and *advocates that the system be fundamentally changed*." [1] Almost invariably, *radical* is equivalent to proletarian, and especially in the American Thirties. Several points need to be observed here: The aesthetic of the proletarian novel adjusted to the local circumstances (the phenomena of a depression society); it also adjusted to an ideology which had had a European history of at least half a century and had become the philosophical guideline of the Russian Revolutionary society; there was a romantic dedication to leftist thought, which led to several kinds of melodrama in the writing of the decade.

To put the issue in its simplest terms, perhaps the best sourcebook is an anthology published in the middle of the decade, *Proletarian Literature in the United States* (1935). [2] In his "Introduction," Joseph Freeman admits that art "is not the same as action; it is not identical with science; it is distinct from party program. Nevertheless, artists are and must be aware of "the revolution." In any case, they are in spirit *engagé*, and the most dramatic events of their times are those of the class conflict. "War, unemployment, a widespread social-economic crisis drive middle-class writers into the ranks of the proletariat. Their experience becomes contiguous to or identical with that of the working class; they see their former life and the life of everyone around them with new eyes; their grasp of experience is conditioned by the class to which they have now attached themselves; they write from the viewpoint of the revolutionary proletariat; they create what is called proletarian literature. There is some magic transformation: the "poet" observes the conditions of a depressed industrial society, and he transmutes his feelings into art. The stock-market collapse of 1929 awoke many writers to the realization that our society was by no means classless. Once they were aware of classes, they saw these classes in a position of basic hostility to each other. So that the context of proletarian literature is both the proletarian condition and the conflict between the lower and the ruling classes. The general attitude of this mid-Thirties collection is optimistic and axiomatic. The novelists of the time, said Granville Hicks, in an essay called "American Fiction: The Major Trend," solved the problem of their own involvement "by placing themselves on the side of the proletariat, working for and with them and seeking to see life as they see it."

The truth is more complex. Much that was seen then as "proletarian" literature designed with an ideological or a political attack in mind comes through to us now as part of the texture of the lives of a people down on their luck, suffering from malnutrition and even starvation, organizing in the hope that political action would bring an end to economic deprivation. The genre of the novel was much concerned with presenting "things as they were," and only part of the time was engaged in the ideological melodramatics we are accustomed to associate with literature of this time. There was much Stalinist fatuity, but even that diminished as the decade proceeded and the local circumstances began to edge out the drama of the Russian conflict. Explaining the change that occurred in *Partisan Review*'s politics in the Thirties, William Phillips said, "Politically, this meant a stand for morality in politics. In literature, it meant a radicalism rooted in tradition and open to experiment, and an awareness that the imagination could not be contained within any orthodoxy. It meant that one could not rule out any literary beliefs or forms as incompatible with socialist aims." [3]

In short there was as much resistance to an "imported ideology" as there was attention paid to it. The American proletarian novel was often a strange mixture of native realism and sudden dips into ideological editorial or melodrama. Very few novelists were spared the awkward hesitation that a commitment to leftist necessities seemed to cause. There were pity and anger, and these were distributed predictably. The victims of the economic debacle were almost invariably from the same class; the villains belonged generally to another; and there were opportunities for editorializing, which usually took on the native hue of a general Marxist disposition toward history. The sense of ideological responsibility varied from writer to writer, even from book to book. Perhaps the most outspoken critic of the matter was James T. Farrell, who tried hard much of his time to throw out the bath water without risking a loss of the baby. In *A Note on Literary Criticism* (1936), he pronounced several times on the issue. Working in terms of the rather arbitrary dualism of "art for art's sake" (which is limited to a narrow sphere of artistic interests) and leftist writing, he defined his views. The latter, while not quite so arbitrarily limited, nevertheless demands "a literature of simplicity to the point of obviousness and even of downright banality." When a literature follows economics, Farrell says, the literature suffers, because "The basic weaknesses of the economic situation in any period produce weaknesses in the literature of that period."

Farrell spares the leftist ideology and its attendant economics from a total indictment. He opts for the literature of "social structures," of large designs and significant derivations. This literature must also make provision for "the individual," for this individual "is a person with resemblances to all the other members of that class, and with a difference from all the other members of that class." Literature can be made to "perform an objective social function," and to serve as "an instrument of social influence," but discriminations must be preserved, between it and propaganda. Ultimately, the greatest literature, for him, is fiction which provides for an inclusive view: "I assume that there is a unity in society as I have defined it, that there are many manifestations from a given set of objective conditions, and finally that the more deeply one is aware of these manifestations, emotionally as well as intellectually, the better one will succeed in understanding contemporary society."

James T. Farrell's intentions, however obscured they may be by his style, are genuinely and natively "American"—as are those of John Dos Passos and John Steinbeck, the other two major novelists of the Thirties. Lesser artists like Edwin Seaver saw the issue much more simply. To the First Congress of American Writers, Seaver spoke of the basic dis-unity in a capitalist culture, a distinction between what he called "the ideological superstructure and the materialist base. . . . That is why, when you have the dis-unity, as in the United States today, it is so necessary to understand the matter of political orientation as basic in any consideration of the proletarian novel. When, on the other hand, as in the Soviet Union, you have eliminated this dis-unity and have new writers immersed in a generally accepted new ideology, then many of the peculiar problems which confront the novelist in our country automatically disappear." [4] What must today appear as arrant nonsense and one of the most naïve readings of history was at the least seriously considered in the Thirties. Yet the native American resistance to extremes of arbitrary ideological statement seems remarkable from the perspective of three decades. A "very sharp distinction" marks the difference between the earlier socialist novels and the proletarian novels of the Thirties. So Walter Rideout cautions: "Where almost all of the Socialist writers had expressly rejected violence in favor of parliamentary methods of change, almost all of the proletarians insisted that the coming struggle for power between capitalist and working class would be of the 'cataclysmic' nature described in their favorite handbook of revolution, *Toward Soviet America*, published by William Z. Foster in 1932."

The "violence" is largely a matter of melodrama; it is also verbal, and energetically argumentative. But, accepting it as appropriate to a limited number of "radical novels," some seventy of which pass the muster of Rideout's rather stringent definitions,[5] it may be useful to discuss the classes of proletarian novel and their relationship to the proletarian aesthetic. First, there was the strike novel, perhaps the most successful use of leftist dramatics. In it, as Rideout points out, there is a "trajectory" of movement and action "aptly designed for artistic expression. The storm gathers, the initial clash occurs, the struggle veers back and forth, producing suspense as the advantage goes now to this side, now to that; the climax is reached when the strike succeeds or is broken, and the action thereafter drops swiftly." This type of novel is obviously an ideal "set up" for proletarian dramatics, if we look at the novel in terms both of action and of quick, radical changes. Few strike novels possessed the objectivity of Émile Zola's *Germinal* (1885), in which neither striker nor manager emerged heroic and the ideological dynamics were reduced primarily to a psychological "symptom." There were some interesting American parallels: Mary Heaton Vorse's *Strike!* (1930), William Rollins' *The Shadow Before* (1934), Robert Cantwell's *The Land of Plenty* (1934) and Meyer Levin's *Citizens* (1940). The most successful literary uses of the type were Levin's and Cantwell's. Perhaps the most overtly dramatic application of the strike's literary possibilities occurs in Rollins' novel.

At the end of this novel, the movement of the strikers toward the barrier is slowly anticipated, with the word STRIKE! recurring in capitals as a means of emphasizing the stages of the journey. The word acts as a punctuation not only of the movement of strikers but also of the "Internationale," the sound of which increases as the men move toward the gate:

> It rose here and there in the crowd. In English, Portuguese, French, Greek, Polish. Some remembered it dimly from the past and hummed it; some followed and hummed it; everybody made some kind of sound. And it blended, rose to the listening watchers at the windows, to the lowhung clouds that scuttled darkly, silently by:

> "THE INTERNATIONAL SHALL BE THE HUMAN RACE!"

> They crowded through the gate, singing, yelling, whistling through their teeth. Someone jerked the watchman's cap over his nose, and when he raised it another jerked it down, and then another jerked it down. They swept along the street behind their leaders, a dark formless unwieldy mob, fiercely exultant.

It is hard to believe that this kind of melodramatic wish-fulfillment was once taken seriously, but the fact is that the details and the movement are exactly what suited the requirements of the strike novel on their simplest level. The "good guys" are victims; the heroes appear in the mass; the dramatics attend the movement of victim toward exploiter; the gate is the symbol of all that stands between the masses and the right expropriation of management facilities. This is, of course, the most simplistic of novelistic maneuvers. The superior novel of this class is John Steinbeck's *In Dubious Battle* (1936); it is, so far as it can be, an objective literary equivalent of the dramatics shown in *The Shadow Before*. Steinbeck had difficulty placing it with a publisher because leftist critics, assigned to read the manuscript, were puzzled over its not really settling upon a point of view.[6] As for the Communist ideology, Steinbeck said, in a letter to his literary agents, "My information for this book came mostly from Irish and Italian Communists whose training was in the field, not in the drawing-room. They don't believe in ideologies and ideal tactics. They do what they can under the circumstances." The novel is a balance of an objective account (though there are certain sympathies that are almost instantly elicited) and a dramatic development of the situation's possibilities. Unlike the uses made of them in Vorse and Rollins, the strategy here is to play the characters and situations out, to let them go as far as they can go, then (in an effective sense) to draw in the lines. Ultimately Mac and Jim, the two prototypes, become extreme cases of ideological hagiology, beyond either personal or doctrinaire understanding. "[Mac] stood up and faced the crowd. His hands gripped the rail. . . . He moved his jaws to speak, and seemed to break the frozen jaws loose. His voice was high and monotonous. 'This guy didn't want nothing for himself—' he began. His knuckles were white, where he grasped the rail. 'Comrades! He didn't want nothing for himself—' "

Rideout's second class of proletarian novel is the "conversion novel," the hero of which follows a developmental progress, from "being out" to "being in." He begins by trying to rise above his class, but with no specific guidelines. He asks himself basic questions about conditions that are a part of the depression world, and is finally (on most occasions) alerted to some form or other of ideological understanding of his predicament. Perhaps Jack Conroy's *The Disinherited* (1933) is the best example, though it is interesting for other reasons as well, not the least of which is that it is a Thirties predecessor of the "On the Road" literature of Jack Kerouac and others after World War II. Down and out for reasons of economic depression, the hero becomes a drifter, moves almost without motive or incentive from place to place, becomes acquainted informally with Marxism, and ends by seeing himself clearly as a member of his class. He hasn't gone the full way at novel's end, but there are suggestions that he will. This is not unlike the progress of John Dos Passos' Mac Williams of *The Forty-Second Parallel* (1930), though the conclusions are different in each case.

Taking his cue from the title of Edward Dahlberg's novel, *Bottom Dogs* (1930), Rideout labels the third division of the proletarian novel as the "bottom dogs" novel, a work which, variously, describes the lower depths world of the Thirties. Included in this group are Nelson Algren's *Somebody in Boots* (1935), an antecedent of *The Man with the Golden Arm* (1949) and *A Walk on the Wild Side* (1956); Henry Roth's *Call It Sleep* (1935), a portrayal of a depression childhood on the Lower East Side; and, of course, Dahlberg's *Bottom Dogs*, which wanders to no end but with a certain effectiveness. The truth is that there is a history of this kind of literature in American fiction, almost from the beginning, though it was certainly much stimulated by the ample evidence of "bottom dogs" life in the Thirties.

The final group in Rideout's classification is the novel that describes the decay and decline of the middle class, and surely this is one of the most important sources of proletarian literature. The drive was always *toward* the middle class in the United States, and it is therefore interesting to see that class analysed in terms of its default of humanistic virtues. Writers of the Thirties were especially active in offering observations of the middle class; most of Clifford Odets' important plays are devoted to it. James T. Farrell's first, and his best, series of novels, the Studs Lonigan trilogy, are concerned with the decline of an Irish middle-class family in south Chicago; and the last novel ends with Studs' death as the sounds of the "new day" and the new judgment are heard in the streets outside the Lonigan home. Josephine Herbst's trilogy is perhaps written along the classical lines of its type: *Pity Is Not Enough* (1933), *The Executioner Waits* (1934), and *Rope of Gold* (1939).

A number of observations need to be made about all of these works of fiction. The first is that any one of these types can yield to a fiction that is quite unideological, and all of them have done so almost throughout the history of literature. In other words, none of these groups of novels derived peculiarly from local social or economic circumstances. On the other hand, these circumstances did encourage the kind of novels we have been looking at, and the lines of their development were especially sharpened because of the times. One of the most important effects upon the novel was the acceleration of its pace as well as, often, the simplification of lines of action. There were few subtleties, though certain novelists, like Robert Cantwell and Meyer Levin, were less simple-minded than others. One of the curiosities of the Thirties novel was Tess Slesinger's *The Unpossessed* (1934), a study of the *déclassé* intellectuals of New York City. It is interesting that the Avon Books editors should recently have chosen it for reissuing, with an "Afterword" by Lionel Trilling. Murray Kempton's review of this new issue, in *The New Republic*, CLV (November 5, 1966), 25–28, quite adequately takes care of this book; it is surprising that anyone should have considered it worth reprinting.

Finally, perhaps one ought to comment upon the contribution of the literature of the Thirties to the comprehension and the depiction of violence. Naturalism began by being permissive concerning the scope and range of the novel's context; such fiction of the Twenties as the novels and short stories of Ernest Hemingway provided refinements, especially in the matter of precision and accuracy of fictional representation. The proletarian novels can be said to have altered the matter in two ways: by accelerating the pace of the violence, and by offering a set of motives for participating in it. However slight its influence may have been in some cases, the fact is that the Marxist theory of history is more than descriptive; it is at least permissive and perhaps at times prescriptive. The fiction written by people affected by it tended to spur the action on, and permitted a number of accelerations in its happening. The Thirties was the first decade in the century in which physical action came close to being a *desideratum* of the novel. There was an entire range of crudities and subtleties involved; American fiction never achieved the excellence of such Europeans as Malraux, Silone, or Koestler. But the novel that was inspired, or whose creation was encouraged, by leftist dynamics, was likely to show some change in its portrayal of physical action, in some testimony or other of the dynamics of doctrinal energy.

The novelist since the end of World War II (there are a few exceptions) is likely to look skeptically and ironically at the more naïve of leftist histrionics. The proletarian novels (at least the seventy of Rideout's listing) of the Thirties now mainly exist as period pieces, to which one refers from time to time, but almost unbelievingly. At the time of their appearance, they were not only tolerated, but warmly debated. The fiction of Farrell, Steinbeck, and Dos Passos survives them, and this largely because it was superior work, less given to formulas and more in the literary tradition of twentieth-century naturalism. None of these is a first-rate writer, but all of them offer a literature that resists the confinement of an ideological source and explanation.

The Marxist Aesthetic Theory
of Louis C. Fraina

LEE BAXANDALL

LOUIS C. FRAINA, known later as Lewis Corey, was one of the earliest Marxist theorists of the arts to appear in America. More than that, Fraina was certainly for many years our most incisive, original Marxist critic and aesthetician. It is perhaps surprising that his analysis of our literature, jazz, and dance, and of new European painting has gone equally unnoticed in accounts of the American critical heritage and of international Marxist aesthetics. Within the total scope of his activities Fraina's aesthetic writings may appear marginal; yet this concern was crucial to his humanistic hopes and values. His method and values transcend their period of origin and still are of great pertinence and interest today. We shall review the aesthetic thought of Fraina, noticing in particular what it reveals about our "proletarian" literature and criticism in the Thirties, which he held in low esteem.

Born in 1892, in the village of Galdo (Salerno), Italy, Luigi Carlo Fraina was brought at the age of three to the United States. The Frainas lived in extreme poverty on the Lower East Side of New York. The father had been an Italian republican with a thirst for freedom; in this promised land, he barely made a living as a waiter and in various odd jobs. As a result, Louis was by the age of six in the street selling newspapers. It was not long before he was shining shoes, or assisting his mother in a tobacco factory. When Fraina's father died he left school for a full-time job, working first as a clerk for the Edison Company; thus ended his formal schooling. He was fourteen.[1]

Fraina had attended a parochial school; now he became an opponent of Catholicism. At sixteen he began to write for an agnostic publication, *The Truth Seeker*. Art Brisbane, the columnist, noticed his work and found the youth a cub-reporter post with the New York *Journal*. Fraina was also developing an oppositional view in politics; believing the large, influential Socialist Party not sufficiently militant, in 1909 he joined the Socialist Labor Party led by Daniel DeLeon.

He proved a vigorous street-corner speaker and powerful writer, and soon was treated as a foremost DeLeonite theorist. When he was seventeen, the general committee of the SLP for New York elected Fraina its secretary. His speeches and writings appeared often in the SLP's *Weekly People*. At the Berkeley Lyceum Hall on December 12, 1909, he gave a forceful summary of Marxist revolutionary socialism. Marxism now provided the context of his continuing attack on Catholicism. Charitable assistance doled out by the Church or capitalism, he declared, would not bring an end to the misery of the four million American children who had no choice but to work. Citing a poem by Victor Hugo, Fraina demanded: "Where is the happy, careless laugh of childhood, the inalienable gift of Nature to all children?"[2]

He developed these views directly, of course, from intensive childhood experience. And, as often happened on the Lower East Side, exposure to literature indirectly helped to form his ideas: "A reading of various radical authors—of whom Hugo, Zola, Shaw, are examples—had engendered in me sympathy for the lowly and oppressed. . . . A vague spirit of revolt imbued my mind . . . it made me susceptible to the Socialist propaganda." In *Weekly People* (1910), Fraina thus explained, at a ripe eighteen years, how the Socialist Party attracted him before he found it too compromising. He recalled in later years that from the age of twelve, besides Hugo, Zola, and Shaw, he read the novels of Dickens, Norris, Sinclair, London, Dreiser, Dostoevsky, and Gorky; the poetry of Burns,

Shelley, Whittier, Whitman, Frost, and Swinburne; and Rolland's *Jean-Christophe*.

We must take particular note of Fraina's experience in organizing the working class. In part, this experience may well explain the acuity and difference of his social and aesthetic views from those of cultural Marxists with middle-class backgrounds (Calverton, Hicks), and Marxists from similar impoverished, émigré backgrounds with no experience of proletarian organizing (Freeman, Rahv, and even Gold, whose views most resemble Fraina's).

He covered the 1912 Lawrence, Massachusetts, textile strike for the DeLeonite paper. Briefly Fraina joined the Wobblies (Industrial Workers of the World), who led the strike; he worked at a succession of jobs and was in the stage hands' union. In early 1914, Fraina broke with De-Leon over the latter's "jesuiticism." By this time he already was a leading contributor to *The New Review*, where he wrote on politics and on the arts.

Apparently the first of his essays in aesthetics is a review of *The Three Daughters of Monsieur Dupont*, a naturalist drama about bourgeois marriage by Eugene Brieux.[3] Fraina displays an astonishing maturity (he was but eighteen); what is more, he employed with incisive result the aesthetic method of Marx and Engels. One is amazed; for in 1910, and indeed until well along in the Thirties, virtually none of the specific views of Marx and Engels on literature were known in the United States, or even in Europe. A rigorous Socialist analysis of culture was all but unpracticed here; generally a few vague sentiments favoring workers' culture were made to serve, as an examination of *The Masses* and *The Comrade* will demonstrate. Yet the young Fraina essentially duplicates the method of Marx and Engels; studying their historical and philosophical works, he derived the implicit aesthetic principles.[4] (Before many of the passages on art and literature by Marx and Engels were in print, a number of individuals in various lands worked out roughly those principles, independently and often in detail, as Fraina did: the connection of Marx's philosophy with aesthetics thus is demonstrated, despite the failure of Marx to write fully on aesthetics as he intended.)

Persuasively, Fraina showed how Brieux fused his rich creative talent and a powerful Socialist perspective. The elements of a Marxist literary approach are deployed, as Fraina writes approvingly that the play: *a*] "indicted" bourgeois marriage; *b*] showed "the social conditions that sustain it"; *c*] the "characters are types of a certain class of people"; *d*] "the types are not of the usually cold and statuesque kind, but imbued with a life and individuality all their own"; *e*] the natural potential of human beings is revealed together with the "artificial repression of natural desires," their alienation in class society; *f*] the fictional method is not moralistic but "ironic," i.e., the critical perspective is *embodied* rather than stated, and so too, the eventual political solution is not stated but merely hinted by the actions of the two daughters who try to escape a bourgeois fate, one by becoming a worker and the other by marrying a worker. ("A worker, a man with a noble aim in life," says Brieux's Caroline.)

Fraina, with Marx, was committed to human progress; therefore an aesthetic of combative realism was not merely possible (this they assumed, on good evidence) but to be encouraged. However both Fraina and Marx laid emphasis on points (*d*) and (*f*); they scorned a crude, inartistic literary method, however Socialist in perspective, and in this sense put art before politics. Marx in a famous letter to Lassalle, criticized Lassalle's play *Sickingen* for its use of a spokesman of the author's viewpoint in the manner of Schiller. Fraina here made the same point, in questioning the method of Bernard Shaw.

> Shaw is the more heterodox, Brieux the more powerful. The first casts his drama in the form of a moral discourse, making his characters disseminate radical thought; and he depends on what they say to ram home an idea into the spectator's mind. The French dramatist, on the contrary, makes his characters say little that could be termed 'revolutionary,' yet their acts are more eloquent than words; his central idea is bound up intimately with the play and he

depends on the plot's development to achieve the desired result. One would have his characters excoriate a certain evil, the other presents it and its consequences to you actually on the stage. In brief, Bernard Shaw depends on radical dialogue, Eugene Brieux on dramatic action.

Notable too is Fraina's lifelong habit, here initiated, of applying the most exacting critical standard to works of progressive reputation especially. French drama had won notoriety for its allegedly radical, realistic treatment of the theme of sex, but Fraina disagreed. While Brieux's work was powerful, revolutionary, and "true to life," he found that most of the French plays arose from and appealed to a decadent, Philistine taste,

> the subject-matter of their sex-dramas is usually adultery and illicit love, glossed over with a thick layer of insipid and vulgar sentimentality. . . . They are disgusting to the thinker and the revolutionist, not because they deal with the theme of sex, but in that their method and spirit of presentation lack the inspiring glow of radical thought. . . . One would expect to see demonstrated in these dramas the blighting influence of bourgeois private property on marital life, and the implied necessity of a Social Revolution, so as to realize a society of free and happy human beings, and love have the opportunity to blossom forth in true sincerity. One would expect to see the dominant idea to be the necessity of natural attraction, physical and mutual, as the basis of a true union; and the necessity of absolute liberty from the trammels of adverse social conditions in the relations between the sexes. All this is lacking; instead we find either brutal cynicism, suggestive and immoral 'realism', or insipid romanticism.

Fraina's Marxism did not flinch before or slight the theme of sex, which he thought "powerful in its irresistible influence." Fraina indeed praises *Spring's Awakening,* the controversial play by Frank Wedekind, for its portrayal of how "ignorance of the 'mysteries' of sex has brought disastrous results in its wake." He cites Nietzsche with approval in this respect. Remarkable was Fraina's ability in extending Marxist aesthetics to such new and problematic areas. It was a hallmark of his gift.

An essay of 1910 shows Fraina's fresh application to the problems of a Socialist intelligentsia, among whom, for this purpose, the Socialist authors were to be considered. The attitude of Marx toward the radical *literati* mixed fondness and reserve (Fraina could not have known this). Marx found that, owing in part to a poet's distant, nebulous relation to the struggle and suffering of the exploited, the poets Heine and Freiligrath were vain personally and unreliable politically, although they were his personal friends. Fraina, too, time and again will express misgivings about the role of a Socialist and Communist intelligentsia; not surprisingly, in Fraina the concern gains more attention than in Marx. The size of that intelligentsia had grown greatly. While in 1910 it virtually had no power, that too was to change, after 1917. Fraina was only, if deeply, concerned to warn in 1910 that, due to their remoteness from practical life, even the most progressive and greatest artists might not be relied upon for the practical answers. He held that poets "are emotional, not scientific; they allow their feelings to dominate their faculty of analytic reason" which, in turn, "lacks a substantial basis." Thus Bernard Shaw "has done valiant work in arousing social discontent; yet he is no more Socialist than is the mythical man in the moon." Victor Hugo, who like Shaw was an early influence upon Fraina, was a "sentimental" and "chaotic" thinker, whose prescriptions were worse than harmless. As for a poet of less ability, he "basks in the pale glow of vacuous sentiment," and is "as often as not . . . an intellectual nondescript, catering to ignorance and prejudice, and therefore, more popular than the real poet. . . . Endowed with a weak mind, he cannot glimpse or purposely ignores the progressive movement in society, and is always acting (consciously or unconsciously, it matters not) in the interest of reaction." Fraina went so far as to say that the function of art was to arouse and could not be to prescribe, except in the most general way: "paradoxical as it may seem, we welcome the poets and their agitation, but, when it is a matter of *action*, we exclaim, 'Beware of the poet!'" "The true poet is endowed with the psychologic power of seeing and experiencing things much more vividly, forcibly, than the ordinary mortal, and, as a consequence, is enabled to describe them in a fervent strain." Dante, Milton, Shelley, Hugo, and Whitman rejected "the sterile theory of 'art for art's sake' " and were "in the thick of the struggle for human advancement," striving "to realize their aspirations into actual practice." The true poet, who can "stir the mentally lethargic mass into activity," is indeed valuable; yet when it comes to a course of action, Fraina finds it fortunate that "seldom are the words of the poet heeded in the course of material development, which alone superinduces social and intellectual progress."

It would be shallow to conclude that Fraina was anti-intellectual. He saw, rather, that in a class society, intellect generally becomes relegated to a social stratum detached from basic and democratic realities and needs.

Even intellectuals from proletarian origins and with experience in the Socialist movement manifested this sort of alienation from the realities of their class or origin, Fraina warned. "The culture that has come out of the socialist and labor movement is petty-bourgeois and in no way proletarian, and has injected a petty-bourgeois spirit among the masses." Even in Russia in 1921, after four years of Soviet power with the nurturing of Proletarian Culture, the only proletarian author Fraina could find was Maxim Gorky; the writing of others from working-class origin—for example, in the United States, Charles Erskine Scott Wood, Floyd Dell, and Upton Sinclair—was shot through with capitalist values and served only to confuse the workers. When would this alienation of thought from social existence end? Only, Fraina believed, when Socialist revolution made every worker an intellectual, and made intellectuals into workers.[5] Marx looked forward similarly to an integration of all human activity in each individual in the future Communist society.

The Paterson textile workers re-enacted their own strike-in-progress at Madison Square Garden, under John Reed's direction, in 1913. "It was human and effective," Fraina later wrote, "because it expressed the humanity and the needs of workers on strike, not the slick clichés which unhappily are the usual thing among labor sympathizers. It was great Labor propaganda whose like I have not since seen." [6] This judgment reflects accurately, and in its affirmative aspect, Fraina's distrust of the alienation of Socialist intellectuals from solid democratic roots.

Fraina was also excited by the New York Armory Show of 1913 when the revolution of European painting was first exhibited to America. He declined to dismiss Cubism and Futurism as pathologic, and those who did, whether conservative or Socialist (and many did), he said were ignorant of

> the social *milieu*, which determines ideas and movements . . . even if we assume that 'decadent' manifestations in art are pathologic, does this account for their *form* of expression, for the movement itself? . . . Art reflects life; it is social and not individualistic. . . . Aspirations continually change with changing social conditions; art changes in harmony therewith, not only in spirit but also in methods. Art appears deadly opposed to pouring the wine of new aspirations into the bottles of old methods. Considered in this light, the New Art expresses capitalism. It is the art of capitalism—not the 'art of decadent and dying capitalism,' as some would have it, but of capitalism dominant (Cubism) and capitalism ascending (Futurism). The aggressive, brutal power of Cubism and Futurism is identical with the power and audacity of capitalism, of our machine-civilization. The New Art is as typical of capitalism as the architecture of the sky-scraper.

Fraina applied a stylistic and sociological analysis to distinguish Cubism from Futurism. Cubism emerged in an advanced capitalist country, France, and therefore could be "definite" in transferring "the technique of machinery, so to speak, to the canvas." Cubism thus "expresses artistically" the capitalist spirit; in contrast, Futurists "are vague and indefinite, failing largely to embody creed in artistic productions . . . not fully materializing" their ideal and projecting instead "the spirit of machinery,—energy, motion, aggression" with "a nervous force and power startlingly vivid, oppressive, characteristic." This distinction is rooted in the fact that "Futurism in Italy, its birthplace, is a utilitarian movement seeking to establish the supremacy of capitalism. . . . In his fight against the remnants of the past, the Futurist expresses the material facts of capitalist necessity as abstract truth. . . . Terrible as are its evils, capitalism is superior to the cemetery-civilization stifling Italy." The ideas of F. T. Marinetti's Futurist Manifesto of 1909 are similarly related to the economic retardation of its land of origin.

Fraina notes the imperialistic rhetoric of Futurism and of Italian capitalism, but terms it "a wild, social passion of the moment, a storm worn out by its own fury." He later was not this sanguine about a Marinetti or Nietzsche. Even now, enthusiastic as he was about a content and form breakthrough in these "superbly capitalist" paintings, Fraina noted that they held "no inspiration . . . for the Socialist." Capitalism's "evil and degrading" nature, fused with capitalism's technique and power, was expressed in them. Fraina looked comprehendingly at these works, and beyond to a yet more modern and human art: "Socialist art must forge its own tools, evolve its own methods to express and interpret the new culture which the Socialist movement carries within its folds." In my judgment Fraina better understood and appreciated modernist painting than had any other Marxist of his time or earlier.

With this historically-relativist perspective, Fraina rejected the charge that a modernist exaggeration of subjectivity was a bad development. Thus he wrote in the same essay that Richard Strauss "expresses the Pagan spirit now transforming our moribund culture. That Strauss does not express the Greek spirit full-orbed is due to the Pagan spirit being immature and corrupted by contact with capitalist degeneracy—a bourgeois and not a proletarian manifestation. Whosoever mentions pathology in this connection must consider pathologic the vital, universal Pagan urge of our generation."

Similarly, Richard Wagner was heroic and revolutionary "in the mold of Nietzsche," expressing a "strident, inchoate revolt amid the discordances of industrial civilization." Byron's Romanticism was a legitimate "revolt against the crushed ideals and conservative reaction succeeding the French Revolution."

After the experience of Fascism and Stalinism, as we shall see, Fraina grew distrustful of romantic energy and subjectivity and emphasized its dizzying corruption, in a Byron and Wagner if not in Strauss. Doubtless Fraina had overlooked, everywhere but in Futurism, those perilous qualities which he later characterized unequivocally as sadistic. Nonetheless, Fraina's later view embodied more than a correction of an unbalanced judgment, and departed, indeed, from a rounded historicism. One must credit as the more historically balanced, for example, this passage written in 1936, when Fraina still located the spirit of romantic literature in "the inspiration of Rousseau's ideals."

> Rousseau's call was animated by faith in life and in what life might be. Cynics may now laugh at his emphasis on the perfectibility of man; but it was a doctrine directed against the stupefying dogmas of original sin and total depravity, against the aristocratic idea that the people were naturally stupid and swinish, and it did not mean the rise of mankind to static perfection but to continuously higher levels of living. The essential meaning of the doctrine is confirmed by modern anthropology, which finds that man is 'unbelievably malleable.'

We may add that the link between Rousseau's ideals, the "strident, inchoate" and rather abstract and errant romantic sensibility in Byron, Wagner, Breton, Marinetti, Mayakovsky, etc., and the "artificial repression of natural desires" mentioned in the Brieux essay and their representation in revolutionary fiction and deeds, is extremely close. Fraina understood it through this period of his life; later, he did violence to its complex, ambiguous character.

In other pre-1917 writings Fraina often and brilliantly located and approved the romantic expression of energy.

He was managing editor for several issues of *Modern*

Dance Magazine in 1914, 1916, and 1917. The magazine featured the photos of young ladies in filmy "Grecian" garb, dancing beneath the trees of suburban estates. For Fraina this was not merely a fill-in job: he believed in the Free Spirit and pagan revival which this magazine urged. He used his platform to advocate also the social revolution as openly as he dared; at a time when war enthusiasm was sweeping through the nation, an editorial suggested that the true "patriotism" of any dancer was, quite simply, to dance. It is remarkable that this 22-year-old Marxist found a cultural periodical with which to project his revolutionary-modernist aesthetics, as had other "rebels" of the time around *Pagany* and *The Seven Arts*, whose pioneering role long has been a matter of record.

Fraina lavishly praised the Isadora Duncan style of dance for finally and lucidly presenting, in a native art, the natural unity of feeling, thought, and expression which in social life was fragmented and crushed. Of an exemplary dancer whom he interviewed, he wrote: "Intellect dominates Lydia Kyasht and her art. Her dances are *idea-dances*; they translate ideas into the rhythm of the dance. . . . Her soul, her brains, her limbs are a unity in her art. And in the dance she is *herself*—not someone else. Self-expression vitalizes her dances." [7] Fraina felt that for depth of feeling to be realized, the intellect had to be agile and controlling: yet it was nothing, without the upsurge of natural desire.

What is more, the dancing of Kyasht projected, not a sentimental invention of her desire, but her own and total being: an *"imaginative reality."* This is a key phrase to much of Fraina's aesthetic thought. He cared little about art that soared beyond or wide of the misery of capitalist life; he was passionately devoted to having individual lives assume the characteristics of artistic achievement. Revolution itself, to a Fraina or a Lenin, was a "drama" to be created and shaped. Here Fraina writes of what is possible to a single life, through art, realizing its imaginative reality in circumstances short of social revolution. A tradition in Marxian theory abroad prepares us for the following incisive passage, which is scarcely anticipated or seconded by another American Marxist:

> *Each of us must be a creative artist.* Art is life vividly expressed. The artist *lives* and *expresses his living in terms of art.* The poetry of Life inspires the poetry of art. Art-forms are *not* art. *Art is the spirit of Life* which art simply interprets. And all human beings who *live* intensely, who *feel* vividly, and who *express their individuality freely in living, are artists,* though they never produce a scrap of art in the conventional sense. . . . The dance is an elemental form of art. *The Modern Dance is the only universal medium of popular art-expression.* . . . 'Men and women may become artists of their own lives' thru the new dances.[8]

This passage bears not only upon a theory of creativity, but also, and directly, upon the latest forms of modern dance (e.g., the Judson Church group in New York), the role for young people of discothèques, and such new and determined inter-relating of life and performance as the Happenings. A movement of self-conscious young men and women, desiring to become the "artists of their own lives," has commenced on a scale Fraina long hoped for. Its ultimate effect on social structure cannot be foreseen.

In the same potent vein, Fraina wrote in defense of the new Negro music. Jazz, he argued, was contemporary and *vital,* unlike anything else in the American arts, which he generally thought snobbish and provincial. Fraina rejected the onus attached to jazz by Philistines because of its Negro origin and sexual suggestiveness. "The feelings exist," he insisted; "they are, perhaps, crude and ugly, because they have been shamefacedly repressed." [9] Fraina was one of the first and most enthusiastic endorsers of the jazz movement; and his discussion is almost certainly the first anywhere by a Marxist.

He wrote also on American literature in the pre-war years, but sparingly: he could locate little vitality. He ascribed this state of affairs to the obscenity laws, and to the writers' fear of life and remoteness from reality:

Think all, feel all, experience all, express all—that is the mission of the artist. Why hurl the puerile charge of obscenity? . . . The disease of American literature . . . is that it is not 'obscene' enough, 'lewd' enough, 'lascivious' enough to possess virility and vitality comparable with the literature of the ages. . . . The American public never tolerated frank analysis of life. . . . *Genuine* immorality is rampant in American literature—the immorality of unreality, of hidden meanings, of pandering to the debased and debasing demands of ignorance.[10]

Literary criticism and history was in as bad a state. Reviewing John Macy's *The Spirit of American Literature*, Fraina found it "the first approach to an adequate study of American literature." Nonetheless it was quite deficient: Macy, being "a pragmatist," had little grasp of the social determinants of literature, and offered instead "an over-emphasis on literary lineage."

Vitality did characterize four young poets reviewed by Fraina in 1915. They were Robert Frost, Edgar Lee Masters, Vachel Lindsay, and James Oppenheim. (Fraina later maintained that he was the first American to write an appreciation of Frost, a statement I cannot verify.) He did not at all praise the four because they took a revolutionary line: on the contrary, Oppenheim, whom Fraina thought "least vital," made the mistake of being "so definitely radical, so overtly revolutionary." Fraina sought the representation of American energy in its concrete, many, diverse expressions. If this was lacking, a critical or combative distancing by the poet meant nothing: "They do not shrink away from drunkards and prostitutes, 'niggers' and 'hired help', automobiles and advertising, 'movies' and vaudeville—all the crudity, hysteria and apparently disgustingly meaningless characteristics of American life. All these things contain a new art and a new world." While he never wrote for the *Masses* (edited by Max Eastman), he did believe that it "in many ways captured and expressed the human elements of the struggle for a new world." [11]

Fraina was quite critical of his fellow Marxists, on the

whole, and on more than cultural issues. His polemic turned time and again to the need to reach, understand, express the specific stuff and psychology of contemporary life, if the social revolution and radical literature and art were to be made possible.

> In spite of Marx's appreciation of the importance of the individual, Socialist propaganda has developed a rigid determinism which minimizes and often totally suppresses the psychological factor. . . . Culturally Socialists are notoriously conservative [seeking] their cultural inspiration in Pagan Greece and the Renaissance. . . . But these ideals of Athens and the Renaissance must be transfused with a new meaning. This meaning can be interpreted and developed through a psychological study of the new individual being produced by social transformation.

For almost twenty years, from the Bolshevik revolution until the mid-Thirties, Fraina did not write on the arts, with the exception of one essay published in 1921 in German.[12] Fraina was hardly inactive. His articles filled *The New Review* until early in 1916, when that journal suspended. He concentrated chiefly on a demand for the formation of a third Communist International, to replace the Second, which in America and all over Europe was acceding to the war preparations and hysteria of the ruling classes. In America, Fraina was the first to seek this organizational break with the established Socialists. Lenin, in Geneva, was voicing the same proposal in the same isolation.

A mere handful of revolutionaries, including Fraina, met with the Russian exiles Trotsky, Bukharin, and Madame Kollantai in New York in January 1917, to plan a new Left Wing Socialist Party for America. Fraina was named the editor of its organ, *The New International,* and he and two others founded and edited a theoretical bimonthly, *The Class Struggle,* for the embryonic organization.

Early in 1918 this grouping next set up the American Bolshevik Bureau of Information; its director was Fraina, and he also edited the first American volume of the post-revolutionary writings of Trotsky and Lenin, published in the same year. He was jailed in 1919 for a month, with Ralph Cheyney, on the charge of war-resisting.

Fraina was in the center of the activities from which the American Communist Party emerged; no one was more persuasive or instrumental than this young man who chaired the crucial National Left Wing Conference in June 1919. He next became the International Delegate of the Conference to the meetings of the Communist International in Petrograd, where he then travelled. Three times, charges of disloyalty were lodged by American comrades; he always was exonerated, the last time by Lenin, who praised the "extremely useful literary works" of Fraina.

Present in Soviet Russia during some of the early days of epochal revolution, Fraina shared with John Reed a developed and heady appreciation for the aesthetic dimension of great events. He later recalled a re-enactment of the Revolution through the streets of Petrograd: "The pageant itself was magnificent. I sat next to Reed and he was literally lifted out of his seat with enthusiasm. That was the real Jack Reed. Can't you have more on the pageant and on Reed's reaction, which means his capacity to link up revolution with the dramatic and the artistic?" [13]

The debates of the Comintern elicited a rather different response from Fraina; even as he took part, his old reservations about abstract Marxist thinkers seemed to find some fresh relevance, and he had not expected it here. He was assigned to tasks in Mexico, and he went, but felt his energies were being misapplied. In Petrograd he had met a Russian girl who translated for the Comintern. Fraina was now deeply involved with her; he often had written of the joy in an equal and enduring bond between a man and a woman, but apparently had not ever fully experienced one, having been so involved in politics. He returned from Mexico to Berlin where his wife-to-be joined him; he hesitated, then resigned from his Comintern responsibilities.

He had bought a film in Berlin on his first trip out of Russia, *The Arabian Nights*, so that he might pose as a film distributor on his voyage to Montreal. He left Berlin this time with his bride and 4200 dollars in Comintern funds, which he used to travel to Mexico and to settle in a new life with the intention, he later said, of repaying the funds in installments. However, the Comintern proclaimed him an embezzler and the public career of Louis Fraina came to an end.

Out of politics, he relaxed and enjoyed a family life which now included a daughter, Olga. When eventually he returned to the United States he did not enter organizational politics; he prepared economic studies of American capitalism and used henceforth the name Lewis Corey. Corey supported his family with proofreading and kept away from the old comrades who might accuse him should they not have forgotten him. About 1930 Corey's *The House of Morgan* appeared. He was an associate editor of the *Encyclopedia of the Social Sciences* between 1931–34; he called it his university—"It filled in all my gaps."

With others, such as Edmund Wilson and Sidney Hook, in 1932 he signed the Communist Party election appeal issued by the League of Professional Groups for Foster and Ford, and he planned to participate in League forums and publications. The League collapsed. He published in 1934 *The Decline of American Capitalism*, at first favorably received by the Party, then criticized. But Corey's *The Crisis of the Middle Class* (1935) was warmly reviewed in *The New Masses* and offered free with new subscriptions, and its author agreed to edit a special Middle-Class issue for the periodical. Corey was, in fact, probably the outstanding American Marxist economist of the Thirties.

The Moscow Trials dampened Fraina / Corey's rather revived hopes for the Communists. He did not join the Party, although invited to do so. He declined to enter the fellow-travelling League of American Writers. He was offered and refused the editorship in economics with *Sci-*

ence and Society, founded by a group of pro-Communist Harvard intellectuals. Finally he joined Sidney Hook, Bertram Wolfe, Louis Hacker, and Corliss Lamont in starting *The Marxist Quarterly;* but the publication failed when Lamont pulled out his financial backing, after the editorial majority decided to question the Moscow Trials. Corey worked for six months as a WPA economist in Washington; then as educational director of Local 22 of the ILGWU in 1937–39.

Corey returned to problems of literature, with his massive economic studies under his belt and having found acceptance among the fresh generation of Communists, few of whom may have known that he had been Fraina, or may even have heard of Fraina.

He made a beginning in *The Crisis of the Middle Class,* where he briefly evoked Walt Whitman as a poet with an egalitarian vision of community which, unfortunately, was not prophetic, as he believed, but in fact hearkened back to a small-crafts epoch of American history which even then was vanishing under the impact of industrial growth.

At 43 as at 23, Corey saw expression of the specific reality as a writer's first and essential task. In this spirit, he wrote a letter to the newly-acclaimed author of *Studs Lonigan:* "It's sweepingly impressive within the terms of its own integrity and logic. The realism is authentic (I was myself a slum child), almost overbearing. Yet it arouses sympathy, the feeling which it is so important to arouse; what a waste of life. I think this is more important than the mechanical propaganda which is at fisticuffs with the integrity and logic of life. More power to you!" [14] Mixed with the praise, one catches a description of Farrell's realism as "almost overbearing." Corey still preferred and wished to encourage literature which was not merely authentic in the Zola naturalist tradition, but achieved also a sufficient perspective or scope of action in story and character so as to bespeak the *historical meaning* of the events, as well as gaining sympathy for them. Asserting this optimum requirement, Corey now confirmed and elaborated his view from the essay on Brieux: independently, he arrived at the classic distinction between naturalism and critical realism stated by the great Marxist aesthetician George Lukacs.

In this sense he wrote three years later in *Partisan Review*, describing Farrell's method as a "static" realism. One had to recognize that Farrell was a captive of the Chicago Irish mentality he depicted. Indeed the method fitted "the milieu and its people. They do not revolt" but destroy themselves with drinking, fighting, and whoring; *Studs* did give a faithful picture of "that peculiar 'revolt' which refuses to accept conditions passively and yet knows nothing of the creative thing to do about it." Farrell, to develop, must discover a way to understand and depict characters who attempt actively and consciously to master their destinies, who "react upon their environment and are not merely acted upon." Would he? "Toward the end of the Lonigan series Farrell is already moving away from the limitations of naturalism, moving from mere sensory impressions to the creative inner life, from the one-dimensional writing where we simply *see* people to that three-dimensional writing where we begin to understand." And Farrell's Danny O'Neill sequence offered a positive hero, an author's prototype, which bore "promise" of affording soon a literary method whereby Farrell could more profoundly interpret life.

Corey planned a novel of his own in these years, and one feels great regret that it was never written; perhaps it might have provided a model of his aesthetic in practice.[15] We know only that it was to be a panoramic novel of 350,000 words with "the movement and changes of American life from the 1890's to the 1930's" as its subject. The characters, as he wrote in his outline, "will not be considered as the embodiment of social forces and ideas; they simply express social forces and ideas and react upon them. Nor will characters be black and white. . . . The novel will be written in straightforward narrative style, no experiments."

What we do have is Corey's thorough appraisal of the Thirties' "proletarian" cultural movement, written for

Martha Foley's *Story* magazine in 1936, where Corey defines very firmly what he means by "mechanical propaganda." He saw in the new vogue an affirmation of "faith in life against the contempt for life of the smart boys and girls of the 1920's." Its difficulty lay in being mainly the product of intellectuals who mistook the role of human consciousness in social development and expression. His own view of the role of consciousness was stated as follows in 1917: "A man *is*, and then he thinks; he *feels*, and therefore acts. Man has tried to make intellect the ruler, but it has been a marionette ruler with instinct and feeling pulling the strings. Our artificial civilization crushes instinct and feeling, and any power that vitalizes them develops the vigor and the beauty of the race." [16] Again in 1936, he writes that in a given situation "the whole of life" sets up the options of consciousness, and "the whole of life" will define the development of the situation. On the one hand, man is "an active player in the drama"; on the other hand, the situation is what primarily directs man in his activities toward "creating new attitudes toward life and imposing on them his hopes and ideals." An example, of course, was the creation of the attitude of the "proletarian" writers by the shock and reality of the Depression. Man's conscious option lies, then, in his relative success at "imposing" the most lucid ideals and analysis and action possible on a situation which has authentically created his attitude. The difficulty of achieving lucidity is complicated by the limited experience to be gained of "the whole of life"; for a class role does restrict one. Moreover, a lucid attitude must include an attentiveness to the *process* by which the meaning of social life becomes conscious; for that process, too, is part of the "drama." In this sense, Corey wrote of the aesthetic of revolutionary literature:

> A definite point of departure is necessary, a philosophy or theory of social change capable of organizing the experience of life as it is becoming and giving it coherence and meaning. The revolution is as broad and deep as life itself. Its theory is not an artificial creation, as it arises out of the understanding of social change and action. Revolutionary

theory becomes life by seizing upon great masses of people and setting them in motion—human, emotional, dramatic. And theory is always only a simplified picture of life, never life itself. When all the leading members of the Bolshevik party, in April, 1917, accused Lenin of having changed his theory of the character of the Russian Revolution, he answered that not his theory but life had changed, and threw at his critics the words of Goethe:

> *Theory, my Friends, is gray,*
> *But Green is the eternal tree of life.*

If that is true of theory in the realm of social action, it is still truer in the realm of literature. Theory is no substitute for the creative understanding and expression of life.

Thus Corey affirmed the necessity of creative Marxist theory to the revolutionary writer; the understanding gained might "liberate the artist and broaden and deepen his vision of changing life."

However, little of this creative theory was apparent in the writing from the Left that Corey knew. Farrell was at least a faithful observer, if he lacked the theory. But *Paradise Lost*, by Clifford Odets, showed "neither the elemental sweep of life nor the understanding that comes of social theory"; it was a play "weakened by ignorance of the social composition of the middle class, its contradictory consciousness and ideals, its relation to present struggles and the oncoming new order of socialism." On the other hand, theory must not be simple-minded. H. G. Wells had spoken in a prewar novel of a new realism as the depiction of life as it is becoming; but Wells held a mechanical idea of "a necessary and irresistible movement toward higher things" which ignored that "retrogression may appear instead of progress"; the rising tide of Fascism, and Wells' own deterioration, evinced the fallacy of a mechanical theory of progress.

Corey did not wholly regret the abstract nature of the depiction in the typical product of the "proletarian" school. The moralizing propaganda novel or play had a "legitimate" importance, he held; but he added: "The call

to action is not the only function of revolutionary literature, and it may be the most limited one. *It must concern
itself primarily with consciousness and values, with attitudes toward life.*" In other words, the real job is not to
state positive values or demands; it is to show how values
and demands, of all kinds, are developed in social relations. The revolutionary must study how to "evaluate
types of action other than his own," Corey held; from the
depiction, an audience will be most deeply informed
about the sweep of life and its theory, and most moved to
creative activity. "Revolutions are not made by one type
of action nor by the action of the most conscious and
militant rebels: their decisive action becomes possible only
in a situation that is eventually created by many different
types of action." Here is one further reason, then, beyond
the practical obtuseness of the artist which Fraina noted
in 1910, for prizing the creator of "dramatic action" above
the author as "excoriator."

Doubtless the corollary of this aesthetic, to be understood by the theorist, will be evident; "the Marxist critic
must evaluate all types of literature, not by mere praise or
blame or categorical pigeonholing, but in terms of the
whole of changing life, social consciousness and culture,
and of revolutionary aspirations." It was especially important for Marxism to "absorb within its outlook and activity" the most masterful literature reflective of "capitalist
disintegration and decline." The creative understanding in
Proust was wholly adequate to its scope and theme:
"Proust's masterpiece *Remembrance of Things Past* is
not in any sense revolutionary, but its magnificent portrayal of the decline and disintegration of the old culture
and attitudes toward life is an extraordinarily vital expression of social change. It tells more of capitalist decay in
fifty pages than the 500 pages of Briffault's *Europa*, which
is neither a novel of living men and women nor a novel of
living ideas." Thus the crucial element of Corey's notion
of realism is not a revolutionary personage whose correct
conduct defines historical meaning. His aesthetic of literature did demand characters with a "creative inner life"

who react on their environment, trying to master it some-how.

From such conflict, "fundamental human values and defense of those values" would necessarily emerge. Corey saw, moreover, a complementary and peculiar importance in literature which, seeking to conserve the enduring human values, ignored revolutionary change. He prized Maxwell Anderson's *Winterset* for having this implicit creative theory, which also provided the basis for evaluating literature from periods before the Marxist outlook existed, and literature about situations where revolt was not an operative reality. Furthermore, Socialists might themselves lose sight of the enduring basis of their outlook, and such literature served to measure and correct them.

> Life . . . goes on . . . it will go on in spite of revolutionary struggles . . . while injustice has changed its class-political forms, there has always been injustice; and there will be injustice under socialism, especially in the earlier stages. It is necessary not to forget the 'eternal' aspects of injustice. If *Winterset* is unsatisfying, it is not the fault of the theme but of the treatment. . . . Marxist criticism must evaluate and absorb within itself any defense of the values that are threatened by capitalist decline and fascism. . . . The revolutionary forces may themselves, in the stress of the struggle, forget human values, the very things they are fighting for.

Optimally, of course, literature should combine a revolutionary point of view and an organic concern with enduring values; "one of the major tasks of revolutionary literature is to emphasize those values, to insist in terms of life itself that they shall not be forgotten." Corey offers the example of a tale by Ignazio Silone, in which a fascist spy manages to betray and destroy a group of radical workers because they are too humanly decent to defend themselves effectively against him. "The moral is: you cannot be decent against the indecent. But Silone conveys more: that it is terrible to abandon decency, *even necessarily and temporarily*, because our fight is to make life decent."

Corey could find no American work which offered a model of revolutionary fiction. The novel which for him combined "the understanding of theory and the sweep of life into a magnificent symphony" was Silone's *Fontamara*. Philip Rahv and William Phillips, similarly exploring the revolutionary novel in America, had also to point to a European work (*Man's Fate* by Malraux) to explain what might be achieved but had not here been accomplished.[17] While Corey believed that our "proletarian" school was not wholly futile, he insisted that it missed the highest purpose and opportunity of revolutionary literature, which he found in "the novel or play that transmutes immediate issues and struggles into universal values. Revolutionary literature can create another Prometheus epic out of the newest and most magnificent struggle of man to liberate himself. . . . Not oppression and not misery are the major themes of revolutionary literature: but the whole of life, awakening, struggling, romantic: the drama of man's effort to fulfill himself." He termed "most American 'Marxist' cultural criticism" a "caricature," for misunderstanding the role and nature of consciousness and attitudes. Fraina's essay on Farrell had a final word on the "proletarian" movement, condemning its pretenses for drawing it into the "most amazingly unreal conceptions." We do not possess a more intelligent, sympathetic but critically informed appraisal of these writers than Corey's.

Into the late Thirties, Corey apparently was convinced that the Soviet Union was essentially following a progressive course, for he did not make his criticisms and disagreements public. At last the indecency and deceits of the Stalin epoch persuaded him that the USSR and its American enthusiasts were enthralled to values he had opposed all his life. He attacked in 1940 the new totalitarianism and dogmatism "which was unjust to Marx himself because the system denied his emphasis on the historical relativity of ideas." A full statement of this view, *The Unfinished Task*, he published in 1942.

From 1942 until 1951 he was a professor of economics at Antioch College, and advocated gradual change rather

than revolution, with the Communists and the Right both
seeking to discredit him and deprive him of his position.
He built a personal collection of art books and classical
recordings. In 1943 he brought an ILGWU Labor Art
Festival to Antioch. In 1945 he described to the student
body his revised analysis of social stagnation and change.
This analysis, conditioned by the Stalinist example, was
still anti-capitalist and in essentials Marxist, while locating
the greatest obstacle to change in the discouragingly low
quality of both bourgeois and Socialist consciousness.

> Economic vested interests are not the greatest barrier to
> human progress. . . . Vested interests in ideas are even a
> greater barrier. . . . I still believe that the economic short-
> comings of capitalism call for new economic institutions
> and new economic policies. . . . But now I believe just as
> firmly that any economic changes must be made within the
> framework of the procedures and values of liberal democ-
> racy . . . , that we must separate liberal democracy from
> the economics of capitalism. . . . There is much in Marx-
> ism that is usable for this purpose, but orthodox systematic
> Marxism must be abandoned. Its fatal flaw is the misunder-
> standing of liberal democracy and of values.[18]

In 1951 he left Antioch for Chicago to become the educational director of the Amalgamated Meat Cutters and
Butcher Workmen.

Unfortunately Corey overestimated the soundness of
American liberal democracy. McCarthyism undid him. He
was visited by the FBI, and persuaded to talk (although
he apparently informed on no one). He was persuaded to
do foreign broadcasting for the Department of State. To
no avail. He was served with deportation papers under the
McCarran Act, at Christmas of 1952. Corey's union employers immediately fired him. He moved to New York,
worked on his legal defense, outlined two books: an autobiography, and *Towards Understanding America*. Now he
wrote for *The New Leader* to demand the invasion of
North Korea and a showdown with Russia. His time ran
out. He had no breathing space to appraise the extent of
the appalling reaction which swept America. He did not

allow for the possibility of the rebirth of liberal values which Stalin's death brought in the USSR.

Corey died of a cerebral hemorrhage on September 16, 1953.

The last writings of Corey manifest a collapse of perspective beneath pressures which weighed on an entire generation of intellectals, who were drawn to Marxism, but then capitulated to establishment "liberalism" at the very juncture when the need to rework the temporal Marxist analysis became inescapable. The Marxism of Fraina was long sustained; first by a slum childhood offering substance and necessity to a revolutionary attitude pinned upon the proletariat, later by the American Depression and the relative success of the Russian experiment. When realities and consciousness of class in the USSR and America took directions which this Comintern Delegate could not derive from his early analyses, he mistrusted his whole frame of reference. Vanished from America was the native socialist vitality of pre-1917; nor could the Stalinist inhumanity and dogma, nor the liquidation of incisive Party theory under Browder at home, sustain or stimulate a creative reappraisal. His life drifted to middle-class environs; and he died at a nadir of lucidity, for the United States, the USSR, and himself. Corey had embraced wholesale the ideology of liberalism, with its vaunted "end of ideology."

Corey was exhausted. In aesthetics, too, he no longer dealt with problems of creativity. As a Cold War liberal he excoriated a lineage of artists who, as he now thought, represented the dangerously romantic trend of the arts in society. The "totalitarian Wagner" was fighting "the humanist Verdi" for "the soul of man," and Corey, forgetting the objective study of actual artworks, wished to be the referee at the sidelines. He set at his side Marx's friend, Heinrich Heine, who offered (he asserted, in lieu of evidence) a "chilling prevision" of the influence of Marx in society.

He felt that capitalism was "fumbling" but pragmatic, and progressively more humane; and that it was encum-

bered by " 'absolute' radical critics" who refused "to see
anything good in American life" and, with their "ideological abstractions," despised and disrupted a steady popular
progress.[19] Sartre, if European, was typical. He had "joined
the Communists" and had written "a fantastic stereotype
of the South as much as the 'mammy' songs," *The Respect-
ful Prostitute*. Some of these "thwarted and distorted"
critics did end in "the circles of 'esthetic' nihilism and
elite reaction (e.g. Ezra Pound, T. S. Eliot)"; more com-
monly, they landed in "the swamp of communism (e.g.
Arthur Miller)." He did trace the aberrations of intellectuals, as he had earlier, to a denial of full democracy
within the society. He held that the individualism set
afoot by the French Revolution "ingrew as it was denied
political expression and became almost wholly personal
and cultural, degenerate, ripe for a totalitarian mythus."
But now all his ire was heaped not upon society but upon
some of its victims, this "impatient elite." Indeed, the
middle class had become "the class of the future, not the
proletariat as Marx argued," and this " 'crowd' has money
and power to get what it wants"; therewith, the definition
of Corey's liberal democracy. (Only in passing, and curso-
rily, did he note the "danger" of "technical-managerial
despotism and manipulation.")

His fears were all focused on "despotic" social critics
and artists who, he affirmed, "never flocked to Lenin,
when it seemed as if their class was being exterminated,
but they flocked to Stalin when it was clear that *their* class
was the ruling power in Russia." Against the "super-
intellectuals and power-intellectuals" he proposed "Populism" as a healthy alternative. But the Populism which
was preferable to any kind of Socialism was no more than
capitalist renewal, exemplified as he said in the New Deal
and Wilson's New Freedom. No more than he now questioned the premises of a capitalism which had increased
its middle class and survived, did Corey question whether
the culture consumed by his class was of its own creation
or genuinely humane. Omitting mention of mercantile,
consumer-manipulating elites, he only attacked "elites

who despise the people and its culture." In this abdication from perspective on capitalism, and while he fought his deportation, he expressed regret that there were "only a few good novels on American business leaders and labor leaders, and these fault-finding, satirical and condemnatory."

An unfinished essay sees the Marquis de Sade as a prototype of the socially-estranged critic, activist, and artist. Sade's personal and literary "erotic indulgence and wish-fulfillment," his "*degradation* of the sexual objects with whom he disports," are attributed to a line of radical thinkers (Rousseau, the *philosophes*, Danton, Mirabeau, Robespierre, Babeuf, Cabet, the Saint-Simonians, Fourier) whom Corey finds revealingly despotic towards women. Sadism is also credited as the psychology of a line of romantic writers, from Byron and Musset to progenitors of Fascism (Wagner, D'Annunzio) and admirers of Stalin's Communism (the French Surrealists and Russian Futurists): all are linked to a "pretense of aristocratic superiority, and their yearning for revolutionary violence, destruction, and despotism." Much the same sickness, but reversed into masochism, Corey finds in Baudelaire, Beardsley, Wilde, Lautreamont, Joyce, Mallarmé, Rimbaud, and Apollinaire. Such is the psychology of the harsher critics of existing society, while the populaces "took the 'radical' ideas of the early nineteenth century and brought them down to liveable human size." So certain of this idea is the Corey of 1953 that he does not analyse the relevant art or lives; he fits them to his new categories.[20]

Had Corey offered analysis, he could doubtless have proven, and rightly, that there were inhumane or despotic aspects in some of these artists and political thinkers whom he condemned so severely and absolutely. Does it matter, therefore, that he neglected to make a historical and situational analysis? Indeed, it makes every bit of difference. The difference between an abstract and a concrete understanding. These are desperate and also errant times for humanists and creators; there scarcely is an unblemished saint among us; still, Corey had always known this. The difference is that earlier he had not yet lost his capacity for historical and balanced perspective on the creative, erratic process whereby a society produces the emotions and theories it needs to develop.

No longer, now, did he concentrate on a creative social thought and a creative aesthetics. He acquiesced to the one-dimensional outlook he had long recognized as in the interests of capitalist power and survival, as against an outlook which uncovers, presents, and fulfills the human needs which capitalism thwarts. One may imagine that had Corey avoided deportation, and lived to see his nation's atrocious policy from Santo Domingo to Vietnam, his concern with "technical-managerial despotism and manipulation" might have grown; he might have recovered emotional and critical distance on liberal America. It would ill behoove us to accept Corey's loss of perspective as an excuse for abdicating the study of his earlier and pioneering originality. Though he reneged, and though his social and aesthetic theory do need fresh appraisal, because conditions are much changed, we shall find his earlier perspective to be worthy of our recovery and development.

The Education of Michael Gold

MICHAEL BREWSTER FOLSOM

MICHAEL GOLD was 37 years old when *Jews Without Money* appeared in 1930, and his best imaginative work was done. He was not, properly speaking, a writer of the Depression, but rather a literary figure of that decade, a busy columnist in the party press and a semiofficial Communist spokesman. As an imaginative writer, the later Gold is of small interest. What he did and meant in the Thirties and after, how he accrued a reputation as the pariah of American letters, and why his "promise" failed him will be fully understood in time. But that understanding must rest upon some evaluation of Gold's formative years, and to those years I devote this essay. I am concerned with Gold's education in the broadest sense— cultural, social, political, as well as institutional— everything which shaped the man.

Michael Gold was a second-generation American literary radical, one of that handful who grew up in the shadow of the old *Masses* magazine and the Provincetown Players and who stuck it out through the Boom to become elders of leftist literature after the Crash. His roots sank into the soil of virgin bohemia in the prewar Village, as well as into the rich muck of the Jewish ghetto. He was mixed up in an inkpot as much as in the "crucible of struggle." By 1930 he was as much an acknowledged character as an accomplished author.

Through the later Teens and the Twenties, Gold was the angry boy of the left. He started out an anarchist and

I.W.W. sympathizer. The "man on an East Side soap-box" who first proclaims news of the Workers' Revolution to the boy at the end of *Jews Without Money*, was in fact the Wobbly orator, Elizabeth Gurley Flynn. That was 1914. For the rest of the decade Gold consorted with the most militant and leftist of radicals, bohemian, and working class. The two poems he contributed to the *Masses* were defenses of the Village and of three anarchists who were killed by their own bomb. Gold met Vanzetti. In 1917 he was invited to lecture a class at Wellesley about the Russian situation, and he informed the girls that the Revolution had come to free the working class—from bondage to the machine. By 1920 or thereabouts he had learned a little better. He joined the Communist Party in its romantic infancy.

Gold was a radical's radical, an appealing vulgarity among polite rebels, a disciplined revolutionary in devil-may-care bohemia, an irresponsible bohemian among party wheelhorses. He was the arch *proletaire*, with an equal dose of the sociological fact and cultural affectation which that Whitmanesque term implies. Memoirs of the period recall the defiant, troubled eyes, the chaos of black hair, the soiled workshirt, red tie, and foul stogie of Gold's youth. The callow rebel pleased to spit on the carpets of pink parlors was somehow always better than a boor. There was something engaging, generous, endearing about him. Even Max Eastman in his late, reactionary years remembers fondly the young "fanatic" who had a "rare gift for writing."

The wonder of Gold's early career is that he ever made anything of himself at all.

Itshok Isaac Granich was born, April 12, 1893, to immigrant parents on Chrystie Street in poverty. As a schoolboy, Gold adopted Irwin for a Christian name; he wrote as Irwin Granich until 1921; during the Palmer Raids he took Michael Gold for a protective pseudonym, and it stuck. Unofficial records, including some of Gold's own, usually state or suggest that he was born in 1894; 1893 is correct.

Gold was born to poverty, reared in poverty, and educated by poverty. The one other thing the Jewish ghetto had to offer him was an abiding respect for literature and learning, and Gold was a gifted boy who thrived on that respect. "I [was] a precocious pupil in the public school, winning honors not by study, but by a kind of intuition. I graduated sooner than most boys. At the exercises I was valedictory orator." Gold's teacher told him she had never read better English composition than his. But his brilliance and the "cultural advantages" of the Jewish ghetto turned sour on him. Poverty.

Gold refused to continue his education because of the economic burden on his family. Before he was a teen-ager he was a dropout, and his ardor for learning turned to animus: "For years my ego had been fed by everyone's praise of my precosity. I had always loved books; I was mad about books; I wanted passionately to go to high school and college. Since I couldn't, I meant to despise all that nonsense." His teacher gave him a lecture about Abe Lincoln and a copy of Emerson's essays for a goodbye gift: "I thanked her for the book, and threw it under the bed when I got home. I never read a page in it, or in any other book for the next five years. I hated books; they were lies, they had nothing to do with life and work." These recollections are quoted from *Jews Without Money*. Almost thirty years after it was published, Gold returned to this anguish with even more piteous candor. Moved by the inquiry of a Soviet high school student, put to him, a famous author in his sixties—"Comrade, can you tell us what you are studying now?"—he wrote in his column in the San Francisco *People's World,*

> Education haunts me. At the age of 12 I was forced to leave school and work in the hot hell of a New York factory making the gas-mantles of the time. Whatever education I later acquired was paid for with sweat and confusion. There were too many difficulties, it seems.
>
> . . . .
>
> I was no Lincoln, unfortunately. I was just one of the many who try and fail. But I always wanted an education, and kept trying and failing again and again.

It filled me with a sense of guilt not to be using my mind. I remember how in another attempt to pull myself up by my bootstraps I registered at a night school [at C.C.N.Y.] supposed to cram you with a high school degree in a tenth of the usual time.

I had to pay tuition for two months in advance. But I never finished the two months. I was working then for an express company [Adams], out in the streets on a wagon 12 hours a day. When I sat down in the hot classroom at night I simply couldn't keep my eyes open. Night after night I slept through it all, until in a final humiliation, again I quit my struggle for an education.

But that was *not* the final humiliation.

The mood in which all books seemed "lies" and all education "nonsense" did not last, as Gold's botched return to high school indicates. In spite of his disappointments, he was a voracious reader again in his late adolescence. After that try at high school he took up with a group of C.C.N.Y. students (among them Lewis Mumford) who kept his mind alive with college talk and who encouraged him with assurances that his wit and wide, if haphazard, reading made him their peer. Some of them were going to Harvard, and he should come, too. It was a quixotic venture.

Gold set out to amass a fortune. From his wages and small gifts which he shamelessly accepted from his impoverished relations he put together $300. With that bundle and no high school education he took the boat for Boston. His only other asset was *chutspe*. He walked into the admissions office and started talking eloquent self-advertisement, relying heavily on the Abe Lincoln tale. Rather to his surprise, Gold was admitted to Harvard College as a provisional student in the autumn of 1916.

The student on trial was delighted with Harvard—with the atmosphere, his classes, and himself. He found the work easy enough, studied assiduously, and, as he remembers it, did well in his courses. What excited him most was the discovery of intellectual discipline, which had been quite lacking in his ragged attempts at self-education. As a fervent anarchist, traveling to Boston Common on Sundays to orate, he found much to defy in the genteel English lectures of Bliss Perry. But he does not seem to have been fundamentally alienated by the content or procedures of the academy. It was giving him everything he most desired: knowledge, discipline, and a sense of intellectual achievement.

What a glorious land is America, where even a Jewish immigrant's son can rise from the ghetto to attend Harvard College!

If he has the cash.

Tuition took a big bite out of Gold's hoard. The rest soon slipped away. By mid-semester Gold was selling his books and clothes, living on doughnuts. Then he went looking for work. He cajoled $15 a week from the editor of the Boston *Journal* for a daily column, "A Freshman at Harvard." But Gold found it increasingly difficult to keep up with his studies after he had finished his column and returned from the city each day. His diet had weakened him. He was plagued by his moody temperament and a sense of insecurity in a new world where he needed so desperately to make good. Both column and studies faltered, then failed, and before the end of the semester he was out of school and work, wrestling with a nervous breakdown. His formal education was finished, and he was finished with it.

Gold's reaction to this ultimate failure is recapitulated in one of his most telling pieces, "Love on a Garbage Dump," which he published in 1928, almost ten years later, in *The New Masses*. The story opens notoriously: "Certain enemies have spread the slander that I once attended Harvard college. This is a lie. I worked on the garbage dump in Boston, city of Harvard. But that's all." Gold's critics like to cite this passage to expose his "anti-intellectualism," especially since it seems so patently disingenuous. They fail, however, to note that "Love on a Garbage Dump" is a fiction, specifically labelled "32nd Attempt at a Short Story" on its first publication. They ignore, or are ignorant of, the reasons for Gold's hostility. And, confusing Harvard with the bounds and seat of the human intellect, they are unable to credit such hostility with any humane motive.

The June after Gold dropped out of Harvard, another young man graduated, his maw heaving with pent-up revulsion:

> All the thrust and advance and courage in the country now, lies in the East Side Jews and in a few of the isolated "foreigners" whose opinions so shock the New York *Times*. They're so much more real and alive than we are anyway—I'd like to annihilate these stupid colleges of ours, and all the nice young men, therein, instillers of stodginess—every form of bastard culture, middle-class snobism.
>
> And what are we fit for when they turn us out of Harvard? We're too intelligent to be successful businessmen and we haven't the sand or the energy to be anything else.
>
> Until Widener is blown up and A. Lawrence Lowell assassinated and the Business School destroyed and its site sowed with salt—no good will come out of Cambridge.

So wrote John Dos Passos who was, like Gold, much less an "anti-intellectual" than an emotional literary rebel, sick of the impossibility of nurturing a manly intellect in an American academy.

The literal untruth of Gold's blunt asseveration about his attendance at Harvard is irrelevant, but the animus was real and deserves more serious attention than haughty blame. This rejection of Harvard establishes the mood and point of the story to follow.

The pattern of "Love on a Garbage Dump" is familiar and serviceable: "I was 19 years old, a fool, and in love with two women." One is a Portuguese who works on the dump, the other an unseen girl of Beacon Hill whom he hears playing Mozart as he walks home at night. Sociology and aesthetics tumble with sex in his mind. He lusts for the working girl, and is (wrongly, he acknowledges in retrospect) ashamed of his physical desire; he is appalled when she asks a dollar for her services. In contrast, he pines for the "pure" form he sees silhouetted in the Beacon Hill window: "This was the world of spiritual beauty, of music, and art, and ethereal love."

The boy's conflict reaches crisis one night when he realizes at last that he, reeking of ordure from the dump, can never enter this world. His first reaction is maudlin: "I wanted to cry for yearning and self-pity. I was ready to give up the endless futile struggle for a living." But a cop, who tells the bum to move on from his vigil, proves catalyst for more fruitful emotion: "Anger boiled up in me, anger to save me from mushy self-pity, harsh, clean anger like the gales at sea." As the boy walks home in fury, he thinks: " 'Mozart and candlelight and the spiritual values, to hell with you all.' . . . It's more honorable to work on a garbage dump than to be a soulful parasite on Beacon Hill. 'If Concha needed a dollar, she had a right to ask for it!' " The story ends with his dreaming of a revolution to set the workers free.

The literary device—conflicting aspirations revealed in terms of conflicting loves—is commonplace, but the experience it orders was essentially, symbolically, Gold's own. Gold added a significant variation to one of the crucial tales of modern literature: the struggle of working-class youths—Jude, Martin Eden, Paul Morel—to enjoy the life of the mind in a society where that life, its content, and the institutions which foster it are class-bound.

Gold's version is nearest and most diametrically opposed to London's. Both men had compulsions to barge into an establishment that wouldn't accept them; variously foiled and twisted, both men had appalling capacities for hatred and self-pity. Gold's hatred made a man of him; London's self-pity a corpse. London was always terrified by the degradation of the "abyss"; Gold found honor, if not love, on a garbage dump.

Gold's reaction to his last failure of formal education was intense. "Love on a Garbage Dump" suggests schematically the kinds of his emotions, but not their real riot or duration. His bohemian slovenliness in the Twenties was somewhat studied; his filth and obscene rags in Boston were pure poverty and utter demoralization. He panhandled to keep alive between odd jobs. Only after his return to New York in 1917, to the ghetto and the Village that were home, did he begin to gain control of himself again. Home and anger kept him whole.

In his fury Gold subsequently found words to damn what he loved or could have loved. Harvard for one thing. For another: "Mozart and candlelight and the spiritual values, to hell with you all!" (In 1954, when Gold prepared the text of "Love on a Garbage Dump" for republication, he cut Mozart from the imprecation.) But is it difficult to understand the young man's hostility? As surely as Jude in Christminster, he had been excluded from the university, from everything he wanted most. Like Jude, he was gifted with more intellectual passion and skill than most of the academically privileged. American cash worked as efficiently as British snobbery. The difference between Jude and Gold is that Gold fought back. Gold saw opportunities which were closed to Jude (and Hardy) for building a counter-culture and for abolishing the whole system which had maimed him. And, if he sometimes acted like a *sans culotte* sacking Versailles, do the shocked proprietors of our culture and its institutions have, like Marie Antoinette, anyone but themselves to blame?

Gold continued to write, and he built a theory to explain his practice and his experience and to solve his problems. The one fundamental fact about Gold's career is that, in spite of his monumental chagrin, he did not forswear his commitment to the life of the mind and of the imagination, but rather revised it in a way which the custodians of our culture can scarcely conceive.

Gold's subsequent success, such as it was, and his literary theories can only be explained historically. It was his fortune to have suffered as he did *when he did*—when there were men and institutions, political and cultural, to nurture his talents and his dreams in spite of the failure of the dominant society to offer him what he needed.

Politically, there were the various radical organizations—the Wobblies, the anarchists, the Socialist Party, and then the Communist Party—to make seem not only desirable, but also credible, the building of a society and a culture by men like himself, which would answer to the needs of working men.

Culturally, there were the *Masses* and *The Liberator* and the Provincetown Players to publish and perform his work, and men to encourage and edit that work. These, too, were Gold's education.

At that same Union Square rally where Gold first heard of the revolution from Gurley Flynn, he first saw and bought the *Masses*. He had been trying to write poetry, but he had no idea that anyone would publish stuff about what it is like to be poor and mad. The *Masses* astonished him with its artwork; it delighted him with its guts and articulate revolutionary vision. That was April. In August 1914 the *Masses* printed Gold's first public work, a prose poem, "The Three Whose Hatred Killed Them." He had mailed some manuscripts to the magazine, and he got in reply an invitation from Floyd Dell to drop around. With fond respect, and in spite of a bitter falling-out in 1929, Gold remembers Dell's patient solicitude for the bushy-tailed novice who came around the office, and kept coming around, hardly believing that anyone would publish his untutored works. Apparently Max Eastman was a similarly generous editor. In his memoirs, he takes credit for exorcising the worst bathos and sentimentality from Gold's stories. Today Gold is loath to thank the Goldwaterite, but Eastman, like Dell and John Reed, was a god to him. In 1918 he wrote an adulatory character sketch of Eastman for the *New York Call*. In 1926 he recollected that Eastman and Dell were "the best teachers youth could have found during those years."

For twenty years "the paper" was Gold's schoolroom. In 1916 and 1917 he was contributing fairly regularly to the *Masses* and had become a familiar of the "group." He was in Mexico, avoiding Wilson's draft, during the first years of *The Liberator*. On New Year's Eve, 1920, he was elected to its editorial board. In 1922, Gold was sharing full editorial responsibility with Claude McKay and Joseph Freeman. After a year or so, he took off for California, exhausted. Still concerned that the Left encourage the work of its literary intellectuals, he strongly opposed the gift of the prestigious *Liberator* to the Workers (Communist) Party to be merged in 1924 with two failing party publications and turned into the preponderantly political *Workers' Monthly*.

Gold was ever constitutionally unfit for the money-grubbing, contributor-coddling responsibilities of editorship. And yet, after the original "*Masses* group" had lost its impetus, he found himself one of the few who would accept that responsibility. Increasingly he took a large part in sustaining and creating the very kind of anti-Establishment cultural institutions which had saved him from defeat. And in doing so he had often to fight not only his temperament and the bourgeoisie, but also many of his comrades. Gold learned that the Revolution, at least in the U. S., did not always appreciate its poets. Soon after the demise of *The Liberator*, Gold began agitating for a new *Masses*. He wrote Upton Sinclair, as paraphrased by Daniel Aaron in his *Writers on the Left*, "Did this sound like Greenwich Village talk? He hoped not. He was simply 'reflecting much of what is going on in Germany, Russia and other countries,' simply insisting that 'artists are a vital part of a revolution, and the intellectuals.' Only American Marxists considered poetry a vice."

The New Masses was born handsomely in 1926 by virtue of a large subsidy and proceeded jauntily for several years very much in the spirit of its predecessor—a nonpartisan, left-liberal coalition of talented intellectuals. When the money gave out, most of its editors gave up, and willingly handed it over to Gold. Now he was pretty much his own boss. He made a virtue of the magazine's poverty and revised it in his own image, attempting to rely wholly on the contributions and ideals of radical workers. The late Boom period was unpropitious for radicalism, for the working-class Muse, and for middle-class intellectual sympathy towards such a blunt leftist approach to the arts. It took a new generation of radical professional writers in the

Thirties to make *The New Masses* again a force in American cultural life, and by then Gold was no great force in the magazine. When in the mid-Thirties the Left became respectable again and respectable writers sought it out, the raggedly proletarian Gold found himself something of a liability as a cultural warrior. In the end, what literary ideals and practices Gold's experience taught him did not suit him either for the conditions of American cultural life or for the necessities of party cultural policy.

Gold's development in the theater recapitulated his early magazine career, though there were significant disparities. His passion was to become a successful playwright, and his deepest regret is that he failed. The theater was the great cultural gift Gold's father and his ghetto had to offer, and it was the literary form Gold most closely identified with his familial and social origins. The language was Yiddish, but the experience catholic. In one of his several recollections of the cultural life of his neighborhood, he wrote,

> When I was a boy on the East Side the Russian-Yiddish-American culture . . . was in full bloom. My father, humblest, poorest of workers, was a lover of the stage, and took me to see all his great heroes perform. . . . Before I was twelve, I had seen Jacob Adler and Mogelescue and other great figures act on the Yiddish stage *King Lear* and *Othello*, also Gorky's *Night Lodging*, *Resurrection* by Tolstoy, *The Robbers* by Schiller, plays by Chekhov and Hauptmann.

After he learned of life in the Village in the mid-Teens, Gold hung around the Provincetown Playhouse, attending its productions and watching from a distance his heroes— Reed, Eastman, Dell, George Cram Cook—and their girls wistfully. He walked home across town to the ghetto to write plays of his own. He was working ten to twelve hours a day on an Adams Express wagon, and the plays took the place of sleep.

As with the *Masses*, Gold screwed up courage and posted a manuscript to the Players. As Dell had, Jig Cook called in the unknown author. He plied the thunderstruck youth with whiskey, praised his play, and told him to keep at it. In 1917 the Provincetown produced Gold's *Down the Airshaft* and *Ivan's Homecoming*. In 1920 it did his Gorkyesque *Money*. All one-acters. Nowhere else could a revolutionary expect to have his plays seen.

For the next six years after *Money*, Gold seems to have written no drama. The spark left the Provincetown when Cook took off for Greece and the past. Gold became involved in *The Liberator*, then in trying to write a novel about his childhood. He spent two years in California (1923–24), then left for Europe and the Soviet Union in 1925. Of that trip he wrote, "My own visit to Soviet Russia, and contact with its new life and art, gave me the sense of direction I had needed. Soviet Russia cured me of sentimentality, and gave me courage to persist in a land where the proletarian writer has no friends." Specifically, that visit brought him in contact with Meyerhold and the Moscow Art Theater. The daring of Meyerhold's "constructivist" stage tactics—the break with the conventions of "realistic" theater, the pageantry, the exploitation of vertical space—astonished him. Homesick, broke, and itching for the theater, Gold hastily returned to the States.

It was hot summer, 1926, when Florence Rauh, sister of Ida, Eastman's first wife, went on vacation leaving the newly returned Gold her Village apartment and credit for groceries in return for a promise that he would write, write plays. Gold recalls he had no plan. He wrote, it seemed to him, "in a trance," furiously. In a month or so he had completed two pieces, his first full-length plays, and virtually his last, *Hoboken Blues* and *Fiesta*. (In the mid-Thirties Michael Blankfort picked up and polished *Battle Hymn*, a play about John Brown on which Gold had been working fitfully for some years; in the early Fifties Gold wrote a tired play about the life of Pete Cacchione, Brooklyn's sometime Communist city councilman.)

Hoboken Blues is a belligerently "constructivist" fantasy of Harlem life, a loose adaptation of the Rip Van

Winkle tale. Ridgely Torrence's *The Rider of Dreams*, which Gold had seen years earlier, was inspiration for the Negro content, Meyerhold for the style, "American" legend for the plot. Still entranced, Gold bundled it off to Lewis Mumford who was then, with Van Wyck Brooks and Paul Rosenfeld, collecting material for their first *American Caravan*. With that characteristic naïve incredulity, he received Mumford's enthusiastic response (and a check) and saw the play published.

Production was another problem. Paul Robeson, who was then acting for the Provincetown, refused to play the easy-going, banjo-strumming lead, because it was not a "positive," heroic character. The Theatre Guild was not interested. His agent sent him to see Otto Kahn, the financier and rebellious angel. Kahn liked the play and increasingly disliked the tepid Theatre Guild which he had been backing. Word spread around the Village that Gold, the *proletaire*, was seen strolling on Fifth Avenue with a capitalist and his dachshunds, but Gold got something like $30,000 out of Kahn to establish what became the New Playwrights' Theatre and that was compensation enough for his chagrin.

Together with Dos Passos, John Howard Lawson, Francis Faragoh, and Em Jo Basshe, Gold spent the money well, if not wisely. In something over a year they put eight plays on their boards, including *Hoboken Blues*. Gold was again trying to re-establish the kind of institution which had nurtured him. But, unlike *The New Masses* in its phases, which pleased either the middle-class intellectuals or the proletarian politicos, the New Playwrights pleased neither—Gold included. There was too much flip fancy to appeal to those working people who did attend this "worker's theater," too much flaunting of half-cocked revolutionary bravado for the uptown crowd. Long before Genet, Gold's script called for an all-Negro cast, playing the several white characters in whiteface. The director put together a white cast in blackface, which only exacerbated the latent stereotyped quality of Gold's characterizations. And Gold "just about puked" when he discovered the actors directed to mingle with the crowd during intermission distributing—balloons. He took both life and art too seriously for such inane high-jinks. The New Playwrights folded, apparently much to nobody's grief.

Fiesta was accepted by the Provincetown, which had struggled on *sans* Cook, turning more "commercial." After numerous delays and revisions, it was performed in 1929. Otto Kahn, who was cheerful about throwing good money after bad, had put up $15,000 for the production. He had his doubts from the start, and, after the play folded, he said something about wishing he could have written the panning reviews himself.

Fiesta is based on Gold's experience in Mexico during the war. In violent contrast to *Hoboken Blues,* it is indebted mainly to Broadway, and is the work of which Gold is most ashamed. In his effort to write in a popular medium for a proper New York theater audience about the peons and revolution of Mexico, he came to feel that he was untrue to his subject, the people, and their possibilities.

Stark Young's review of *Fiesta* in *The New Republic* is a generous assessment of Gold's weaknesses as a playwright and of his gift. Young notes a lack of craftsmanship and "a lack of maturity in meaning," but praised Gold's "genuine poetic instinct for types, fresh feeling, contrasts of personality, raw color, youth and pressing life." Though neither *Hoboken Blues* nor *Fiesta* deserves an audience today, they do offer some good insight into the man whom most people know only as a dolorous ghetto-haunted Jew without money. In both plays Gold has a characteristic ear for melancholy, but for the special tones of the lamenting Latin and of the blues, so different from the wails of Yom Kippur. And he shows a hankering after gaiety which he tried to find among the poor of other cultures, an *élan* which is quite missing from his urgent, sober book about his childhood. In these plays Gold suggests there is triumph in the very joy of common men. This attitude burst out elsewhere most vigorously in Gold's cordial squabbles, public and private, with Upton Sinclair, who was what Gold disliked most in a radical: a prude. He wrote Sinclair, around 1923,

> Attack the filthy, the blood-stained luxuries of the rich all you want to, but don't moralize against the poor little jug of wine and hopeful song of the worker. It helps him to live and fight. The little pleasure I get out of this wretched world helps me to live and fight. I love humor, joy and happy people; I love big groups at play, and friends sitting about a table, talking, smoking, and laughing. I love song and athletics and a lot of other things. I wish the world were all play and everybody happy and creative as children. That is Communism; the communism of the future. Meanwhile there is a lot of dirty work to do and a dirty world to live in. Let's do it as communistically as we can.

That was Michael Gold, child of the *Masses* and young man of the Twenties.

There was one other figure, a man and an institution combined, who helped bring Gold up and keep him at work: oddly, H. L. Mencken. Ever since 1917, when Gold printed in the *Masses* a scrap of autobiographical fiction, he had been working on a novel about his childhood. Poor training, interruptions, and an inveterate lack of *Sitzfleisch* kept him from finishing it to his satisfaction. At least one manuscript he destroyed. But he kept coming back to it. In the later Twenties he was writing the halting gusts of narrative, local color, reminiscence, and invention which would eventually coalesce into the rhythms of *Jews Without Money*. Some pieces he printed in *The New Masses*, but he despaired of completing a book. Again he trusted the mail with a piece of work, this time trying *The American Mercury*. Again he got an editorial invitation, this time to be lectured gruffly over lunch in a Third Avenue rathskeller. The two men scoffed at each other's politics, and Gold was later to hoist Mencken as the quintessential monster of the roaring, snobbish parvenue-bourgeoisie before the Crash. But Mencken published three of Gold's chapters, and, what was more useful, egged him on with encouragement and criticism.

Jews Without Money was achieved. Mencken did Gold

one more service. He got him a publisher, Horace Liver-
ight. I have written an appreciation of the nature and
success of *Jews Without Money*, with some emphasis on
the argument against calling it either a novel or an autobiography (*The Nation*, February 28, 1966). Several aspects of the book which I could not consider there are
relevant here.

Two of the most difficult passages of *Jews Without
Money* reveal much about Gold's education in the ghetto.
They are difficult, that is, for the critic who would understand Gold; his detractors have an easy time dismissing
the man with little more than reference to these passages.
For one: "Mother! Momma! I am still bound to you by
the cords of birth. I cannot forget you. I must remain
faithful to the poor because I cannot be faithless to you.
The world must be made gracious for the poor! Momma,
you taught me that!" The sentimentality is egregious.
Indeed, except when Gold wrote in moods of wrath, there
is usually a strong undertow of sentiment in his work, but
the bathos here is uncharacteristic. Gold or a helpful
editor more often kept that mood in firm control.

The reasons for excess are two. First, Gold in his young
manhood did tend to forget his mother and to abhor the
ghetto. He was at least ambivalent. When he decided to
try exile in Mexico to avoid dying for Wilson's democracy,
he left without informing his mother, nor did he write her
for a year or so. His trip was illegal, and he had good
reasons of policy to keep quiet, but it hurt. He felt faithless. In the Twenties he would visit his mother on Chrystie Street (his father was long dead), more out of duty
than desire, but he desperately resisted her importuning
him to stay the night. He would not be dragged back so
intimately into the role and memories of his childhood
nightmare.

But one cannot read *Jews Without Money* through
without understanding Gold's real love and respect for his
mother and her world. She is the largest figure in the
book; in a 1935 introduction, Gold calls her its "heroine."
What Gold lacked in his ambivalence and in the exacer-

bated passion of this passage was *distance*, a distance which, in fact, he more usually achieved. Two paragraphs earlier: "My humble funny little East Side mother! How can I ever forget this dark little woman with bright eyes, who hobbled about all day in bare feet, cursing in Elizabethan Yiddish."

The other reason for emotions running amok in this passage is that it expresses the one fundamental principle of Gold's troubled career. With wisdom or bravado or whatever mistaken policies, Gold's one conscious purpose has ever been to make the world gracious for the poor, to "destroy the East Side and build there a garden for the human spirit."

That dream is the burden of the other "difficult" passage, the concluding paragraphs of the books, about Gold's "epiphany," his revolutionary "conversion." (One difficulty about the passage is that, in two recent editions, it was exorcised; Avon, N. Y., second printing, 1966, includes the full text.) After a brief characterization of his aimless, desperate, lonely adolescence, drifting from job to menial, thankless job, Gold concludes:

> A man on an East Side soap-box, one night, proclaimed that out of the despair, melancholy and helpless rage of millions, a world movement had been born to abolish poverty.
>
> I listened to him.
>
> O Workers' Revolution, you brought hope to me, a lonely, suicidal boy. You are the true Messiah. You will destroy the East Side when you come, and build there a garden for the human spirit.
>
> O Revolution, that forced me to think, to struggle and to live.
>
> O great Beginning!

The first problem, which is crediting this experience at all, is partially obviated by the knowledge that Gold is virtually recording autobiographical fact. Before he blundered into Union Square that afternoon in April of 1914 on his way home from a fruitless day's job hunt, heard Gurley Flynn, and had his head cracked when the cops busted up the rally, Gold did not know there was an "unemployment problem," much less a movement to abolish it. His "conversion" was more like an awakening, for he had been converted from nothing but ignorance, and it was that quick, if not that easy. After the melee he was taken in by the proprietor of an anarchist bookshop off the square. He was soon out on a soapbox himself.

But the passage is unsatisfying because so cryptic. Regardless of its factual truth, Gold relies upon rhetoric, leaving us to take him on faith, rather than upon the patient narrative and self-examination which would allow us to credit his experience implicitly. But Gold was out of patience. This was his way of ending the book somehow, and being done with it. Part of the passage he simply lifted from the foreword to an earlier collection of his short works, 120 *Million* (1929).

But the real tough nut, which more critics spit out than crack, is Gold's characterization of the Revolution as "the true Messiah." Gold thus invites in response the hackneyed opinion that Marxism is but an ersatz religion. For instance, Sol Liptzin; "This irrepressible Jewish Messianism, estranged from its traditional soil, finally discovered a pseudo-religious outlet in communism." Of course, it was not communism to which young Gold first responded so intensely, but anarcho-syndicalism. Nor was it a body of dogma, pseudo-religious or otherwise, which Gold at first knew nothing about, that caught his commitment. It was rather the simple idea of a practical solution to his problems based on communal effort.

There is surely a messianic quality to Gold's vision of building a garden for the human spirit, one which is prepared for through much of the book, but that vision cannot adequately be explained as a mere sublimation or transference of an essentially religious temperament. Revolutionary politics was for Gold not an outlet for a dislocated religious vision, but the fulfillment of a need, both personal and social, which religion, Judaism or any other kind, was by its nature unable to satisfy.

Gold's early education was as much Jewish as it was

"American," and a part of Gold's growth was to learn to assimilate the two cultures, rejecting the dead and the corrupt in both, revering what seemed to him strong and humane in two traditions which gave him pride in the dual identity of an American Jew. (Michael Gold is a characteristic enough "Jewish" name, but he adopted it because it belonged to an old man who had fought in the Union Army, to free the slaves, so it seemed, and to keep the Republic whole.) As a boy, Gold recalls in *Jews Without Money*, every day after "American" school, he attended a *Chaider*: "Reb Moisha was my teacher. This man was a walking, belching symbol of the decay of orthodox Judaism. What could such as he teach any one? He was ignorant as a rat. He was a foul smelling, emaciated beggar who had never read anything, or seen anything, who knew absolutely nothing but this sterile memory course in dead Hebrew which he whipped into the heads and backsides of little boys." Religious services were, to the boy, only less brutal, and hardly more meaningful. At synagogue "mostly the congregation droned through hours and hours of meaningless Hebrew. The synagogue stank with bad air; the windows were always locked. People gossiped, yawned, belched, took snuff, talked business, and spat on the floor. Even the grown-ups were bored. And so a boy wriggled from his father's side and rolled dice for picture buttons with other bored youngsters in the hallway." But a boy could appreciate in Judaism that which was alive and sustained life: tradition, festivity, and drama. There were the holidays, "like having a dozen Christmases during the year," celebrating in joy and sorrow the travails and triumphs of his people; the passion and agony of old men as they "groaned, sobbed, beat their breasts and wailed these strange Oriental melodies, that are two thousand years old, yet still move the Jewish heart." And there was the Messiah. "I believed the Messiah was coming. . . . It was the only point in the Jewish religion I could understand clearly. We had no Santa Claus, but we had a Messiah."

The same "American" education which taught the boy

about Santa Claus spurred his imagination with another, more awful folk figure with which to compare his God. The child goes to ask Reb Samuel about His coming:

> Would he look like Buffalo Bill? I asked.
>
> No. He would be pale, young and peaceful. He would not shoot people down, but would conquer them with love.
>
> I was disappointed. I needed a Messiah who would look like Buffalo Bill, and who could annihilate our enemies. I had many talks with Reb Samuel about this.

Such were the fancies of a boy who was reared in an oppressed enclave within a hostile society.

In his adolescence Gold's private faith became more serious and desperate: "I developed a crazy religious streak, I prayed on the tenement roof in the moonlight to the Jewish Messiah who would redeem the world."

All his early life, Gold had nothing but hope in the Jewish Redeemer, as he conceived Him, to grasp for solution to his problems. When he stumbled on a new means of solving these problems, revolutionary politics, it was easy to conceive these means in familiar terms, and easy to cleave to those means because they were so conceivable. But Gold's text and his character make evident enough the crucial difference between the Jewish Messiah and the Revolution in his mind.

In organized Judaism, he could find no community, for reasons explained at some length in *Jews Without Money*. The boy praying on the roof, like the bored congregation, lived in hopes only of some mysterious agency solving his problems for him. And, alone, he was demoralized in spite of his faith. Anarcho-syndicalism, then communism, offered him community not only of attitude, but also of effort—a program of action in which he could participate toward a practical solution of his problems. And, not least, it offered a view of the world in which, for the first time in his life, the enemy ceased to be the *goyim*, and in which the chosen people were replaced by the People. Revolutionary politics was Gold's release, not only from despair, but also from that parochialism which has never done a Jew any good except as quietistic mental defense against oppression.

In the end, *Jews Without Money* is more about the moneyless than about the Jews, and Gold's faith is precisely the opposite of religion—a faith in the ability of his people, the poor, to solve their own problems in deed.

The conclusion of *Jews Without Money* is pat. But the Revolution hardly solved Gold's problems. Rather, political activity gave him a reason for persisting—"to think, to struggle and to live." His moody, unstable temperament persisted, too, his neurotic insecurities, the extravagance of enthusiasm and apathy. The nervous breakdown in Boston two years later was more disastrous than any of his preradical anguish, and in the later Teens and early Twenties he suffered other nervous crises. Commitment to the Revolution in fact added troubles, as Gold suggested when he spoke of the direction and courage which his Soviet trip gave him "to persist in a land where the proletarian writer has no friends." Nor did a few months in Moscow in 1925 cure his *Angst* (or his sentimentality), however much it helped.

Jews Without Money had to conclude pretty much where it did, though not necessarily as it did, to keep the book whole. But Gold never could pick up where he left off. He wrote imaginative work best about his own life, and he could hardly bring himself to write about his experience after 1914. He published a few vignettes, like the story about the Boston dump, which built upon subsequent periods of manual work. But, after 1917, he was principally a journalist, editor, and reporter. The private traumas of an insecure radical intellectual carousing in bohemia and bucking his comrades were tough to handle, even veiled in fiction. The life was hardly subject matter for the proletarian literature his theories demanded.

Gold tried one novel, with the working title, *Reborn in Tampico*, about his time in Mexico as a "slacker." He made the central character a liberal, middle-class pacifist who left the country for pure conscience and was to return a confirmed revolutionary, but Gold couldn't sustain the character, the narrative, or the notion. In the early Thirties he began a novel about life in the shanty "Hoovervilles" of the unemployed. Edward Dahlberg encouraged him with a parcel of newspaper clippings about "Hoovervilles" and with the assurance that Defoe built great works out of research. But Gold was no researcher and no shanty stiff. After numerous false starts he distilled his manuscript into one short story.

Only *Jews Without Money* worked. It was possible, and it fit his theories neatly.

Gold's "Towards Proletarian Art," which was printed in *The Liberator* in 1921, was not the first radical literary manifesto in America, but it was, with one previously unpublished exception, the first to speak of literature wholly from the point of view of the working class. Most earlier radical theorists (and many later) were middle-class rebels who demanded literature variously schemed *for* the working class or *about* it, with socialist ideals in view. In contrast, Gold's theory bears the clear mark of his class origin and of his experience trying to educate himself and to make himself a writer in spite of his origins.

That one earlier argument for art entirely *of* and *by* the proletariat was not published until 1927 and never received much attention: William D. Haywood's gentle harangue in Mabel Dodge's salon, as reported with embellishments by Max Eastman in his novel, *Venture*. Haywood's ideas bear comparison with Gold's. Eastman remembers, "the first thing he wanted to call [the guests'] attention to about proletarian art was the fact that there isn't any."

> "The only problem, then, about proletarian art," he continued, "is how to make it possible, how to make life possible for the proletariat. In solving that problem we should be glad of your understanding but we don't ask your help. We are going to solve it at your expense. Since you have got life, and we have got nothing but work, we are going to take our share of life away from you, and put you to work."

He smiled in a fatherly way, as though he were explaining a somewhat complicated punishment to a child.

. . . .

"I suppose you will want to know what my ideal of proletarian art is," he continued, "what I think it will be when a revolution brings it into existence. I think it will be very much kindlier than your art. There will be a social spirit in it. Not so much boasting about personality. Artists won't be so egotistical. The highest ideal of any artist will be to write a song which the workers sing, to compose a drama which great throngs of the workers can perform out of doors. . . . The important thing is that our side, the workers, should fight without mercy and win. There is no hope for humanity anywhere else.

Gold's theories rested upon much the same attitudes and principles as Haywood's defiance of middle-class parlor folk: alienation from the dominant culture, a trust in the ability of the deprived to solve their own problems, and an insistence that the health of all culture depended on the solution of those problems. But the frustrated scholar and literary aspirant lacked Haywood's lofty calm; his vehemence buried a wistfulness which the older Wobbly did not feel. More important was their theoretical difference. Gold insisted that a literature of the working class is possible, now, in America, without a revolution. When he reviewed Trotsky's *Literature and Revolution* ecstatically in 1926 in *The New Masses,* he differed with that Leonardo da Vinci of the Revolution about one matter only: Trotsky's idea that the attempt to create a distinctly proletarian literature is in error since the proletariat is a transitory class intent on destroying itself along with all other classes.

Haywood was an organizer (and no poet) talking about pre-revolutionary conditions. Trotsky was a highly literate theoretician looking at a post-revolutionary society. Although Gold did not altogether catch the drift of the latter's remarks, he virtually answered both Haywood and Trotsky in his reply:

I do not agree with this [Trotsky's theory]. Even if for only fifty years the proletariat remains in subjection to [or,

Gold should have added, "in post-revolutionary conflict with"] capitalist society, will there not be some art growing out of this mass of intense, tragic, active human beings? Will they not sing, and need cartoons, plays, novels, like other human beings? Are they not studying, groping, reaching out hungrily for culture? It is not a matter of theory; it is a fact that a proletarian style is emerging in art. It will be as transitory as other styles; but it will have its day.

It was for Gold a *fact*—precisely. Unlike Haywood and Trotsky, he was a working writer in capitalist society, as much committed to his métier as to his politics and people. His first attempts at poetry were made with paper, pencil, and time stolen from his employers. His theory of "proletarian art" of 1921 was essentially an explanation of his own experience and practice blown up in bombast:

> What have the intellectuals done? They have created, out of their solitary pain, confusions, doubts and complexities, but the masses have not heard them; and Life has gone on.
>
> . . . .
> The tenement is in my blood. When I think it is the tenement thinking. When I hope it is the tenement hoping. I am not an individual; I am all that the tenement group poured into me during those early years of my spiritual travail. Why should we artists born in tenements go beyond them for our expression? Can we go beyond them? "Life burns in both camps," in the tenements and in the palaces, but can we understand that which is not our very own?
>
> . . . .
> The masses are still primitive and clean, and artists must turn to them for strength again. The primitive sweetness, the primitive calm, the primitive ability to create simply and without fever or ambition, for primitive satisfaction and self-sufficiency—they must be found again.
>
> The masses know what Life is, and they live on in gusto and joy. The lot of man seems good to them despite everything: they work, they bear children, they sing and play. But the intellectuals have become bored with the primitive monotony of Life—with the deep truths and instincts.

The boy in the ghetto must not learn of their art. He must stay in the tenement and create a new and truer one there.

There was no more flagrant individualist on the Left than Gold, no more passionate lover of the world's past literature in parlor or school, no lifelong Communist who attacked anti-intellectualism in his party more vigorously. What did he mean by denying his individuality, rejecting "their art," and vilifying "the intellectuals"?

Gold's "anti-individualism" makes sense in historical context and as a reaction against what Haywood called the boasting and egotism of bourgeois art, what Gold called the crabbed confusions of solitary pain—in other words, against what they considered the antisocial individualism of middle-class society, with its twin aspects of dog-eat-dog and poor-little-lonely-me. Gold was quite in step with the changing history of Marxist aesthetics. It was the period of "masscult." He would for a while repeat ineffectual notions like Haywood's about the ideal of an art which was communal in performance as well as in spirit. In the Twenties he tried his hand at writing "mass recitations." This extreme aspect slipped from Gold's work and thought, but not the idea of an art which is communal in spirit. To the extent that *Jews Without Money* is autobiographical, it is perhaps the most self-effacing autobiography ever written. The individual is there in the narrative and in the informing sensibility, but he serves mainly as the perceiver of and relater of that community life which is the subject of the book. *Jews Without Money* is the autobiography of the tenement in Gold's blood, a record of the tenement thinking.

Gold's argument against going to the school of the bourgeois writers was a less orthodox and more cramping injunction. Gold was to gain some of his notoriety by maintaining his position through the Thirties and defending it hotly—against, among others, Joshua Kunitz and, as Kunitz pointed out, Lenin, who urged the workers to expropriate for their own benefit the cultural heritage of class society—and against the Politburo of the CPSU. But Gold was still intimately at war with that society, and he had been painfully denied those benefits. Like the black militant today who argues that "integration" means assimilation into the dominant and corrupt white culture, and with as much justice and necessity, Gold was hell-bent on establishing his own forceful identity as a child of the ghetto. His effort was, in turn, to urge his people to find themselves in unique, imaginative expression, indebted in no way to their masters. On this point Gold differed most fundamentally from the norm of American radical writers, who came to the Left with their middle-class cultural debts established, and whose identification with the working class was more wishful (and temporary) than lived. This is not to argue for Gold's position, but to account for it.

Gold's rejection of "bourgeois" art was, however, more apparent than real. Though his wild, early rhetoric was hardly clear, he did not mean to include all past literature in "their art." Shakespeare, Heine, Shelley, Schiller, Whitman, Dickens, Thoreau he revered. It was the likes of Thornton Wilder, "prophet of the genteel Christ," and the idea that such writers had anything to offer his kind that exercised his indignation.

Similarly, to fault Gold with "anti-intellectualism" because of his deprecation of confused, doubtful, complex "intellectuals" in that 1921 essay is to engage in a semantic quibble—though, Lord knows, a quibble which Gold's sloppy rhetoric and often simplistic thinking demand. To comprehend what Gold meant is perhaps quite as difficult for proper academics as it is for white liberals of good faith today to grasp what SNCC means by Black Power. Gold was not condemning thought and knowledge in themselves, but rather using the term "intellectual" to denote those thinkers whom he considered cut off from the life of working men, and whom he thought, thus, in their isolation, bogged down in *fruitless* confusions. Prince Hamlet is, indeed, not mankind's only hero.

Gold was simply (and sloppily) trying to say that the

men whom the dominant society respected as "intellectuals" did not have anything to say to the people of the ghetto. Like SNCC, Gold, in his struggle to solve his own problems, learned that respectable ways were impertinent. He set out to found his program wholly on the needs and aspirations of the people he considered his own. Harvard had now as little to offer Michael Gold as Max Lerner to Stokely Carmichael.

Gold's decorum or his good sense may be questioned, but not his fundamental and continuing commitment to both the life of the mind and to the intellectual and cultural flowering of the mass of his countrymen, who never heard of Harvard.

A year after that essay on proletarian art, *The Liberator* printed Gold's "The Password to Thought—to Culture," a story. Its central character is a young sweatshop worker who is troubled by confusions, doubts, and complexities—and by solitary pain—because he would rather read Ruskin than to succeed in business. The boy's employer and, more generously, his parents are studies in philistinism. They understand *thought* only as "common sense," commercial practicality, and *culture* only as "fairy tales." The boy is essentially Gold, and the story ends where Gold was: a young man wandering alone in the night of a world which was hostile to and uncomprehending of the passions of his mind.

In 1921 Gold's novel theories were tolerated by, even congenial to, his fellows on the literary left, but most of Gold's comrade writers were hardly proletarians or tenement children. He was talking to himself. In 1929 Gold felt confident enough to be descriptive rather than prescriptive in his *New Masses* editorial, "Go Left, Young Writers!"

> A new writer has been appearing: a wild youth of about twenty-two, the son of working class parents, who himself works in the lumber camps, coal mines, steel mills, harvest fields and mountain camps of America. He is sensitive and impatient. He writes in jets of exasperation and has no time to polish his work. He is violent and sentimental by turns.

He lacks self confidence but writes because he must—and because he has a real talent.

He is a Red but has few theories. It is all instinct with him. His writing is no conscious straining after proletarian art, but the natural flower of his environment. He writes that way because it is the only way for him. His "spiritual" attitudes are all mixed up with tenements, factories, lumber camps and steel mills, because that is his life.

There is as much wishful thinking here as truth. Gold was describing himself and encouraging similarly ill-educated children of poverty to make something of their lives in words—as he would soon do with *Jews Without Money*.

In this implicit description of himself—and I don't suppose a better has ever been written—Gold lists many of the stylistic limitations which social origins, education, and temperament imposed upon him, and he makes virtues of them, as he made virtues of them in his best work. In this passage and in the earlier essay on proletarian art, other limitations are implicit.

The life of factories, steel mills, lumber camps, fields, mines—in other words, the life of the industrial proletariat—were mostly beyond Gold's intimate ken. As an adolescent he worked in light and service industries. A stint on a Pennsylvania railroad section gang in 1916 was rather a lark. He well knew the hell of menial work for starvation wages, but not that "heroic" industrial labor which many a fair-weather radical writer awkwardly idealized in the Thirties. Gold mentions the tenements in 1929 as one center of working-class life among many. In the 1921 article, closer to the experience and less ideologically adept, he trumpeted the tenement as *the* center of life.

All of which is simply to define sociologically the limits within which Gold himself was able to work in creating "proletarian" art. *Jews Without Money* succeeds because he stuck within those limits. And perhaps these limits suggest why *Jews Without Money* has a special appeal today, when poverty looks like an isolated urban ghetto phenomenon, and when so many liberals and young radicals are contemptuous of the industrial working class

which has won its way into the suburbs. When Gold
spoke his faith in and commitment to the "poor," he
meant the working class; we make a distinction. (It should
be noted that Comrade Kunitz, reviewing *Jews Without
Money* in *The New Masses* at the time, criticized Gold
for his failure to make precisely that distinction.)

In the 1921 essay several of the crucial influences on
Gold's mind and sensibility coagulate. Gold's debt to and
reverence for the American cultural past is evident in its
Whitmanesque prose. The essay ends with a paean to
Whitman and an argument that proletarian art is to be
the completion of Whitman's great but illusion-warped
beginning. Most of Gold's poetry follows Whitman's
flabby example. Later, Gold's critical writings are laden
with praise for the writers of the "American Renaissance,"
and his frequent defenses of the literature of the Depression decade rest on the argument that it was a second and
comparable native flowering.

Perhaps more evident in that 1921 essay is Gold's romanticism. (As well call the conclusion of *Jews Without
Money* "romantic" as "messianic.") A robust romantic
flair and lilt and impracticality runs through much of
Gold's work and career; many of his failures result from
the failure of that spirit, the aging of the natural child of
the old *Masses*. But nowhere I know in Gold's work does
the intellectual heritage of European Romanticism show
itself more clearly and more oddly than in that 1921 essay:
"The masses are still primitive and clean, and artists must
turn to them for strength again. . . . But the intellectuals
have become bored with the primitive monotony of
Life—with the deep truths and instincts." This was the
inspired nonsense of Gold in midpassage. His fiction, before and after that wild essay, usually suggested his sense
of the dignity, strength, and humanity of the urban
poor—most notably in the person of his mother in *Jews
Without Money*—but in that same fiction Gold demonstrated his sure knowledge of the noisy, sophisticated depravity bred by poverty out of need in the slums. He built
his hope in spite of and as a remedy for that depravity.

In his desire to establish and argue for a font and root of value and art in utter defiance of the dominant culture, he invented what looks like a twentieth-century urban version of the old pastoral, noble-savage, feudal-commune motif, though it was a unique effort at that. There were, however, fundamental differences between Gold on the one hand and Wordsworth, Rousseau, and Carlyle on the other. Gold was romanticizing his own milieu, his own people. He grounded his idealization on a system of thought and a political program which seemed to promise the actual creation of a world in which this people might flower and this community be realized triumphantly. The Marxist romantic had none of the frivolous nostalgia of his romantic predecessors, who never dreamed of Michael or the virtuous red man or Jocelin mastering the world.

Gold's ecstasy, in long bitter years, was damped. His hope remains a dream, but it remains. *Jews Without Money* lives, a testament and honest record of his people and their frustrated possibilities. His dream is fixed in the needs of the poor. More than fifty years after Michael Gold learned his lesson in Union Square, speaking for blacks without money, Stokely Carmichael said: "The society we seek to build . . . is not a capitalist one. It is a society in which the spirit of community and humanistic love prevail."

The Brief Embattled Course
of Proletarian Poetry

ALLEN GUTTMANN

ALTHOUGH Edwin Rolfe's *First Love and Other Poems* did not appear until 1951, proletarian poetry as an American literary movement of permanent importance began in 1929, with the publication of Kenneth Fearing's first book, and ended—to assign an arbitrary date—in 1939, with the start of World War II. A political event, the Seventh Congress of the Communist International, quite appropriately divides the period into two parts. Before the summer of 1935, when the Seventh Congress called for a Popular Front of all anti-Fascist elements, proletarian poets were a tiny group of self-conscious militants who wrote off Archibald MacLeish as a "dirty Nazi" whose *Frescoes for Mr. Rockefeller's City* entitled him "to first place among the incipient Fascists of American poetry." [1] After the summer of 1935, the emphasis shifted from the creation of a Communist society to the defense of bourgeois democracy against the increasingly fearful threat of Fascism. Vilification of liberals ceased. MacLeish, especially valued for his eloquent defense of the Spanish Republic, was among the featured speakers at the Communist-sponsored American Writers' Congress of 1937. Isador Schneider, who had spoken on "Proletarian Poetry" at the first writers' congress in 1935, was not on the program. Communists continued to write poetry through the late Thirties and Forties, but it was hard, after *Poetry* magazine turned over an entire issue to Horace Gregory for a "Social Poets Number" and the Yale Younger Poets series included three of their number, to feel that they were the persecuted apostles of an unrecognized gospel. Cold War application of the dormant Smith Act revived the genre in the work of Walter Lowenfels, but proletarian poetry remains a *movement* of the Thirties.[2]

This movement can now be seen with a fair degree of clarity. Speaking of his contemporaries, men who came of age in the late Twenties and early Thirties, Edwin Rolfe described a discontinuity not only between Communist and bourgeois society but also between his generation and its predecessors within the world of radical politics. Rolfe and his friends had taken the Writers' Workshop at the Workers' School on East 14th Street, "but when we turned to the writing of revolutionary poetry, we had nothing to guide us. . . . Michael Gold and Joseph Freeman, the only two living poets with whom we had occasional personal contact, could give us nothing through their work and very little through their talks." An examination of the poems Gold and Freeman wrote in the Twenties would indicate that the discontinuity between generations was overstated by Rolfe, but the point he made is emotionally valid; he, Sol Funaroff, Alfred Hayes, Ben Maddow, Isador Schneider, and the rest *felt* that they had completely to break with the past in order to create a wholly new kind of poetry appropriate to a wholly new kind of society.

Within the ranks, there was very nearly a critical consensus on the new poetry. The poet had to write as one consciously committed to Marxism. The significant poet, argued Rolfe, had to "leave his mark on the world in which he lives and in which other men will live," and to do this a correct political position was necessary.[3] In his introduction to Granville Hicks' anthology, *Proletarian Literature in The United States* (1935), Joseph Freeman urged a modest view of what Marxism could do for the poet: "No party resolution, no government decree can produce art, or transform an agitator into a poet. A party card does not automatically endow a Communist with artistic genius." Most of those involved in proletarian poetry, as poets and as critics, attempted to discriminate among poems and to avoid what might be termed the partisan fallacy, the assumption that political orthodoxy suffices for artistic success. But the temptation was almost unbearable. Granville Hicks argued, for instance, that the conversion to Communism transformed Isador Schneider's work: "In the revolutionary poems there is self-confidence; the assurance of a man who has found allies and has come to terms with the world. He no longer needs to tear himself to pieces to find his theme; he has been released from sickly subjectivism and has learned to contemplate fearlessly the men and movements of his day." [4] Schneider himself testified to the therapeutic value of Communism, but the literature upon which this praise was lavished seems unworthy: consider Schneider's poem for the tenth anniversary of the *Daily Worker*:

Ten years ago:

> *Boss America was fat,*
> *belched across the world and was applauded.*
> *His drippings lined the paunches*
> *of priests, professors, editors, hacks;*
> *even of poets, if they smoothed out lies,*
> *steaming the news, and rouging ads,*
> *there was grease enough to slide them on to Paris*
> *to take the arms of Gonorrheal muses. . . .*

The title of Schneider's book—*Comrade: Mister*—contains the ideological contrast, but the ineffectiveness and abstractness of Schneider's ill-will refutes the argument that versifiers who "joined the side of the workers . . . must thereby become better artists." [5] As Rolfe regretfully concluded, journalism was not literature. Marxism meant, for some men, perceptions they might otherwise have lacked, and these perceptions made possible poetry better than the poetry they might have written, but dedication to revolutionary thought and action were no guarantee.

The necessity of the "correct" political position was the essence of the thematic part of the program. There was almost the same degree of consensus on poetic forms. Almost everyone admitted that a slovenly lack of interest in form could ruin a poem. Harriet Monroe, charging that "poems ineffective as art probably also prove ineffective as propaganda," merely echoed the laments of the proletarians themselves.[6] But the forms *had* to be simple, almost ballad-like if rhymed, almost prose if in the form of free verse. Otherwise the poetry would fail to reach its intended audience—the great mass of the working-class population. "We are agreed," wrote John Yost, "that the poetry written to be read and remembered by our side in the American class struggle will have to be simple."[7] Stanley Burnshaw, who has achieved immortality as a critical antagonist of Wallace Stevens, proclaimed the virtues of clarity and directness. "A Marxist poet has no reason to be obscure."[8] The argument behind the statement ran something like this: Marxist thought outmodes the complexity of bourgeois poetry as Copernican thought superseded the fantastic epicycles of Ptolemaic astronomy. Marxism simplified the world and made complexity unnecessary.

Oversimplified poetry, i.e., doggerel, was the obvious opposite extreme, and Newton Arvin warned against a too strenuous attempt to break away "from the excessive indirectness and allusiveness" of the previous generation of poets.[9] The best of the proletarian poems managed to find a middle way between the jingles published in the *Daily Worker* and the experiments of Muriel Rukeyser's first book, *Theory of Flight* (in which a very loose syntax combines current history, allusions to English literature, and an unusually large amount of aerodynamics).

The first poem of Kenneth Fearing's first book—*Angel Arms* (1929)—refutes those who have abused proletarian poetry for its alleged humorlessness. St. Agnes' Eve is not as Keats imagined it.

> *The dramatis personae include a fly-specked*
> *Monday evening,*
> *A cigar store with stagnant windows,*

> *Two crooked streets,*
> *Six policemen and Louie Glatz.*
> *Bass drums mumble and mutter an ominous*
> *portent*
> *As Louie Glatz holds up the cigar store and*
> *backs out with*
> *$14.92.*
> *Officer Dolan noticed something suspicious, it*
> *is supposed,*
> *And ordered him to halt,*
> *But dangerous, handsome, cross-eye'd Louie*
> *the rat*
> *Spoke with his gat,*
> *Rat-a-tat-tat—*
> *Rat-a-tat-tat*
> *And Dolan was buried as quickly as possible.*

Five police chase Louie and go Blam, Blam, Blam! Louie's demise is cinematic:

> *Louie's soul arose through his mouth in the form*
> *of a derby hat*
> *That danced with cigarette butts and burned*
> *matches and specks of dust*
> *Where Louie sprawled.*
> *Close-up of Dolan's widow. Of Louie's*
> *mother.*
> *Picture of the fly-specked Monday evening*
> *and fade-out slow.*

Whatever else this poem is, it is *not* solemn. It has comic-book qualities which today would earn it commendation as "pop-art" parody. Fearing himself, in another poem, answered those who want to know if the point of view is Marxist. In "Cultural Notes," Maurice Epstein protests against a symphony by Beethoven and Otto Svobada rebukes him.

> *"He's crazy! Them artists are all crazy,*
> *I can prove it by Max Nordau.*
> *They poison the minds of young girls."*
> *Otto Svobada, 500 Avenue A, butcher, Pole,*
> *husband, philosopher,*
> *Argued in rebuttal: "Shut your trap, you!*

> *The question is: does the symphony fit in with*
> *Karl Marx?"*

That is certainly not the question in *Angel Arms*.

Despite his irreverence, Fearing was considered ortho-dox enough for publication in *The New Masses*, the Par-ty's journal of cultural affairs. *Poems* (1935) was the first of a series published by *Dynamo: A Journal of Revolution-ary Poetry*. This volume was devoted, in the introductory words of Edward Dahlberg, to "the sleazy cinema dreams, the five and dime loves and frustrations, the mystery pulp heroism and furnished-room microcosm of the pulverized petty bourgeois." The poems, more overtly political than those of *Angel Arms*, are written in a stanza-form almost regular, a kind of free-verse reversal of the Alexandrine in which a long first line, often melodic, is followed by a series of short unmetrical lines that undercut the original statement. "Obituary," for example, begins, "Take him away, he's as dead as they die," and moves into an absurd, pathetic catalogue of the dead man's effects, to be distrib-uted to Standard Oil, People's Gas, The D.A.R., J. P. Morgan, Al Capone, Gene Tunney, the I.R.T., and other worthy recipients. Comedy abounds, but the book ends with "Denouement," a dank, chilly image of disaster.

> *And all along the waterfront, there, where rats gnaw into*
> *the leading platforms, here, where the wind whips*
> *at the warehouse corners, look, there, here,*
> *everywhere huge across the walls and gates "Your*
> *party lives,"*
> *where there is no life, no breath, no sound, no touch,*
> *no warmth, no light but the lamp that shines on a*
> *trooper's drawn and ready bayonet.*

Kenneth Patchen is another writer whose range bewil-ders those who think of proletarian poetry as a string of slogans produced by resentful hacks who see all things through "the lenses of class conflict." [10] *First Will and Testament* (1939) contains poems like "Street Corner College," which does seem in its bitter starkness to repre-sent a genre.

Next year the grave grass will cover us.
We stand now and laugh;
Watching the girls go by;
Betting on slow horses; drinking cheap gin.
We have nothing to do; nowhere to go; nobody.

Last year was a year ago; nothing more.
We weren't younger then; nor older now.

We manage to have the look that young men have;
We feel nothing behind our faces, one way or other.

We shall probably not be quite dead when we die.
We were never anything all the way; not even soldiers.

We are the insulted, brother, the desolate boys.
Sleepwalkers in a dark and terrible land,
Where solitude is a dirty knife at our throats.
Cold stars watch us, chum
Cold stars and the whores.

But that is only one side of Patchen. The other side can
be seen in the transition to tenderness of "23rd Street
Runs into Heaven."

You stand near the window as lights wink
On along the street. Somewhere a trolley, taking
Shop-girls and clerks home, clatters through
This before-supper Sabbath. An alley cat cries
To find the garbage cans sealed; newsboys
Begin their murder-into-pennies round.
We are shut in, secure for a little, safe until
Tomorrow. You slip your dress off, roll down
Your stockings, careful against runs. Naked now,
With soft light on soft flesh, you pause
For a moment; turn and face me —
Smile in a way that only women know
Who have lain long with their lover
And are made more virginal.

Our supper is plain but we are very wonderful.

Fearing and Patchen are still familiar names. Their
work is easily available and they have received some critical attention. The poets who appeared in We Gather

Strength (1933) have worn less well, but when their collection was published Herman Spector and Joseph Kalar were greeted as the heralds of a new era in poetry, and their poems were treated as a bountiful harvest. Spector, whom Michael Gold characterized as "the raw material of New York Communism," seemed a proletarian version of the Man with a Hoe: "I am the bastard in the ragged suit / who spits, with bitterness and malice to all." Kalar, a lumberjack and papermill worker from northern Minnesota, shared Spector's bluntness. "Papermill," his best known poem, had already appeared in *Unrest*, 1931, the third volume in a series edited by Jack Conroy and Ralph Cheyney. The poem begins with the image of an idled mill and ends with the disbelief of the unemployed men:

> *The fires are banked and red changes to black,*
> *Steam is cold water, silence is rust, and quiet*
> *Spells hunger. Look at these men, now,*
> *Standing before the iron gates, mumbling,*
> *"Who could believe it? Who could believe?"*

Spector and Kalar were both included, along with twenty-seven other poets, in Granville Hicks' important anthology, *Proletarian Literature in the United States* (1935). The best poems in the anthology were, however, by Horace Gregory and Muriel Rukeyser, two poets whose careers, like those of Fearing and Patchen, transcended the radical movement. Rukeyser's poem, "City of Monuments," is probably the best of the many poems that surveyed symbolic cities and warned of the old order's doom:

> *Blinded by chromium or transfiguration*
> *we watch, as through a microscope, decay:*
> *down the broad streets the limousines*
> *advance in passions of display.*
> *Air glints with diamonds, and these clavicles*
> *emerge through orchids by whose trailing spoor*
> *the sensitive cannot mistake*
> *the implicit anguish of the poor.*

The throats incline, the marble men rejoice
careless of torrents of despair.

Split by a tendril of revolt
stone cedes to blossom everywhere.

Gregory's dramatic poem on Dempsey's defeat, a poem
which ought to have been illustrated by George Bellows,
makes of the fighter a symbol for beaten men everywhere
as the speaker begs for Dempsey not to quit and appeals
to God to help Dempsey to his feet. At the end of the
poem, the speaker confuses himself with the defeated
Dempsey and prays, in a sense, for all of us.

Publication of the anthology and of radical magazines
devoted to literature—*Dynamo, The Anvil, Partisan Review*—make 1934 and 1935 the time of the movement's
intensest activity—but not the time of its best poetic
achievement. With the exception of Gregory and Rukeyser, few of the really talented poets were represented by
samples of their best work. Sol Funaroff and Edwin Rolfe
both published poems in *We Gather Strength* and in
Proletarian Literature in the United States. (Funaroff's
were published under the pseudonym of Charles Henry
Newman.) Ironically, however, Funaroff's best poems appeared, and Rolfe's were written, in the late Thirties,
when the Party's attempts to form an anti-Fascist literary
front meant that emphases were changed and consciously
proletarian poets received somewhat less than their due.
By the time Norman Rosten became Yale's "Younger
Poet" in 1940, the Party's enthusiasm for poetry of any
kind was at less than record heights.

Sol Funaroff, who rates exactly one paragraph in Horace
Gregory's history of twentieth-century American poetry
and is not even mentioned in Daniel Aaron's *Writers on
the Left,* certainly deserves more attention than he has
received. Although friends gathered material for a posthumous book after his death in 1942, *The Spider and the
Clock* (1938) is the collection Funaroff ought to be remembered by. "Uprooted" is perhaps the best of a group
of imagistic poems that dramatize the desperation of the
Great Depression.

The shadows of silent machines
spread on the walls of the city.
Amid uptorn pavement of the broken street
a blanketed steamroller,
stranded, waits.
Hands in pockets, he stands at the corner, waiting,
or walks, a brooding figure through the streets.

"Uprooted," "Factory Night," "Unemployed: 2 A.M.,"
and "The Worker" resemble Kalar's "Papermill" or
Patchen's "Street Corner College," but the first and last
poems of the book show a wider range. In "The Bell-
buoy," Funaroff sees himself in images not unlike Baudelaire's; he is a voyager in "this human deep" where "the
derelict's dreams are drowned / in absinthe solitudes."
He is, like Cain, the Wandering Jew, Ishmael, and other
symbols of Romanticism, an exile. But with a difference.
"I am that exile / from a future time, / from shores of
freedom / I may never know. . . ." Nor would Funaroff
have agreed that "les vrais voyageurs sont ceux-là seuls
qui partent / Pour partir." For him, there was a new
Atlantis to be found.

The title poem, which is both satire and affirmation,
takes its imagery from a news item: "A . . . biologist has
been studying the battle of a hairy black arachnid to
harness the moving hands of an alarm clock in its silken
web." History, as Marxists understood it, moved inexora-
bly, and there was no Joshua to stop the sun. Like Muriel
Rukeyser's "City of Monuments" ("Split by a tendril of
revolt / stone cedes to blossom everywhere"), "The Spider and the Clock" is a hymn to inevitability, an affirmation of natural rather than mechanical images.

Can all the holy waters of christendom
drown this conflagration in the east
where morning's firelings flame?
Does man walk upward down a hill?
Will the sun
            stand
                still?

The sun moved, but there were many stones that refused
to cede to their appointed blossoms. Poems of triumph

became harder to write as the momentum of Fascism increased and seemed almost to have an inexorability of its own. "Two thousand years we have been taught renewal," wrote Boris Todrin in a poem on the destruction of Austrian socialism, "Now put your ear to European earth / And hear the armies marching." [11]

Joy Davidman, the last to appear of the important proletarian poets, won the Yale Younger Poets award, 1938, with a book so gloomy that it sometimes seems a collection of dirges, elegies, and laments. *Letter to a Comrade* is dedicated to Ernst Thaelmann, the murdered leader of the Kommunistische Partei Deutschlands. His death is commemorated in "Spartacus 1938." The title poem concludes, after a mind's-eye survey of America, with an affirmation so melancholy that it seems almost to echo Ecclesiastes:

Only remember,
wanderer, under the murdered and slender trees
white bodies given over to slaughter, remember
only the fireweed, comrade, the glory in burnt places,
the sharply colored torchbearers, the new warriors,
the green and flowery resurrection, the fireweed
marching over burnt hills down to the sea's edge. Remember
resurrection riot among the roots of the birches, resurrection
out of the white and black bones of burnt trees, resurrection.
    Remember
with what a brave necessity the fireweed
answers birdcry down the desolate beaches
speaks to the aimless wind the heart's red syllable,
blooms on our bones. Let the fireweed answer,
comrade, and so we may lie quiet in our graves.

The appropriate literary reference for "Dirge for the Living," in which Miss Davidman asks to be delivered "out of the hand of pain," is probably *Measure for Measure.*

> *Sever up the bone annihilate the sinew*
> *stop up the nostril choke the mouth and let us*
> *drift out of matter on wings, and let this bird*
> *this breath, this little air, go loose upon air,*

> *an eddy of wind, a swirl among the stars;*
> *and let us come to nothing.*

When Miss Davidman praised the things of this world,
her praise became a reminder of sorrow. Here is the complete lyric, "Snow in Madrid."

> *Softly, so casual*
> *Lovely, so light, so light,*
> *The cruel sky lets fall*
> *Something one does not fight.*
>
> *How tenderly to crown*
> *The brutal year*
> *The clouds send something down*
> *That one need not fear.*
>
> *Men before perishing*
> *See with unwounded eye*
> *For once a gentle thing*
> *Fall from the sky.*

"Near Catalonia," another poem of the Spanish Civil
War, sets men against bombers and achieves, now that we
know how it all ended, pathos.

> *If we had bricks that could make a wall we would use*
> *them,*
> *but bricks will break under a cannonball;*
> *if we had iron we would make a wall,*
> *but iron rings and splinters at the bomb*
> *and wings go across the sky and over a wall. . . .*
>
> *We have only the bodies of men to put together,*
> *the wincing flesh, the peeled white forking stick,*
> *easily broken, easily made sick,*
> *frightened of pain and spoiled by evil weather;*
> *we have only the most brittle of all things the man*
> *and the heart the most iron admirable thing of all,*
> *and putting these together we make a wall.*

But the wall was broken.

The Spanish Civil War, about which Miss Davidman
and scores of other poets wrote,[12] was the war to which
Edwin Rolfe went. Leaving behind wife and work in the

summer of 1937, he went clandestinely to Paris, to Perpignan, and then to Albacete, in Spain. He was sent to Madrid to be the second editor of *Volunteer for Liberty*, the newspaper that the "Lincolns" shared with the British and Canadian battalions of the XVth International Brigade. Although he was given the job to spare him the fate of many poets on the battlefield, he "deserted" and joined the battalion in the crossing of the Ebro River, the last major offensive before the withdrawal of the Internationals by Premier Juan Négrin (in a useless effort to bring about a change of policy in the democracies).

At the instigation of Bennett Cerf, Rolfe wrote what is still the battalion's best history. He also wrote, in Spain, a series of poems which have never had even the minimal attention given to the work of Funaroff and Davidman. The poems were simply published in the wrong place by the wrong publisher, at the wrong time. *First Love and Other Poems* did not come out until 1951—in the midst of the Truman-MacArthur controversy and in the heyday of McCarthyism. The book was published in an edition of only 375 copies by The Larry Edmunds Book Shop in Los Angeles. The poems were the fulfillment of a career.

Rolfe was only twenty-four when he joined Spector, Kalar, and Funaroff in *We Gather Strength* (1933). The seven poems are clearly apprentice work, but the last eight lines of "Asbestos" are effective.

> *John's deathbed is a curious affair:*
> *the posts are made of bone, the spring of nerves,*
> *the mattress bleeding flesh. Infinite air,*
> *compressed from dizzy altitudes, now serves*
>
> *his skullface as a pillow. Overhead*
> *a vulture leers in solemn mockery,*
> *knowing what John had never known: that dead*
> *workers are dead before they cease to be.*

Rolfe placed two new poems, "Unit Assignment" and "Poem for May First" in Hicks' 1935 anthology of proletarian literature. Already considered by many to be the most talented of the proletarian poets, he was on the original editorial board of *Partisan Review* when the John Reed Club of New York began that journal as a "Bi-Monthly of Revolutionary Literature" early in 1934. Rolfe published poems in *Partisan Review*, in *The New Masses*, in the first issue of Jack Conroy's magazine of proletarian stories, *The Anvil*, and even in *Poetry*. His first book, *To My Contemporaries*, was brought out by *Dynamo* magazine in 1936. (Kenneth Fearing's *Poems* was the first in *Dynamo's* series; Sol Funaroff's posthumous *Exile from a Future Time* was the third and last publication.)

To My Contemporaries, which apparently included most of the poems published to that date, sold well (for poetry), but was not a very successful book. There was in it the same tendency to sloganize that Rolfe had condemned in others of his generation. The mind, he wrote in "Credo," must "renounce the fiction of the self / and its vainglory."

> It must learn
> the wisdom and the strength and the togetherness
> of bodies phalanxed in a common cause,
> of fists tight-clenched around a crimson banner
> flying in the wind above a final, fierce
> life-and-death fight against a common foe.

Harriet Monroe singled Rolfe out, in 1936, as "the best poet among those inflammatory young men and women," but she chided him for admitting in "To My Contemporaries" that his poems were often "stray, fugitive thoughts."

> Here I am not surrendered to my poem
> nor master of its words and images;
> too great's the doubt in me to synthesize
> fragmentary feelings, thought-lines that balk,
> grow twisted, fade before they reach their ends.

In *Four Quartets*, T. S. Eliot could get away with this kind of fret over his problems with language; Rolfe couldn't. Even Harold Rosenberg, a friendly critic reviewing for *Partisan Review*, insisted that Rolfe was not yet able to do what he had set out to do: "What he does too often is to take the stuff which forms the atmosphere of the revolutionary movement in America and to give an emotional rendition of it, without adding anything to the concrete image in the reader's mind."

The poems written in and about Spain cannot be charged with this kind of vagueness. Experience has made them invulnerable. The first poem of *First Love and Other Poems* describes the entry of the volunteers into Spain. The poem is *there*, thick with images of the voyage, with loaves of bread, tinned sardines, *gauloises*, chocolate, snatches of foreign languages. Even the thoughts of the men are vivid. The second poem, "City of Anguish," is for Madrid. There is the same density of detail. Amid the ruins of the city, a beggar sings his lament:

> All night, all night
> flared in my city the bright
> cruel explosions of bombs.
> All night, all night,
> there, where the soil and stone
> spilled like brains from the sandbag's head,
> the bodiless head lay staring;
> while the anti-aircraft barked,
> barked at the droning plane,
> and the dogs of war, awakened,
> howled at the hidden moon.

Rolfe writes now as war's *aficionado*. War, the abstraction, is embodied, flesh and blood. Rolfe is almost scornful of inexperience:

> No man knows war or its meaning who has not
> stumbled from tree to tree, desperate for cover,
> or dug his face deep in earth, felt the ground
> pulse with
> the ear-breaking fall of death. No man knows war
> who never has crouched in his foxhole, hearing
> the bullets an inch from his head, nor the zoom of
> planes like a ferris wheel strafing the trenches. . . .
>
> War is your comrade struck dead beside you,
> his shared cigarette still alive in your lips.

Ernest Hemingway, speaking at the American Writers' Congress in the summer of 1937, insisted that the task of the writer was to discover what was true for his time and his place, and to make his readers feel that truth. Rolfe had always shared this definition of the writer's task. Now he shared with Hemingway a chance to write of what was important for his time and place. Rolfe's success was attested to by Hemingway, who sent him numerous letters of encouragement and congratulation.

Another poem, "Survival is the Essence," adopts Conrad's language to praise the destructive element: "Survival is the essence, but only after submergence / completely in chaos, in combat as clearest eyes see it." In this poem, consciously or not, Rolfe uses songs sung by the Thaelmann Battalion very much as Eliot, whom he had studied, used Wagner's *Tristan* in *The Waste Land* — to communicate the homesickness of exile. *Die Heimat ist weit.*

The next to last poem of the book is "Elegia," devoted to the city of Madrid. The name is used as a refrain. The poet's hunch is that the name itself, like that of Carcassonne, is enough to move the reader. "Who is not true to you is false to every man / and he to whom your name means nothing never loved."

> *And if I die before I can return to you,*
> *or you, in fullest freedom, are restored to us,*
> *my sons will love you as their father did*
> *Madrid   Madrid   Madrid.*

Rolfe's third and last book of poems, *Permit Me Refuge*, was published by *The California Quarterly* in 1955, a year after his death.[13] Thomas McGrath, Rolfe's friend and an important poet in his own right, noted in the foreword that these poems represented a new poetic style. Rolfe refused, wrote McGrath, "to repeat the easy successes of an earlier time and fought stubbornly for the way to name the new thing that a degenerate age had created. This brought a new wryness and toughness into some of his poems. He had crossed the cold summit, the height-of-land, had found the best way for his speech." Up to a point, McGrath was right. The poems, careful and sometimes even intricate in their forms, are a world away from the declarative verse of *We Gather Strength*. The lyric, "Many an Outcast," is certainly good enough to merit McGrath's enthusiasm. Nonetheless, Rolfe was clearly in no position to rival, technically, a poet like Richard Wilbur. He will be remembered for his first love—and that is as he wanted it.

Perhaps Rolfe wrote his own evaluation in the last poem of *First Love and Other Poems*:

> *Again I am summoned to the eternal field*
> *green with the blood still fresh at the roots of flowers,*
> *green through the dust-rimmed memory of faces*
> *that moved among the trees there for the last time*
> *before the final shock, the glazed eye, the hasty mound.*
>
> *But why are my thoughts in another country?*
> *Why do I always return to the sunken road through corroded hills,*
> *with the Moorish castle's shadow casting ruins over my shoulder*
> *and the black-smocked girl approaching, her hands laden with grapes?*
>
> *I am eager to enter it, eager to end it.*
> *Perhaps this one will be the last one.*
> *And men afterward will study our arms in museums*
> *and nod their heads, and frown, and name the inadequate dates*
> *and stumble with infant tongues over the strange place-names.*
>
> *But my heart is forever captive to that other war*
> *that taught me first the meaning of peace and comradeship*
>
> *and always I think of my friend who amid the apparition of bombs*
> *saw on the lyric lake the single perfect swan.*

The young men of the Thirties who milled about at Congresses and sent their radical magazines hopefully to press revolutionized neither poetic forms nor—what was much more important to them—the consciousness of their generation. Robert Penn Warren wrote their epitaph in 1939 when he noted that they "failed to achieve the popular appeal to which [they] aspired." [14] Measured in this way, which they themselves suggested, they failed. But popular appeal is not, after all, much of a criterion for poets, not even revolutionary poets. They tell us a great deal about their time, and about our time as well. At moments, they move us as all good poets must. The standard literary history of the United States, by Robert Spiller and others, includes Fanny Fern and Kimball Flaccus and excludes Joy Davidman and Edwin Rolfe. Reassessment is necessary.

Edward Dahlberg, Early and Late CHAMETZKY

1. Allen Tate set the terms of the problem and challenge with his usual fine precision: "Criticism as we write it at present has no place for it [Dahlberg's work] and this means that I shall probably not be able to do justice to my own admiration. Mr. Dahlberg eludes his contemporaries; he may have to wait for understanding until the historians of the next generation can place him historically." "A Great Stylist: The Prophet as Critic," *Sewanee Review*, LXIX (April-June, 1961), 314–17.

2. Ihab Hassan does note the "savage joy" in these early books. "The Sorrows of Edward Dahlberg," *The Massachusetts Review*, V (Spring, 1964), 457–61.

The Roots of Radicals KLEIN

1. See Granville Hicks, *Part of the Truth* (New York: Harcourt, Brace and World, 1965), pp. 134–35.

2. The tumult attending Gold's review of Wilder is recorded by Daniel Aaron, *Writers on the Left* (New York: Harcourt, Brace and World, 1961), pp. 241–43.

3. See Harvey Swados, *The American Writer and the Great Depression* (Indianapolis: Bobbs-Merrill, 1966), p. xvi.

4. Nelson Algren, Preface to the Berkley edition of *Somebody in Boots* (New York, 1965), pp. 8–9.

Character and Self in Fiction on the Left EISINGER

1. Irving Howe and Lewis Coser, *The American Communist Party* (Boston: Beacon Press, 1957), pp. 301, 303–5; Philip Rahv, "Proletarian Literature: A Political Autopsy," *The Southern Review*, IV (Winter, 1939), 616–28.

2. Carl G. Jung, *The Integration of the Personality*, trans. Stanley Dell (New York: Farrar and Rinehart, 1939); see especially pp. 16, 70, 91, 96.

3. David F. Bowers, "Hegel, Darwin, and the American Tradition," in *Foreign Influences in American Life*, ed. David F. Bowers (Princeton: Princeton University Press, 1944).

4. Karl Marx and Frederick Engels, *Literature and Art: Selections from Their Writings* (New York: International Publishers, 1947).

5. George V. Plekhanov, *Art and Society*, Critics Group Series, No. 3 (New York, 1937), p. 85.

6. Erich Fromm, *Marx's Concept of Man* (New York: F. Ungar, 1961), p. 44.

7. Meyer Levin, *Citizens* (New York: Viking, 1940), p. 650.

8. Mark Schorer, "Foreward: Self and Society," in *Society and Self in the Novel*, ed. Mark Schorer, English Institute Essays (New York: Columbia University Press, 1955), p. ix.

9. Michael Gold, "Introduction," in *The Way Things Are* (New York: International Publishers, 1938), p. 13.

The Aesthetics of the Proletarian Novel   HOFFMAN

1. Walter Rideout, *The Radical Novel in the United States 1900–1954* (Cambridge, Massachusetts: Harvard University Press, 1956), p. 12. I am indebted to Professor Rideout for much help throughout this essay.

2. *Proletarian Literature in the United States*, ed. Granville Hicks et al. (New York: International Publishers, 1935).

3. William Phillips, "What Happened in the 30's," *Commentary*, xxxiv (September, 1962), 207. Quoted by Harvey Swados in his Introduction to *The American Writer and the Great Depression* (Indianapolis: Bobbs-Merrill, 1966), p. xxi.

4. Edwin Seaver, "The Proletarian Novel," *American Writers' Congress*, ed. Henry Hart (New York: International Publishers, 1935), p. 102. For one of the shrewdest statements of the issue in the Thirties, see Kenneth Burke, "Revolutionary Symbolism in America," *ibid.*, pp. 87–94.

5. One must consider that an average of 1900 fiction titles appeared annually in the Thirties. See Rideout, pp. 170–71.

6. See Lewis Gannett, "Steinbeck's Way of Writing," introduction to *The Portable Steinbeck* (New York: Viking, 1946), p. xvii.

The Marxist Aesthetic Theory
of Louis C. Fraina   BAXANDALL

1. For these and other biographical facts, I am much indebted to Theodore Draper, *The Roots of American Communism* (New York: Viking, 1947); and to Esther Corey, "Lewis Corey (Louis C. Fraina), 1892–1953: A Bibliography with Autobiographical Notes," *Labor History* (Spring, 1963), pp. 103–31. Unpublished biographical data was obtained from the Corey Papers, Columbia University Library.

2. "Charity," *Weekly People* (September 4, 1909), p. 4.

3. For a bibliographical listing of Fraina's essays on art and literature, see Lee Baxandall, comp., *Marxism and Aesthetics: A Bibliography* (New York: Humanities Press, 1967).

4. For a presentation and discussion of Marx's aesthetic views, see *Marxists on Art and Literature*, a forthcoming anthology coedited by Stephan Morawski and Lee Baxandall.

5. "Emporkömmlinge," *Forum* (Berlin), October, 1921, pp. 6–14; apparently never published in English. Fraina perceived the bourgeoisification of the working class as early as the 1910 Brieux essay: "The 'ideals' of a ruling class cannot be held guiltless of some effect upon the ruled class as well. The concept of a marriage controlled by material gain has made its impression on the proletariat as well."

6. Corey Papers: Unpublished manuscript on John Reed (ca. 1948).

7. "The Spirit of the Dance," *Modern Dance Magazine*, (August-September, 1917), p. 20; signed "Charles Louis." The widow, Mrs. Esther Corey, in a letter to the present author, states that Fraina was responsible for unsigned and pseudonymous materials in the issues produced under his tenure. The extensive editorial section—all articles unsigned—often sounds like Fraina, writing floridly and in accessible language against censorship, religion, literature imitative of Zola, the "boring" past-invoking Tagore and the "empty," technically-facile Swinburne, and for spontaneity, the tango and "music which inspires, which interprets, which makes the individual *one* with the soul of life!" Perhaps also the "Story of the Dance" series, stressing utilitarian purposes of primitive dance, is his.

8. "Why Damn the New Dances?" *Modern Dance Maga-*

zine (March, 1914), pp. 6–7. Unsigned but certainly by Fraina.

9. This subject was first discussed by Fraina in above item. Includes view of the artistic nature of the Negro, with W. E. B. DuBois cited.

10. "What's the Matter with American Literature?" *Modern Dance Magazine* (April, 1914), p. 20.

11. Papers: Unpublished manuscript on John Reed (ca. 1948).

12. See note 5. This essay may be read as an indirect expression of his disillusionment with the quality of Bolshevik thought, as he prepared to break with the Communist International. Presented in a case study of the bourgeoisification of a working-class author.

13. Corey Papers: Letter to Granville Hicks, December 30, 1935, answering a query in respect to Hicks' forthcoming Reed biography.

14. Corey Papers: Letter to James T. Farrell, February 19, 1935.

15. Corey Papers: Outline for a novel.

16. "The Spirit of the Dance," *Modern Dance Magazine* (August-September, 1917), p. 20.

17. "Literature in a Political Decade," *New Letters in America*, ed. Horace Gregory (New York: W. W. Norton, 1937), pp. 170–80.

18. *Labor History* (Spring, 1963), p. 127.

19. Corey Papers: Outline, *Toward Understanding America* (1953).

20. "Marquis de Sade—the Cult of Despotism," *Antioch Review*, XXVI (Spring, 1966), 17–31.

The Brief Embattled Course
of Proletarian Poetry GUTTMANN

1. Margaret Wright Mather, "Der Schöne Archibald," *The New Masses*, X (January 16, 1934), 26; Stanley Burnshaw, "The Poetry Camps Divide," *The New Masses*, XII (July 31, 1934), 22–23.

2. On Lowenfels, see my essay, "The Poetic Politics of Walter Lowenfels," *The Massachusetts Review*, VI (Autumn, 1965), 843–50.

3. Edwin Rolfe, "Poetry," *Partisan Review*, II (April-May, 1935), 37.

4. Granville Hicks, "A Study in Comparative Literature," *The New Masses*, XIII (December 4, 1934), 23.

5. Burnshaw, "The Poetry Camps Divide," p. 23.

6. Harriet Monroe, "Poetry of the Left," *Poetry*, XLVIII (July, 1936), 221.

7. John Yost, "On Revolutionary Poetry," *The New Masses*, XVI (August 27, 1935), 23.

8. Stanley Burnshaw, "Notes on Revolutionary Poetry," *The New Masses*, X (February 20, 1934), 22.

9. Newton Arvin, "A Letter on Proletarian Literature," *Partisan Review*, III (February, 1936), 13.

10. For one of the most abusive essays, see Charles L. Glicksberg, "Poetry and Democracy," *South Atlantic Quarterly*, XLI (July, 1942), 254–65.

11. Boris Todrin, *Five Days: Austria: February 12th to 17th, 1934* (Chicago: The Black Cat Press; 1936), p. 34.

12. For comment on some of these poems and novels, and for a bibliography, see my book *The Wound in the Heart: America and the Spanish Civil War* (New York: Free Press, 1962), pp. 167–95, 269–75. Much of the present information on Rolfe is derived from an interview with his wife, Mary Rolfe, on December 27, 1966.

13. After a brief stint in the U. S. Army (1942–43), Rolfe moved to California and made documentary films, the best of which is *Muscle Beach* (with music by Earl Robinson). He also wrote a novel, *The Glass Room* (1946), with Lester Fuller. He died in 1954, of the heart condition which had led to his discharge from the army.

14. Robert Penn Warren, "The Present State of Poetry in the United States," *The Kenyon Review*, I (August, 1939), 386.